D1404708

THE MAURICE
AND LAURA FALK
FOUNDATION

Maurice Falk—1866–1946

Laura Falk—1867–1928

Portraits painted by Charles C. Curran,
1861–1942, New York City, member of
National Academy of Design.

THE MAURICE AND LAURA FALK
FOUNDATION

A PRIVATE FORTUNE—A PUBLIC TRUST

Agnes Lynch Starrett

*To the American people we shall hold ourselves
constantly accountable for the trust we have
accepted.*—J. STEELE GOW

THE HISTORICAL SOCIETY
OF
WESTERN PENNSYLVANIA

❧   ❧   ❧

Pittsburgh, Pennsylvania

THE MAURICE AND LAURA FALK FOUNDATION

A PRIVATE FORTUNE—A PUBLIC TRUST

LIST OF ILLUSTRATIONS

FOREWORD

The story of The Maurice and Laura Falk Foundation is the story of the imagination and leadership of one man—J. Steele Gow—who was the Foundation's Executive Director for the thirty-five years of its existence.

The Foundation's Board had great confidence in Mr. Gow and never hesitated to confront him with searching questions. The first question asked him was what the Foundation could do about the Great Depression of the 1930's. His reply was the development of an economic research program to get and evaluate the facts, analyze policies and practices, and report the findings, conclusions, and recommendations in important places. This program did much to improve this country's understanding of the forces at work and their effects on the economy. Later, he was asked what the Foundation could do to help bring about improvement in government. His answer was a broad program of teaching and research in political science with a strong emphasis on the role of politics in government—a program that observers have credited with initiating a new "movement" in higher education. And so it went from one field to another, with the Foundation undertaking to pioneer and develop each field until methods were so well established that others were willing to carry on.

The Board of the Foundation is proud of the record that Mr. Gow has made for the Foundation which is recorded in this volume. We hope it will be useful to others in the field of philanthropy.

Leon Falk, Jr.
Chairman, Board of Managers

AUTHOR'S PREFACE

Writing the history of The Maurice and Laura Falk Foundation has been for me an exciting experience. I hope that some of the matters which have made it exciting show in the text. Others I want to mention here.

Not least rewarding has been the opportunity to work on the thirty-third floor of an office building in the heart of downtown Pittsburgh. My windows look out on the Monongahela River winding to "the Point," where the Monongahela meets the Allegheny and, with it, flows out of sight as the Ohio. Tow boats *pushing* fleets of barges, many kinds of pleasure boats, and other craft pass up and down, heralded suitably by whistles or calliopes or horns. Along the river stretches the busy world of trade and manufacture. Motor cars and buses cross back and forth over a web of bridges and along highways parallel to the river on both sides; long lines of freight cars shake and grind along the river's southwest margin; and funiculars, which we Pittsburghers call "inclines," carry travelers up and down the hills across the river. With the changing seasons the view outside contracts and expands—sometimes closing in with mist or snow or rain, or widening out again with sunlight and air so clear and bright that roof tops, church steeples, and radio towers, miles away, are etched sharply against a very blue sky where white clouds reflect in moving shadows on the hills. Always, outside the windows, vibrates the world of busyness and beauty which is Pittsburgh.

Inside the office, too, there has been drama and enchantment, quieter but no less dynamic. Rows of files and broad shelves gather and hold the archives of The Maurice and Laura Falk Foundation in order characteristic of all Foundation activity. Papers and books and pamphlets store and record the work of the Foundation itself and the accomplishments of the research and educational and cultural institutions which through thirty-five years have received Falk Foundation grants.

Measured only in statistics the Foundation history is exciting. Maurice Falk set up the Foundation with $10,000,000 in 1929, a year of economic depression. By the close of its thirty-five years the Falk Foundation had made grants totaling more than $33,000,000 in three major fields important to human welfare; approximately $6,000,000 to economic research and $4,000,000 to political education. More than $20,000,000 was given in grants to Pittsburgh education, medicine, and culture. The Foundation helped distribute publications resulting from the study and activities of those who received the grants to the amount of about $1,000,000.

People are a rich part of the experience of writing the history. For the history of the Falk Foundation is woven of people and facts into a fabric designed by the hopes, the ideas, and the energies of men and women engaged in an adventure of purpose, plan, search, and accomplishment, carrying out the wish of Maurice Falk to use, entirely and within the limit of one generation, the surplus of his earnings, both income and principal, for the "welfare of mankind."

And if at times the author's enthusiasm should in this writing embarrass the self-effacing gentlemen who have carried so well their trust of selecting fields to support and their work of administering the funds, the author takes full responsibility. But written history, for good or ill, and however factual, is limited by an author's attitude and understanding. I am sure the enthusiasm of the Board, the Director, and the Staff in the performance of their work has been no less than my enthusiasm in the recording of it—however much each individual might, in modesty, understate his own contribution.

There are many individuals I should thank. I am grateful to the Board members Arthur E. Braun, Louis Caplan, Eugene B. Strassburger, and Leon Falk, Jr. for information they gave so willingly. I thank Trudy Pokras, secretary to the Director, and Evelyn Reeves, Jean Taylor, and Jean Froelich of Mr. Falk's staff for many kindnesses. And I thank Dorothea Paulat and Eleanor Montagna for their careful typing of notes and manuscript. To Margaret Happel, assistant to the Director, must go a special accolade for patience and for sharing the ready, copious knowledge of her many years with the Foundation. I am beholden for the helpful criticism of my husband, C. V. Starrett, Stanton C. Belfour of The Pittsburgh Foundation, and most of all, for the wise counsel and encouragement of J. Steele Gow. The friendliness and help of these people have been a rich and lasting part of writing the history of The Maurice and Laura Falk Foundation.

Agnes Lynch Starrett
December 1965

THE MAURICE
AND LAURA FALK
FOUNDATION

❧ ❧ ❧ ❧ ❧

Part One

THE BEGINNING

❧ ❧ ❧ ❧ ❧

*It is my firm belief that any surplus
of material wealth which may come to
a man is properly to be regarded as a
trust to be employed for the welfare
of mankind.* —MAURICE FALK

Original Board of Managers of The Maurice and Laura Falk Foundation with Maurice Falk and Attorney A. Leo Weil at the signing of the *Articles of Agreement*, in the office of A. E. Braun, Farmers Deposit National Bank, December 14, 1929. Seated, left to right: Arthur E. Braun, Maurice Falk, Israel A. Simon. Standing, left to right: Nathan B. Jacobs, Frank B. Bell, Eugene B. Strassburger, Leon Falk, Jr., Ernest T. Weir, A. Leo Weil.

Signatures on *Articles of Agreement,* December 14, 1929: Board of Managers, depositary representative, attorney, and witnesses.

ARTICLES OF AGREEMENT

The Maurice and Laura Falk Foundation has completed its destined thirty-five years. These years began with a document called *Articles of Agreement* signed by Maurice Falk and seven of his friends and business associates and dated December 14, 1929. The real beginning of the Foundation, and even its end, cannot be limited by dates on a calendar. Measured by the influence of its performance, its end is unpredictable. Its beginning was in the heart and mind of Maurice Falk.

The language of the *Agreement* reveals that heart and mind, and it honors the legal philosophy of the commonwealth and nation which protects the nobility of Maurice Falk's intent. The very word "trust" and the phrases of the first paragraph hold the author's faith and reliance in the integrity and justice of the law and of the gentlemen whom he named Board of Managers.

The second paragraph tells even more about the man; it "dedicates and devotes" a portion of his estate as a "memorial" to his wife Laura, "whose comfort and encouragement made his life happy" and whose "memory is lovingly enshrined in his heart."

The third paragraph defines his own philosophy, personal and sincere: "The creator of this trust believes that one who by good fortune has accumulated wealth beyond his personal economical requirements should hold in trust that wealth to be expended for the benefit and helpfulness of mankind."

This is followed by his humane purpose, "the uplifting and upbuilding of the unfortunate, the amelioration of the sufferings of the afflicted, and the encouragement, improvement, and betterment of mankind."

And there are sagacity and skill and foresightedness in the advice, which he says is not to be binding, for administering the funds—to hold back for a time spend-

3

ing of the principal so that "income may accumulate and become part of the principal"; in his allowing the Managers freedom to invest and reinvest, "as though they were the owners," and to receive gifts for the Foundation, "if they do not conflict with its purpose"; in his limiting the life of the Foundation to thirty-five years, lest its direction restrict generations with new problems and fresh needs, which, he was confident, they would be able to take care of in their own way.

A homely wisdom shines throughout the *Agreement*— the wisdom of Maurice Falk, citizen of a great community—a strength born of life in his native Pittsburgh and perhaps even of ancestors faraway and in ancient lands.

The *Articles of Agreement* are printed fully in the Appendix.

CHAPTER ONE

Maurice Falk and Laura Falk

Maurice Falk was born December 15, 1866 in Old Allegheny, when it was a city in its own right across the Allegheny River from Pittsburgh, to which it was officially joined in 1907. He was always proud of Pittsburgh. Throughout his lifetime he contributed much to its leadership in industry and culture.

His parents, Charles and Sarah Sanders Falk, came to America in the 1850's from Erpol, a village near Frankfort, Germany. They had been childhood sweethearts and were newly married when they migrated in a second wave of Germans, Jewish and Lutheran, seeking wider opportunities and freedom. Allegheny, Pennsylvania, their new home, was a community where Germans had been citizens for half a century among neighbors who were earlier "Scotch-Irish" pioneers.

Allegheny was a pleasant town, with tidy rows of small brick homes on well-gravelled side streets, large houses set back in spacious lawns along tree-shaded cobbled main streets, and green commons which are still unmarred by crowded building and parking. The Civil War, ended just before Maurice Falk was born, brought a prosperity to Pittsburgh and to Allegheny, which were arsenals and manufacturing centers of supplies for the Union. Allegheny was a patriotic town, cherishing the ideals Charles and Sarah Falk were seeking.

The town had a water system, a gas works, a rolling mill, a very busy market house, fire engines, a post office where letters went back and forth to the old country, and a good public school and high school. The Butler Pike, the Pennsylvania Canal, and three rivers—the Allegheny, the Monongahela, the Ohio—with the covered bridges over the Allegheny linking Allegheny City to Pittsburgh, made Allegheny a busy center for trade and for the musical and other cultural events prized especially by citizens of German heritage. It was a town where Charles and Sarah Falk could make the kind of home they wanted.

Charles Falk was an expert tailor, and with two friends also newly come from Germany he formed a partnership in a clothing store known as "Strassburger, Falk, and Hirsch." Two children were born in the Falk home on Cedar Street, Tillie and Maurice. And within a few years, after the family left the clothing business for larger opportunity in suburbs east of Pittsburgh— in Greensburg and what was then called Irwin Station— five more children were born: two more sons, Leon and Sigmund, and three more daughters, Carrie, Jessie, and Amy. They were all educated in the local public schools.

Maurice, Leon, and Sigmund, taking advantage of the resources in Western Pennsylvania and West Virginia, returned as young men to invest their imagination and energies in Pittsburgh, bringing their parents with them. There was prosperity for many who, like the Falks, were willing to work hard and try their luck in new enterprise. No longer was it necessary for the children of new Americans to make only a modest living by skilled handicrafts of their European ancestors. There was better livelihood, even a fortune, to be earned through the exploitation of the rich resources of the mines. Railroads opened up new and faster transportation than the rivers had afforded. A foresighted man could invest and reinvest his earnings and build a better future for his children and have some to spare for others.

In 1893 Maurice Falk went into business with Henry Weiskopf and established the Duquesne Reduction Company, smelters and refiners of copper, brass, and other nonferrous metals. It became the largest enterprise of its kind in the Pittsburgh district.

In the 1920's the Falks created the Federated Metals Corporation for secondary refining of nonferrous junk metal, a joining of the two older Falk companies: the Great Western Smelting and Refining Company of Chicago and the Duquesne Reduction Company. They also owned the American Chemical Company of Newark, New Jersey.

The Falk brothers had not only skill and foresightedness in business operation, but they had what was even more important, the sensitiveness to select men of vision and industry as leaders for the businesses in which they invested their earnings. With Isaac W. Frank and John Phillips they acquired a plant in West Virginia known as the Phillips Tin Plate Company. Mr. Falk and Mr. Phillips, in turn, went into business with Ernest T. Weir and John Williams to form Weirton Steel Company (later National Steel Corporation). Maurice Falk was a large stockholder in all these companies and in Blaw-Knox Company, Reliance Life Insurance Company, and the Farmers Deposit National Bank in Pittsburgh. National Steel stock was the broad base of assets for the Foundation, to which later Mr. Falk willed his stock in Edgewater Steel, a company of which Mr. Frank Bell was president. Both were independent steel companies.

During World War I the Falk brothers, as a patriotic effort, financed a potato flour industry. The flour was shipped abroad and throughout the United States for the military services. The industry was a financial loss to the Falks but a contribution to the war effort.

Meantime, in 1888 Maurice Falk had married Laura Klinordlinger of Pittsburgh. His brother Leon had married Fannie Edel of Virginia. Both wives encouraged their husbands in their work and kept alive in their homes the spiritual heritage of Jewish family life and the tradition of sharing any means beyond that needed for the family's independence with others less fortunate —first with those in the Jewish community, and then with those in the larger community which made good fortune possible. And they fostered, too, the understanding, old in Hebrew lore, that the good life included, beyond material wealth, learning and freedom and love for one's neighbor.

Gifts to Pittsburgh philanthropic and public-spirited causes were made by the Falks before Maurice Falk created the Foundation. In 1910, as a tribute to his wife, Fannie Edel Falk, Leon Falk, Sr. donated a recreation and teaching wing for the Rodef Shalom Temple in Shadyside, Pittsburgh. Its classrooms, swimming pool, library, and recreation facilities were the first institution of its kind in the city. And in 1912 Maurice Falk and his brothers helped Rabbi J. Leonard Levy organize the Pittsburgh Federation of Jewish Philanthropies, to which they were always generous contributors. Maurice Falk was a director of the Montefiore Hospital, which stands in the first rank for research and nonsectarian medical care.

In 1928 Maurice Falk's wife and his brother Leon died. Both losses cut deep into the sensitive spirit of Maurice Falk. He had no children. His wife Laura had been an invalid since the death of their infant son. His brother's two children, Leon, Jr. and Marjorie Levy Falk, were like his own. Leon, Jr. filled his father's place in the community, and he became his Uncle Maurice's closest business associate. Leon Falk, Sr. had been a trustee of the University of Pittsburgh. His son succeeded him there and has become vice chairman of the University's Board of Trustees.

Because of their friendship with Chancellor John G. Bowman of the University of Pittsburgh, and their recognition that good health care was a fundamental need in Pittsburgh, Maurice Falk and Leon, Sr. had given to

8

the University, just before Leon, Sr. died, $1,000,000 to establish in Oakland, the civic center of Pittsburgh, the Falk Clinic, outpatient unit for what has become the great complex of hospitals, medical research, and teaching departments for physicians, nurses, pharmacists, and dentists which is Pittsburgh's great Health Center.

In his loneliness following the death of his wife and of his brother, Maurice Falk talked often with Chancellor Bowman. Mr. Falk was recuperating from an illness on his nephew's farm, "Falklands," in Bedford County, next to "Waterbrooks," the farm which was the country home of Chancellor Bowman. He told the Chancellor he was always regretful that it seemed impossible to do enough to alleviate human ills. And he was always earnest in wanting to help make his native city prosperous, fair, and good. Leon Falk, Jr. gives Chancellor Bowman credit for suggesting that a foundation would give order and plan to carry out these deeply humanitarian interests.

Another strong influence which helped direct Maurice Falk's plan for his foundation was his admiration for his friend Julius Rosenwald (Sears, Roebuck, and Company) and the philosophy upon which Mr. Rosenwald founded his philanthropies. This philosophy Mr. Rosenwald expressed in interviews with the public press and in magazine articles and occasional speeches. He was opposed, he said, to the permanent or never-ending endowment "because it tends to lessen the amount available for immediate needs." He believed that future generations would be as humane and enlightened as his own, and he added, "The generation which has contributed to the making of a millionaire should be the one to profit from his generosity." And there were many who thought that the contribution of these ideas to philanthropic giving was of even greater value than the contribution of wealth. The character of the Falk

9

Foundation was influenced by Maurice Falk's admiration for these ideas.

          ❦   ❦   ❦   ❦   ❦

And so, after deep thought and consultation with friends and advisors, The Maurice and Laura Falk Foundation began to take form. A somewhat detailed account of its founding and its subsequent grants will follow this brief biography of Maurice Falk.

In 1930, when the Foundation program was yet in the planning stage, Maurice Falk married Selma K. Wertheimer, daughter of Isaac Kahn and widow of the late M. S. Wertheimer. She had been a friend of Laura Falk and Mr. Falk found her a good companion and a loving wife.

Those who knew Maurice Falk well were devoted to him. Mary Kelly, his bookkeeper from earlier business years and until his death, recalls many kindnesses and consistent acts of thoughfulness for the welfare of his employees, in his home and in his businesses. She remembers how regular he was in attending to every duty, from the days when he was driven from his home to the office in a carriage which he bought for his wife and which later, of course, he replaced by an automobile. There were gifts for many on holidays and special occasions.

His colleagues at the Foundation respected Maurice Falk's opinions. But he made it very clear to the Board and to the Director that he would never interfere with their policies or decisions. He attended meetings only as an observer. In fact, although Mr. Falk lunched with Director J. Steele Gow, informally, at the desk in Mr. Gow's office, two or three times a week, he never discussed Foundation matters on these occasions, lest, as he said, any comment he made be given undue weight or seem to influence Board action. His conversation was bright and challenging on significant local and world affairs and people. Mr. Gow always affectionately called him "Uncle Maurice."

Maurice Falk died in 1946, at the age of eighty, when the Foundation had just passed its duration half mark. No biographical record would be complete without some presentation of Maurice Falk's *Will*, which was drawn up at his request by his friend and legal advisor, Louis Caplan. Two of his sisters were living at the time of his death, Mrs. Jessie Forst, a widow with no children, and his sister, Mrs. Carrie Wolf. With his usual loyalty to family ties, he acknowledged with bequests his affection for his second wife's daughter, Mrs. Birdie W. Einstein, along with bequests to those of his own blood. A favorite sister of his wife Laura, Mrs. Minnie Oberndorf, was living too. And there were the children of his brother Leon, and their children. For all of these, his own and his wife's relatives, Maurice Falk provided generously, relying most on Leon, Jr. to hold and administer certain family trusts. His friend Eugene B. Strassburger and his secretary Israel Simon, who were members of the Foundation's Board of Managers, served with Leon, Jr. as executors of his estate. Characteristic of his generous spirit and his careful forethought, Maurice Falk's *Will* first took care of family, close friends, business and domestic employees, and then, to carry out his public trust, made the Foundation residuary legatee of his estate.

☙ ☙ ☙ ☙ ☙

The *In Memoriam* printed below from the Foundation Minutes April 14, 1946, pays tribute to Maurice Falk and to his faith in his fellow man; it expresses well the deep affection of his friends and colleagues for him, and renews their pledge to establish his good works.

IN MEMORIAM

Maurice Falk
December 15, 1866—March 18, 1946

The death of Maurice Falk in Miami, Florida, on Monday, March 18, 1946, closed a life that was good and useful.

Maurice Falk was a kindly man. His kindliness nurtured in him a deep compassion for all who suffered misfortune, so that those in need found him a liberal benefactor.

Seeking neither private commendation nor public acclaim for his many benefactions, his modesty kept him humble in the presence of praise for his good works.

Maurice Falk was a wise man. He was quickly responsive to calls for charity, but he realized that charity alone was less than a cure. He perceived the importance of helping efforts to develop a society so sound that it would rarely breed privation and distress. Great as were his gifts for charity, they were exceeded by his generous subventions for constructive philanthropy to advance the frontiers of knowledge, to broaden and sharpen understanding, to promote tolerance and good will, and in all ways to strengthen the power of man to make enduring progress for himself and for society.

Privileged by a Divine Providence to accumulate substantial means, Maurice Falk counted it his clear duty to draw generously upon his resources to help humanity. When, on December 14, 1929, he created The Maurice and Laura Falk Foundation as a memorial to his late beloved wife, Laura Falk, he stated, "It is my firm belief that any surplus wealth which may come to a man is properly to be regarded as a trust to be employed for the benefit of mankind."

In keeping with that view and to evidence his conviction that men of means should give generously of their wealth during their lifetime, he at once gave the Foundation the major portion of his estate. Subsequently, he provided in his *Last Will and Testament* that the Foundation should receive much of the remainder of his estate, to use "for the benefit of mankind."

Having served by his appointment as members of the Board of Managers of The Maurice and Laura Falk Foundation since its establishment in 1929, we pledge ourselves to continue to give

12

these positions of trust and responsibility our faithful attention, to the end that the resources he has put at our disposal may soundly serve good and useful purposes.

As members of the Board of the Foundation, and as his friends who had for him a great personal affection, we record our profound sympathy for his family in their bereavement.

* * * * *

To this *Memorial* the original members of the Board of Managers of the Foundation and the executive director signed their names. Those who signed were Arthur E. Braun, Leon Falk, Jr., Israel Simon, Ernest T. Weir, Nathan B. Jacobs, Frank B. Bell, Eugene B. Strassburger, and J. Steele Gow.

A GLORIOUS CORNER STONE

Newspapers and magazines over the United States and in other nations featured announcements of the establishment of The Maurice and Laura Falk Foundation in Pittsburgh. This cartoon, a favorite with Maurice Falk, was drawn by Cy Hungerford, *Pittsburgh Post-Gazette,* December 1929.

CHAPTER TWO

The Plan

The deep sense of responsibility to the Foundation and to the community which prompted every action of the Board of Managers throughout the tenure of the Foundation was emphasized in its first deliberations. The opening meeting was held Saturday afternoon, December 14, 1929, in the office of A. E. Braun, president of the Farmers Deposit National Bank.

Maurice Falk and the seven men he had selected as Managers signed the *Articles of Agreement:* Arthur E. Braun, Leon Falk, Jr., Israel Simon, Ernest T. Weir, Nathan B. Jacobs, Frank B. Bell, and Eugene B. Strassburger. Attorney A. Leo Weil, legal advisor who helped draw up the *Agreement,* signed as witness. Mr. Braun signed a second time as representative of the Farmers Bank, which Mr. Falk had appointed to act under instruction of the Board as depositary for the securities, properties, and assets of the Foundation, to keep its books and help gather financial advice on investments.

When all had signed, officers were elected: Leon Falk, Jr., chairman; Israel A. Simon, secretary; E. T. Weir and Frank Bell, vice chairmen. Maurice Falk was elected an honorary member and, at his request, without voting power.

The Board's first official act with Leon Falk, Jr. in the chair was to agree that an executive director be elected as soon as possible. The chairman and Maurice Falk reported talks they had had with J. Steele Gow, executive assistant to Chancellor John G. Bowman of the University of Pittsburgh and dean of University administration. That Mr. Gow was just right for the appointment both were confident. The Board agreed unanimously to engage him as soon as he could be released from his duties at the University, and to withhold any public announcement of his appointment until the Foundation was "more thoroughly organized."

Finally, the Board adopted resolutions which expressed appreciation for the "public spirited aims" of Maurice Falk in creating the Foundation, and pledged to him and to the community their "wholehearted allegiance and loyalty."

❦ ❦ ❦ ❦ ❦

Late in December 1929 newspapers and magazines from coast to coast and throughout the world announced that Pittsburgher Maurice Falk had established a trust fund of approximately $10,000,000 to be expended, principal and income, within thirty-five years, "for human welfare," and that a Board of Managers held "broad powers of discretion" regarding its distribution. Immediately, into the Foundation Board and to Maurice Falk himself came a deluge of letters, three thousand of them, from North and South America, Europe, and Asia. All of them were answered. The answers and further public announcements stated that no grants could be made until the Board studied carefully what the Foundations's program of distribution should be. The Board itself discovered, as Maurice Falk had before he set up the Foundation, that there was great need everywhere, but to make gifts, one by one, to every individual person or institution asking for them would soon exhaust any amount of wealth without reducing the numbers who still had to have help. Obviously, a plan was necessary: how and where to give to strike at the causes of widespread need.

J. Steele Gow, the director, was not able to leave the

University of Pittsburgh full time until September 1, 1930. But in the eight months preceding that date he spent many hours studying the philosophy of foundation giving and talking with officials of older foundations and with members of the Falk Foundation Board.

At the first Board meeting Steele Gow attended, January 11, 1930, one month after the organization of the Foundation, Frank Bell suggested that the director and members of the Board talk with President Frederick P. Keppel of the Carnegie Corporation about effective ways and means for building a program. This was done, and for several months talks with other authorities continued. President Henry Suzzalo, Carnegie Foundation for the Advancement of Teaching; General Director Shelby M. Harrison, Russell Sage Foundation; President Edwin R. Embree, Julius Rosenwald Fund; Mr. Beardsley Ruml, Spelman Fund; Director Charles F. Lewis, The Buhl Foundation; Secretary Henry Allen Moe, John Simon Guggenheim Memorial Foundation; staff members of the Rockefeller Foundation, the Wieboldt Foundation, and the Twentieth Century Fund—all gave Director Gow generous help.

From talks with these men and their associates Steele Gow evolved a basic philosophy for foundation giving: that the only way to do anything of lasting value was to concentrate upon specific limited fields; to emphasize preventive measures—not temporary relief; to supplement and even stimulate other giving, but not to displace it. The essay presenting the philosophy was printed and circulated widely. Literature concerned with foundations at the time was only fragmentary and many requests came into the Foundation for the Gow essay. It stands as a landmark in the philosophy of philanthropic giving.

The next step was to select a fundamental field for the Falk Foundation's philanthropy. Housing, industry, economics, government, law, education, child welfare, and dentistry—these and other subjects were discussed by the Board with experts, local and national. Reports of activities and letters of helpful advice came from many: Dr. James Ford of the President's Conference on Home Building and Home Ownership, Dr. Robert S. Lynd and Dr. M. B. Givens of the Social Science Research Council, Dr. Leon Marshall of the Institute of Law of The Johns Hopkins University, Director W. V. Bingham of the Personnel Research Federation, Mr. T. E. Rivers of the National Recreation Association, Mr. David Lawrence of the *United States Daily,* Dr. Luther Gulick of the National Institute of Public Administration, Director W. F. Willoughby of the Institute for Government Research of the Brookings Institution, Dean H. E. Friesell of the School of Dentistry of the University of Pittsburgh, Dr. E. V. Cowdry of the National Research Council, and scores of others.

One paragraph from the 1928-29 Report of Dr. Charles F. Lewis, director of The Buhl Foundation, Mr. Gow quoted as helping him materially to sharpen the focus of a plan.

Though millions upon millions be paid for social relief and adaptation, if health and education be neglected, misery will breed faster than it can be ministered unto. Though the principal fortunes of the state be paid for the protection of the public health, if education and character building be neglected, social workers may be forever caring for those who, through ignorance and weakness, fail. Again, though we provide the finest and fittest possible education for every child and the best foundation in health and character and culture, how long will he keep his health or respect his training if he cannot, when grown, find a job by which to maintain himself and advance his family?

The Buhl Foundation had been established in Pittsburgh by the *Will* of Henry Buhl, who like Maurice Falk had made his fortune in Pittsburgh. He had directed that the money be spent locally, and Director

Charles F. Lewis and his board, though restricted geographically, had planned their program on a broad base of helping people help themselves. The Falk Foundation was not restricted geographically, and it was seeking, like the older foundation, a way to make the results of its giving fundamental and lasting.

❧   ❧   ❧   ❧   ❧

And so, after eighteen months reviewing other foundations' policies and practices, exploring many fields for possible effective giving, and after much discussion at meetings held regularly every month, in July 1931 the Board agreed to enter, tentatively, the field of economics, and to grant some well-established research institution the means of studying a basic problem. They agreed, too, to move slowly, and for a time at least, to concentrate on this one field.

Thus The Maurice and Laura Falk Foundation was launched on a program sound in plan and purpose. And later, when the Foundation selected other fields for giving, it continued the same responsible program its first step had taken. So that when the last grant was made, thirty-five years later, the Foundation had become a tool, precise and effective, and as its donor intended, "employed for the improvement of mankind."

THE MAURICE
AND LAURA FALK
FOUNDATION

❦ ❦ ❦ ❦ ❦

Part Two

GRANTS TO

RESEARCH IN ECONOMICS

❦ ❦ ❦ ❦ ❦

*To extend the frontiers of economic
knowledge through research, competent,
honest, unbiased—and to make it available in clear and nontechnical language
to the public.*—J. STEELE GOW
Biennial Report 1935-1936

Brookings Institution, Washington, D. C., new buildings dedicated November 1960. Built with support of friends of the Institution, among them The Maurice and Laura Falk Foundation.

Visitors from foreign lands in an orientation session, Maurice Falk Auditorium, Brookings Institution.

CHAPTER THREE

The Brookings Institution

During the year ending December 31, 1931—the Falk Foundation's second year—the study of other foundations' policies and practices begun the first year was completed and decision was initiated to concentrate on support of economic research. Meantime, the Foundation continued to plan ahead how to live as far as possible within income and to defer any large expenditures of principal.

In October 1931 the Foundation paid a fee of $3,000 to the Social Science Research Council in New York to furnish suggestions for a program of research important to the general economic well-being during the next decade. The Research Council staff was engaged in collecting facts concerning the economic status of the country that would spell out problems for further study by other organizations which in turn would interpret the facts and distribute them publicly.

News media had announced the Foundation's concentration of interest in economics, and requests were coming into the office for support of specific projects. These impressed Steele Gow with the desirability of trying to find out just what economic problems were basic and how study of them could be most efficiently supported.

In letters to Dr. Meredith B. Givens of the Social Science Research Council, Mr. Gow made clear that the Foundation's fee was to augment funds from other sources which had already come to the Council's division of industry and trade. He hoped that this additional money might make it possible for the Council to report its findings to the Falk Foundation as early as possible in 1932. And it was understood that whatever information was gathered could be shared with any other groups interested in economic research.

The Board approved the cautious and thorough approach of the Director preceding recommendation or rejection of grants, and they voted to postpone issuing any public report of Foundation activity until the first grant was made.

In entering the field of economic study the Falk Foundation was entering what was practically virgin territory for support. Many other foundations, some limited by their charters, were concentrating in other fields. The Twentieth Century Fund was one of the few which had shown any specific interest in economic study. Later, other foundations and institutions with greater resources than the Falk Foundation were to become interested, and when they did the Falk Foundation directed its funds to other important causes. But throughout the next thirty years, even while making grants to other fields, the Falk Foundation supported economic research by many competent groups and institutions.

A strong reason impelling the Foundation to enter and to concentrate for a time in economics was the financial crisis paramount throughout the country and keenly felt in the industries, manufactories, and market places of Pittsburgh. The country was in the throes of an economic depression, destructive to human welfare, material and spiritual, and demanding immediate remedies to relieve widespread suffering of those without work or income. These remedies could not hope to guarantee that similar crises would not arise again, in recurring cycles familiar throughout past history. Many thoughtful persons saw in the confusion of poverty and distress the dangers of hasty legal and government palliative action that might eventually weaken the funda-

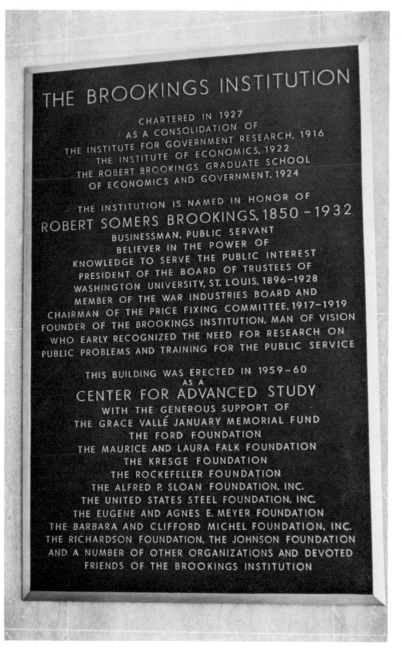

Plaque recording the dedication of the Brookings Institution as a center for advanced study and its donors.

mental structure of political and economic freedom. The greatest need, it seemed, was to know how to gain now and for the future a hale and stable economy.

The result of the advice that came to the Falk Foundation from sources expertly qualified called forth fresh policy: the Foundation would not make its own studies, but would grant funds for the use of recognized experts; it would ask these experts to seek the causes of trouble and, if possible, suggest widely beneficial solutions; it would give utmost freedom in the use of funds, asking only reports or publications, intelligible not just to scholar economists, but to the general public as well.

❧   ❧   ❧   ❧   ❧

The Falk Foundation's first grant was made to the Brookings Institution in Washington, D. C., January 8, 1932, for a study of the distribution of wealth and income in relation to economic progress. Brookings Institution was recognized as one of the most competent organizations in economic research, and was especially well-staffed and well-equipped to make this particular study, which Mr. Gow told the Board, "cut so deeply into economics that it could open additional problems for study which could make helpful and permanent contribution to economic knowledge."

The first study, begun April 1, 1932, was in progress until 1935, when it was published in four volumes: *America's Capacity to Produce, America's Capacity to Consume, The Formation of Capital,* and *Income and Economic Progress.* These volumes were the cooperative work of the Brookings staff, at first directed by Edwin G. Nourse, who was largely responsible for the broad outline of the entire study and primary author of the first volume; the others were under the personal direction of Harold G. Moulton, who also shared in the writing. They appeared as separate volumes, hard bound, and also in a text-book edition which united the four parts in paper binding and somewhat abridged them for classroom use. There was also a small pamphlet digest which sold on newsstands for thirty-five cents.

The first grant was followed by a series of grants to Brookings which extended over most of the life of the Foundation, from the Foundation's first grant in 1932 until the final grant to Brookings was made in October 1959. This final grant was to build an auditorium in Washington, D. C. for the Brookings Institution. In recognition of the long association of the Foundation with the Institution in economic research and of Maurice Falk's contributions to national life the auditorium

Research and writings by Brookings scholars and others were financed by grants from the Falk Foundation, which also helped finance their wide distribution. "Reliable knowledge to make intelligent decision and action possible."

is called The Maurice Falk Auditorium.

To Brookings studies and to their distribution the Foundation made grants of more than $1,500,000. The biennial reports of the Director show how the Brookings studies became a central core around which were built related studies, so that every new grant benefited from a preceding grant. (All these grants are listed in the Appendix of this book with the *Cumulative Record of Grants.*)

The first grant set a pattern for all future grants. At the beginning, and even during the period of study, experts were consulted to test the validity of the research and of its place in the Foundation program. With each step the Foundation learned how to make a grant count most; the public learned and benefited from newspaper and magazine digests and from the use made of the published knowledge by legislators, teachers, lawyers, and others with opportunities to influence improvement of economic welfare. And a basic function of a philanthropic foundation was fulfilled—to help raise the competence of society to do for itself that which so long it was thought had to be done for it by charitable philanthropy.

❧ ❧ ❧ ❧ ❧

Relations with Brookings Institution established friendships based on mutual trust and understanding between officers of the Foundation and the research scholars.

Harold Glenn Moulton, president of Brookings Institution most of the time covered by its association with the Foundation, had been a political economy professor at the University of Chicago from 1911 to 1922, when he became director of the newly established Institute of Economics in Washington, D. C. Under his leadership the Institute, in 1928, was consolidated with the Institute for Government Research and the Brookings Graduate School, also in Washington, to form the Brookings Institution—a research institution and a supergraduate training school for economists. From time to time, as other studies fostered by Falk Foundation grants were published, Dr. Moulton, alone or accompanied by associates, met with officers of the Foundation at Board meetings or at dinner to discuss the research for which grants were being requested, or to report progress on research underway.

When Dr. Moulton retired, in 1952, he retained his interest in the research and was still called upon by the Foundation for advice. His successor at the Institution was Dr. Robert DeBlois Calkins, a graduate of William and Mary College, a Doctor of Philosophy of Stanford University, like Dr. Moulton honored with several doctoral degrees, and like him a competent research scholar.

Edwin Griswold Nourse, graduate of Cornell University, Doctor of Philosophy of Chicago University, and a vice president of Brookings when Dr. Moulton was president, was another member of the staff generous in cooperation with the Foundation and author of some of the studies. Later he was chairman of the President's Committee of Economic Advisors for President Truman.

꙳   ꙳   ꙳   ꙳   ꙳

In 1951 the Falk Foundation had contributed $75,000 in conjunction with a $150,000 grant by the Alfred P. Sloan Foundation to establish an economic education division at Brookings. In 1953 the Foundation granted Brookings $15,000 for conferences with President Eisenhower's Council of Economic Advisors.

About this time Falk Foundation public dinners be-

came in themselves an institution, with a purpose supplementing that emphasized with every grant—soundly
tested information passed on as widely as possible for
the good of society. Among the guests were college and
university executives and teachers; leaders of industry,
trade, finance; and other prominent Pittsburgh citizens.
Each learned to respect the other and, mutually, to
define the economic problems of Pittsburgh and the
nation, and they learned how and where to seek counsel
and guidance. These dinners, where scholar-theorists sat
at table with the practical business and professional
leaders of Pittsburgh, gave each a chance to learn from
the other for the good of all—through a speech prepared
by an expert and through the informal discussion preceding and following the speech.

꙳ ꙳ ꙳ ꙳ ꙳

More than a score of studies were made by Brookings
scholars with the assistance of Falk grants, and from
these came more than fifty publications.

A list of those grants, 1930-1955, shows the wide
range of inquiry into economic problems: *Distribution of
Wealth and Income in Relation to Economic Progress; The
Recovery Problem in the United States; Industrial Price Policies
and Economic Progress; An Evolving and Flexible Program of
Economic Studies; Productivity, Wages, and National Income;
Government and Economic Life; Wartime Control of Prices;
Pricing for Prosperity; Relief and Social Security; Refugee Settlement in the Dominican Republic; Impact of the Defense Program upon the Economic Life of the Nation; Proposed Studies
of the Effect of Governmental Fiscal and Other Economic Policies on the Private Enterprise System; An Economic Program
for Postwar United States; Annual Wage and Employment
Guarantees; A Study to Determine the Need for Changes in
Federal Labor Policy and to Recommend the Changes Indicated;*

30

Concentration in American Industry; Taxes and Economic Incentives; A Study of Social Security Costs and Financing Methods; A Survey of Medical Service in the United States; The Dynamic Economy; The Problem of Pensions; The Price-Changing Process; The Impact of Union Policies upon Industrial Management.

A colophon in all publications states that the study was made possible by Falk Foundation funds but that the Foundation was "not author, publisher, or proprietor" of the publication and was "not to be understood as approving or disapproving by virtue of its grant any of the statements and views expressed." This became the usual colophon in all publications of studies supported by Falk grants.

The studies followed the trends of social change through the 1930's, 40's, and 50's—as the economy geared itself for war, or worked and produced under wartime controls, or struggled with employment, wages, price controls, debts, taxes, relief, social security, pensions— all the problems of postwar recovery. The aim was consistently to find some way of solving the problems of conserving human resources at a minimum of cost. Publications were written by the Brookings staff, or when necessary by others accustomed to translating the technical language of the specialist into language more widely comprehensible.

The Foundation considered that the widest possible communication of the scholars' study should be made. And for auxiliary distribution the Foundation appropriated funds and furnished lists of people who would use the information for intelligent public discussion of the issues the publications raised—for speeches, for articles in journals and magazines, and for a variety of discussion groups. Thousands of copies of the publications went to lawyers, legislators, ministers, editors, writers, teachers, students, housewives. Here the Foundation endorsed the philosophy of Maurice Falk—that with courage and intelligence and hard work and faith in other men, good can be realized.

       ❧   ❧   ❧   ❧   ❧

One grant to Brookings Institution in 1940, although a grant for economic research, was outside the program studying American domestic policy.

In October 1940 the Foundation appropriated $50,000 so that Brookings could meet the request of the Dominican Republic Settlement Association for a study of the economics of the refugee problem in the Dominican Republic. The object was to determine how European refugees being settled there by the Association could establish a sound economy.

The Association had been formed by a group of prominent American citizens, some of them Pittsburghers, following a conference representing thirty-two nations held at Evian, France in 1938. President Rafael Leonidas Trujillo of the Dominican Republic offered the refugees 26,000 acres on the northern coast of the Republic in which he personally invested $100,000. Others eventually contributed about $3,000,000 more.

Dr. Dana G. Munro, dean of Princeton University's School of Public and International Affairs, supervised the study, a book was published, and about seven hundred settlers, by dint of hard work, mostly farm labor unfamiliar to the many whose skills were professional, did for a time make a living. The Brookings study did not find the territory suitable for "general settlement purposes," but admitted that it had the advantage of being immediately available and suitable for a limited number of the many distressed political and religious refugees from Central Europe. Director Gow explained that this was a "token grant, a means of calling attention to the need for constructive philanthropy in the field of refugee settlement"; certainly it was a problem critical among other problems to be studied and solved in this time of economic upheaval.

＊　＊　＊　＊　＊

Even as economic research was emphasized, not only with grants to the Brookings Institution, but as succeeding chapters tell, with grants to other economic research and teaching, the Board remembered other matters important to the "welfare of mankind." In July 1931, when the Board had unanimously and enthusiastically approved the emphasis on economics, Eugene B. Strassburger, Nathan Jacobs, Ernest Weir, and Frank Bell offered resolutions that "whenever the requirements of this program permit, the Foundation consider granting aid to other projects important in the Pittsburgh area, proper to the Foundation's purpose . . . whether or not these projects are related directly to economic welfare." There was consistently kept before those concerned with administering the funds dedicated by Maurice Falk the philosophy that man was not fed by bread alone.

CHAPTER FOUR

The American Law Institute

Between 1944 and 1964 the Falk Foundation made several substantial grants to important projects of the American Law Institute: in 1944, toward preparation of a modern uniform commercial code that, hopefully, would be accepted throughout the United States ($285,000); in 1961, to reactivate the editorial staff of the code and help keep their work up-to-date ($125,000); in the decade 1948 to 1958, for study of federal income and estate and gift tax laws and the improvement of their structure ($620,000); in 1963, for further support to the same purpose ($187,000); and in 1961, for continuing legal education ($37,500)—grants totaling $1,254,500.

These grants exemplify an important function of a foundation: private money spent for private effort supplementing government effort to serve the public good.

The preparation of a uniform commercial code was a project initiated and conducted by judges, lawyers, and law professors to bring about a uniformity and a simplification of the law concerning business and trade transactions in the several states of the United States, and much real progress toward its adoption by the several states has been realized. The grants to study federal income tax and the federal estate and gift taxes made possible the first actual major attempt at much needed, thoroughgoing statutory revision of these laws. Another grant helps guarantee for lawyers, teachers, and others a continuing understanding of the law under which men live. These grants are explained in this chapter. They have potentiality significant far beyond the present.

ᴕ ᴕ ᴕ ᴕ ᴕ

The American Law Institute was organized in 1923 in Washington, D. C. Its nucleus was a committee of prominent American judges, lawyers, and law teachers who had met in 1920 and reported to their fellows that American law in character and expression was uncertain and needlessly complex. The chairman was Elihu Root, respected widely for his legal acumen, and the vice chairman was Attorney-General of the United States George W. Wickersham. Other distinguished members of the committee were Judge Learned Hand; Benjamin M. Cardozo, later a justice of the United States Supreme Court; Harlan F. Stone, later chief justice of the United States Supreme Court; other prominent members of the bar; and celebrated professors from such law schools as those at Harvard, Pennsylvania, and Chicago. These men were authors as well as teachers. They suggested that it be "the concern of the legal profession to simplify the form of expression of the public law, the details of private law, the procedure or administration of law and of judicial organization." This required patient scholarly effort—and financial support.

Several hundred leaders of bench, bar, and law school attended the first meeting in 1923 and began plans for instituting and implementing specific projects. The Carnegie Corporation was asked for funds and granted $2,419,196 for work to cover a ten-year period.

ᴕ ᴕ ᴕ ᴕ ᴕ

There were Pittsburgh attorneys on the Council and the committees of the Law Institute who recognized that the Falk Foundation, because of its focus on the economic field, might be interested in granting aid to the preparation of a modern commercial code. John

Grier Buchanan, a scholarly Pittsburgh attorney, graduate of Harvard Law School, and a member of the Institute's Council, discussed the possibility of such a grant informally with Director Gow early in April 1944. Louis Caplan, able member of the law firm, Sachs & Caplan, also furnished information concerning the Law Institute and its need for support to its work for uniform state laws. Mr. Caplan was not then a member of the Foundation's Board of Managers. Eugene B. Strassburger was a member of the Foundation Board, and he had been prominent in the deliberations of the Institute for several years. His information was helpful, but with the careful approach characteristic of the Foundation management Mr. Strassburger refrained from voting when the proposal for a grant eventually came before the Board.

The request for funds came jointly in 1944 from the American Law Institute of Philadelphia and the National Conference of Commissioners on Uniform State Laws. The National Conference had been founded in 1892 "to promote uniformity in state laws on all subjects where uniformity is deemed desirable and practicable." Director Gow considered that this joining of forces for preparation of a Commercial Code promised success to the project. Also, his consultations with authorities in legal scholarship, such as Roscoe Pound of Harvard, who was not active at the time in either organization, brought to the Foundation disinterested approval.

In May 1944, in Philadelphia, Mr. Gow conferred with President of the Law Institute George Wharton Pepper, a former United States Senator, gentleman of the old school of manners, polished and ceremonious; Third Circuit Court Judge Herbert Goodrich, a native of Iowa, advisor to the Institute for professional relations, later director of the Law Institute; and former Attorney-

General of Pennsylvania William A. Schnader. Mr. Gow, when he reported the conference and presented the proposal to the Foundation Board in the spring of 1944, recommended it as "a first-rate opportunity to aid American business."

To stress the importance of the project the joint application said, in part:

> The economic need for a Commercial Code can scarcely be exaggerated. To unify American commercial law and to state it in terms understandable by businessmen and by lawyers whether trained under our own or a foreign legal system will not only facilitate domestic business transactions but will remove from the path of international commerce obstacles which in the past have proved insurmountable.
>
> To leave this field to pressure groups, each seeking ill-considered legislation in its own area, would be altogether disastrous. The work must be done as a whole and according to a method which combines scholarship, business experience, and practical judgment.

In June 1944 the Board of Managers voted the first grant to support the study—making clear that support was to the study and the framing of the law; for while the Foundation would, of course, watch with interest the progress of adoption in each state, and would consider that adoption the fulfillment of the study, it would not and could not assume any responsibility for that phase of the project.

In 1952 the Law Institute and the National Conference of Commissioners on Uniform State Laws published in Philadelphia their book, *Uniform Commercial Code.* The Editorial Board, with Judge Goodrich as chairman, had as members Professor Karl N. Llewellyn, University of Chicago Law School; John C. Pryor, Burlington, Iowa; William A. Schnader, Philadelphia; Harrison Tweed, New York City. They were responsible for overseeing the drafting and for the editing, and in the final stages questions of policy were considered by them and by the Enlarged Editorial Board consisting of Howard L. Barkdull, Cleveland; Joe C. Barrett, Jonesboro, Arkansas; Robert K. Bell, Ocean City, New Jersey; Robert P. Goldman, Cincinnati; Ben W. Heineman, Chicago; Albert E. Jenner, Chicago; Arthur Littleton, Philadelphia; Willard Luther, Boston; Kurt F. Pantzer, Indianapolis; R. Jasper Smith, Springfield, Missouri; and Charles H. Willard, New York City. Professor Llewellyn and Professor Soia Mentschikoff were chief reporters of the Code, and final editorial preparation was in the hands of Professor Charles Bunn, Wisconsin Law School.

Ten years of work resulted in a publication dealing with all aspects of the law concerning business and trade. There were nine articles: general provisions; sales of personal property; commercial paper; bank deposits and collections; letters of credit; bulk transfers; warehouse receipts, bills of lading, and other documents of title; investment securities; secured transactions. Article Six, bulk transfers, was written by Professor Charles Bunn of Wisconsin Law School and Mr. Eugene B. Strassburger of the Falk Foundation Board of Managers.

The Honorable Stanley S. Surrey, assistant secretary of the United States Treasury, in an address in St. Louis, Missouri, to the Section of Taxation, American Bar Association, August 6, 1961, said: "The 1954 Code was made possible only because the American Law Institute had engaged in intensive technical research." Director Herbert F. Goodrich of the Institute reported that the Right Honorable Lord Justice Denning of England, in an address to law teachers, cited the Commercial Code as a great work of American jurists. Judge Goodrich reported, too, that it had been translated by French jurists as an example of excellent study and performance.

Each year more states are added to the list of those adopting the Code; the large commercial states were among the first to adopt. The names and the year each adopted the Code and the year it became effective for each are printed here as they appeared in the Law Institute's *Annual Report* of 1965.

State	Adoption Date	Effective Date
Pennsylvania	1953	July 1, 1954
Massachusetts	1957	October 1, 1958
Kentucky	1958	July 1, 1960
Connecticut	1959	October 1, 1961
New Hampshire	1959	July 1, 1961
Rhode Island	1960	January 2, 1962
Wyoming	1961	January 2, 1962
Arkansas	1961	January 1, 1962
New Mexico	1961	January 1, 1962
Ohio	1961	July 1, 1962
Oregon	1961	September 1, 1963
Oklahoma	1961	January 1, 1963
Illinois	1961	July 2, 1962
New Jersey	1961	January 1, 1963
Georgia	1962	January 1, 1964
Alaska	1962	January 1, 1963
New York	1962	September 27, 1964
Michigan	1962	January 1, 1964
Indiana	1963	July 1, 1964
Tennessee	1963	July 1, 1964
West Virginia	1963	July 1, 1964
Montana	1963	January 2, 1965
Maryland	1963	February 1, 1964
California	1963	January 1, 1965
Wisconsin	1963	July 1, 1965
Maine	1963	December 31, 1964
Nebraska	1963	September 2, 1965
Missouri	1963	July 1, 1965
District of Columbia	1963	January 1, 1965
Virginia	1964	January 1, 1966
Virgin Islands	1965	July 1, 1965
Utah	1965	January 1, 1966
North Dakota	1965	July 1, 1966
Iowa	1965	July 1, 1966
Washington	1965	July 1, 1967
Nevada	1965	January 1, 1966

Hawaii	1965	January 1, 1967
Kansas	1965	January 3, 1966
Colorado	1965	July 1, 1966
Florida	1965	January 1, 1967
Texas	1965	July 7, 1966
North Carolina	1965	July 1, 1967
Minnesota	1965	July 1, 1966

The Foundation, recognizing that considerable time might be required for nation-wide adoption and that changes in commercial practices from time to time might require revisions in the Code, was pleased to grant an endowment of $125,000 in 1961 to reactivate the editorial board of the Code and help give it a permanent staff to review the Code from time to time and keep it up-to-date as well as uniform. In Director Gow's *Biennial Report of 1961-1962* the grants to the Code were summarized thus:

Beginning with the 1944 grant, the Falk Foundation grants for the preparation of the Code amounted to $285,000. The endowment grant of $125,000 for the work of the Editorial Board brought the total to $410,000, an amount considered modest when the potential importance of the Code for improving the flow of this country's commercial transactions is considered and when the Code's prospect of realizing its potential is as bright as its record of adoptions to date appears to make it.

           .♥   .♥   .♥   .♥   .♥

In 1948 the Law Institute asked the Foundation for a grant of $225,000 to draft an integrated and basic federal income tax statute that would coordinate the law then existing and the considerable body of court decisions, accumulated but not reflected in the law itself. The federal income tax law was then thirty-four years old and no thoroughgoing revision had been drafted in many years. Amendments presented only patchwork which created loopholes of misinterpretation and even occasional inequity. This revision was a job for which the legal profession was particularly suited, and which the Law Institute estimated would require three years to complete.

It became evident before the three years elapsed that because of the complexity of the task an additional year's work and additional funds would be needed. So,

Uniform Commercial Code (discussions and drafts), *Toward Excellence in Continuing Legal Education,* and other studies by legal experts were helped substantially with grants from the Falk Foundation. The Code simplified legal language and broadened understanding of the laws governing commerce; it has been adopted by more than forty states (1966).

in July 1950 the Foundation granted the Law Institute $75,000 more to complete the revision.

In April 1953 the Foundation granted the Institute $150,000 to finance a project to correlate the federal income tax with federal estate and gift taxes, to integrate the revised federal gift tax with the revised federal estate tax. Because of the close relationship between federal estate and gift taxes and the federal income tax this grant, the Board agreed, was a desirable supplement to the earlier grants made to the Institute.

In 1957 the Board voted another grant of $120,000 to support these tax studies for a four-year period, recognizing that continuing study was needed to keep the laws which governed these taxes timely and appropriate, assuring fairness to both taxpayer and government. The total support of the Foundation to the Institute's federal tax studies since 1948 had been $620,000.

And in April 1961 Director Gow presented a request from the Institute to use a balance of $38,000 remaining from the 1957 grant to finance a year's exploration of the possibilities of further constructive studies in estate and gift tax laws. Professor A. James Casner of the Harvard Law School conducted the exploration and in a sizable document of considerable detail illustrated how specific revisions in estate and gift tax laws could effect improvement. He found the tax structure too complex; too easily misinterpreted; favoring certain kinds of property; not allowing control of wealth to move easily from older to younger generations; causing differences in decisions by local law about similar conditions. In other words, considering these objections and others to the laws as they were, his exploration recommended a new and full and fundamental approach to revisions in these laws, and the funds to support it.

Mr. Gow reported that he had consulted with tax attorneys, certified public accountants, trust officers of banks, reliable sources to appraise the application for a new grant. The majority expressed the hope that further support would be given for the urgently needed improvements in the laws. They agreed that Professor Casner's proposal was sound and thorough. Mr. Gow himself brought out the point that someone eventually would make the study—maybe someone less competent than the highly qualified Law Institute—in a field where Foundation funds had been granted throughout fifteen years to help the Institute develop better federal tax laws in all categories.

There was much discussion at the Board meeting of April 5, 1963, led by Mr. Strassburger and Mr. Caplan, the attorney members of the Board, when the request for funds to finance further study was broached. And with the care characteristic always of Falk Foundation deliberation, the Director proposed that the Board meet at dinner with Norris Darrell, Sr., then president of the Law Institute, to hear an explanation of the proposal. And so, on April 24, Mr. Darrell described the project in general and answered specific questions, explaining how the study would be organized and the funds administered. On April 25 Mr. Darrell was officially notified that the Foundation vote would grant the Institute $187,000, to which the Institute might add any balance from the 1957 grant, to finance a three-year study.

The Foundation made clear that this was a final grant for the project and asked that the American Law Institute agree to carry the study to completion with its own financing should support beyond this grant be required.

     ❧   ❧   ❧   ❧   ❧

Eugene B. Strassburger of the Falk Foundation Board of Managers and J. Steele Gow, director of the Foundation, in a Board meeting, December 1961, led a discussion of a request from the American Law Institute for $37,500 to enable the Joint Committee on Continuing Legal Education, an agency of both the Institute and The American Bar Association, to organize and conduct a conference and prepare a report of conference proceedings and recommendations to develop and improve the Joint Committee's program on continuing legal education. The grant was made.

A series of meetings held at Arden House, Harriman, New York, was attended by members of the Joint Committee of Continuing Legal Education—leading jurists and scholar-attorneys from legal educational institutions from every section of the nation.

Harrison Tweed of Milbank, Tweed, Hadley & McCloy, New York, was co-chairman with Ross L. Malone of a Second National Conference. The conference was to measure the value of results of the first conference and make further recommendations. Mr. Tweed reported the results to the Foundation. It was agreed by those attending the Conference that the organized bar had a primary obligation to make continuing legal education available to students of law, that literature, programs, and techniques should be improved by the law schools and universities, that law firms should encourage juniors to take advantage of continuing education, that the newly-admitted lawyer should be provided stronger apprenticeship and clerkship programs, that a central depositary of continuing education publications should be set up and reviewed periodically for improvement, and that the organized bar should assume an obligation to subsidize the program and eventually make it self-sustaining.

Succeeding reports in law journals and in the Falk Foundation's correspondence files indicate that the recommendations which came out of the Second National

Conference are being followed successfully, and also that the Falk Foundation's support to ventures of the American Law Institute has been fruitful and rewarding.

❧   ❧   ❧   ❧   ❧

CHAPTER FIVE

Economic Research in Israel

Blessed art thou, O Lord our God . . . for keeping us alive, preserving us, and permitting us to attain this day.

ANCIENT HEBREW PRAYER

Some of the most important economic research fostered by grants from the Falk Foundation was centered in Israel, a new nation set precariously in the Middle East.

Early in 1952 Alex Lowenthal, Pittsburgh cultural leader, asked Leon Falk and Steele Gow whether The Maurice and Laura Falk Foundation, because of its interest in supporting fundamental economic research, could finance a program in Israel to help the infant nation cope with its difficult and complex economic problems. To set up a sound economic structure would contribute substantially to Israel's survival as an independent nation.

This was a practical need, and it carried deep emotional significance for Jews—those already settled in Palestine and many of their kin throughout the world. For Palestine has always been to the Jews a Holy Land—their land, even when they were scattered over the face of the earth. And now Palestine had become a sanctuary for the dispossessed and the fugitive; it had become, also, depository of their own Jewish institutions, folkways, customs, and language. Visitors returned from Palestine praising the communal colonies, or "kibbutzim" where the intrepid, the resourceful, and the hard working had made barren country blossom. It seemed the time to help set the young nation on the road to self-sustainment.

Only once before had the Foundation supported economic research outside the boundaries of the United States—in 1940, when the Foundation supported a Brookings exploration of the economic possibilities of land in the Dominican Republic for refugees from Europe, with the hope that research would help discover how, at least for the critical moment, settlement there might be possible and perhaps even furnish a pattern for establishing refugees in other lands.

Several steps preceded a grant for research in Israel which was made July 1, 1953. Leon Falk and Steele Gow, early in March 1952, visited Israel's Ambassador Abba Eban in Washington, D. C. for information firsthand concerning the need for economic research in Israel and suggestions for a program that would be helpful beyond just the immediate. The conference was fruitful. An understanding was established that the Foundation was willing to support a preliminary objective survey by experts to determine what kind of research might mean most, with no commitment of support beyond the survey.

On April 4 a memorandum came to the Foundation from Ambassador Eban outlining a possible plan of study for an institute of economic research in Israel. The introduction to his memorandum gave a clear general picture of the situation and the need:

There is a compelling need for an institute in Israel to undertake research in all questions affecting the economy of the country. The recent influx of newcomers and refugees has put a heavy strain on the country's economy. Increased knowledge of economic processes would reveal ways of relieving pressures on the economic structure and thus assure a better standard of living for the country. Ways and means of reaching that end could only be discovered by a systematic and scientific investigation of industry, trade, commerce, and agriculture and of economic trends in other parts of the world and by examining the degree of their applicability to Israel.

Scarcely any work of this kind has been done in Israel. Government and business have thus had to rely upon the expensive method of trial and error, or upon incomplete information, incomplete study, and inferences drawn from incomplete facts. This has had serious ill effects on the economy of the country, on the standard of living of the established population, as well as of the newcomers. An institute which would undertake economic investigation on the spot, studies in the United States, and projects of general research would be a powerful instrument in the country's economic progress, thus fulfilling the declared policy of the U. S. Government in rendering technical assistance to countries that do not yet enjoy full economic development.

Following Board agreement, Mr. Gow, on April 9, replied to the Ambassador, reiterating the Foundation's promise to finance a single preliminary survey of the feasibility and the need for research.

In July a letter to Mr. Gow from Israeli Minister Plenipotentiary David Goitien emphasized the importance of basic study to make Israel eventually independent of other governments for financial support.

And in October 1952, after clearance with Robert Calkins, president of Brookings, the Falk Foundation allotted $10,000 to commission A. D. H. Kaplan, a senior staff member of Brookings, to make the preliminary investigation. At Mr. Gow's request, Brookings agreed to act as fiscal agent for the investigation and granted Dr. Kaplan leave of absence to go to Israel.

Dr. Kaplan conferred with Ambassador Eban and with authorities in Washington, New York, and London before making his intensive survey in Israel.

In Israel, Professor Kaplan met with the leading personalities in the political, economic, and academic life of the country, from Theodore Kollek, director-general in the Office of the Prime Minister, to the junior lecturer on the economics faculty of The Hebrew University. Theodore Kollek was dedicated to Israel and its best future. He had spent his early life in a kibbutz near the Sea of Galilee. His government post was one that survived changes in prime ministers. He was, indeed, a man

United States Advisory Committee for Falk Project for Economic Research in Israel. Seated, left to right, A. D. H. Kaplan, Simon Kuznets, Stacy May; standing, left to right, Isador Lubin, Daniel Creamer.

Office of Falk Project for Economic Research, 17 Keren Hayesod Street, Jerusalem (on the top floor surrounded by balcony). Photograph by Alfred Bernheim.

49

of wide knowledge and outstanding intelligence.

Dr. Kaplan's study reported to the Foundation significant problems for economic research in Israel and their urgency and importance; the type of agency to do the research, either one already existing or to be set up; the staff required to carry out the studies; and cost estimates of the research recommended. He emphasized how vital the study of the economic problems in Israel would be to the United States and to any other country engaged in trade with Israel.

As a result of Professor Kaplan's comprehensive study and his recommendation, Simon Kuznets, professor of economics at The Johns Hopkins University, and Daniel Creamer, senior staff member of the National Bureau of Economic Research, New York, were sent to Israel to work out details for a program. They spent part of the winter of 1953-54 in Israel setting up a plan for what was to be called the *Falk Project for Economic Research in Israel,* a new and independent agency.

The Project, with A. D. H. Kaplan as first chairman of the U. S. Advisory Committee, began its work in Jerusalem, January 1, 1954, with a five-year grant from the Falk Foundation totaling $430,000—which over a ten-year period was increased by a second five-year grant to a total of $814,575. The Falk grants were channeled through Israel Foundations Trustees, set up to receive and disburse philanthropic funds for nonprofit programs in Israel.

In the first annual report of the Falk Project the scope and the purpose were presented clearly:

The scope of the Falk Project is intended to be as broad as the range of economic problems that confront a new nation. These problems relate to population, labor force, national income and its components, the cost structure of agriculture and industry, the supply and price of money and credit, the international balance of payments, and kindred fields. The scope extends also to problems

50

arising out of the position of Israel in the world, especially its relations with other states...

The choice of an independent, nonprofit organization to foster *research* and *training in economic research* was based on well-established precedent. Even in older and richer countries that have eminent records of publicly supported economic research, it is often found desirable to encourage and rely upon private study. The pressures of government tend to limit the resources that can be devoted to objective scholarship, especially to the exploration of new frontiers of knowledge and application. In the universities it is also rarely possible to devote the time or secure the assistance required for the steady and systematic study of economic facts and issues.

The decision to support a private organization was also based on a factor unique to Israel. It is a new nation, with social and economic features that require special study. It has distinctive institutions such as the farm collectives, the labor union system, and the Jewish Agency. This uniqueness means that empirical research in Israel cannot be, if indeed it can be anywhere else, a matter of imitation, of adapting ready tools and models to an entirely new situation. All research findings, no matter how factual, must be studied with the awareness that their meaning and significance for public policy will vary under different conditions. Research on the Israel economy would be futile if it did not take into account the distinctive features of this new society. The task of independent research is to scrutinize the prevalent concepts to see whether they should be modified to portray Israel's reality more clearly and to examine critically the basic data to see how well they reflect the real substance of economic life.

The *Ten Year Report (1954-1963),* published in Jerusalem in September 1964, emphasized the accomplishment of the twofold aim of the plan: (1) publications in both Hebrew and English supplying essential data on the economy of Israel, and (2) selected Israeli scholars trained as research economists to assure in years ahead continued supply of basic data and fundamental analyses needed by individuals and organizations, including the government. The Report described individual studies; listed publications and summarized their content; and presented biographical sketches of the working staff and the advisors in the United States and Israel. (The publications of the research are listed in the Appendix of this book. Their titles suggest the width and depth of the studies and of their possible contributions.)

❧   ❧   ❧   ❧   ❧

During the ten years of study there were, successively, three resident directors of research.

Daniel Creamer, the first director, was a Doctor of Philosophy from Columbia University who had been a civil servant in the United States federal government and an economist on the Social Security Board and the National Income Division of the United States Department of Commerce. In 1944-1945 he had collaborated with Robert Nathan in the preparation of an economic survey of Palestine. This survey gave him background valuable to the 1953 study. Although he had intended to stay with the Project only one year, he was persuaded to stay two years. When he returned to the United States he became a member of the National Industrial Conference Board and he served as a member of the United States Advisory Board for the Falk Project.

Dr. Creamer was succeeded as director for a year by Harold Lubell, another American scholar; he had worked from the beginning of the Falk Project as senior economist. He was a Doctor of Philosophy from Harvard University and had served as a statistician for the United Nations in the United States and in Geneva, Switzerland. Since leaving the Falk Project, his more recent work under Ford Foundation grants has included studies in Vietnam and Malaysia.

Don Patinkin, a Doctor of Philosophy and an assistant professor from the University of Chicago, a research scholar of the Cowles Commission for Economic Research, had been in Israel since the early years after Independence as a member of The Hebrew University

52

faculty. He has become a citizen of Israel and his children have been born there. He succeeded Dr. Lubell and continued as director through the life of the Project. Meantime he was also professor of economics in the Eliezer Kaplan School of Economics and Social Sciences at The Hebrew University in Jerusalem, developing for research in the Project Israeli-born scholars who returned to Israel with American doctorates. Many of them became writers and teachers. He is the author of books and articles in economics, and in 1959 published *The Israel Economy: The First Decade,* which has become an authoritative reference for planning the economy of new nations. He is Israel's foremost and senior economist with a reputation world-wide. His willingness to become director of research is weighty testimony to the value and scholarly level of the Falk Project in Israel.

Simon Kuznets, Columbia Doctor of Philosophy and the recipient of honorary doctoral degrees from the universities of Princeton, Pennsylvania, Harvard, and The Hebrew University of Jerusalem, had been a professor of economics at The Johns Hopkins University. He was made chairman of the program for the Falk Project and later chairman of the United States Advisory Committee for the Project. He was a man of warm human qualities, liberal intellect, and professional skill. He is George F. Baker professor of economics at Harvard University. He continues as a member of the advisory committee for the studies in Israel.

The other members of the United States Advisory Committee for the ten years were American economists. Although advisory, the Committee really acted as a policy-determining body during the period preceding the turning over of the project to an Israeli institution. Besides Drs. A. D. H. Kaplan, Daniel Creamer, and Simon Kuznets, the Committee included Dr. Stacy May, an economic advisor of the International Basic Economy

Corporation, New York, and Dr. Isador Lubin, industrial commissioner for the State of New York, a Brookings postgraduate scholar, and eminent practical economist. These men were economists with a wide range of knowledge and insight. Over the ten years they met frequently, giving service beyond its recompense. A mutual confidence and a warm friendship grew between the Foundation director and this committee. When Director Gow introduced them at the 1962 dinner, announcing an endowment grant to give the Project a permanent status in Israel, he expressed his thanks and his respect for their contribution thus: "The Falk Project could not possibly have had wiser or more dedicated guidance than these eminent economists have given it throughout its ten-year history."

During the second five years of the Falk Project the Advisory Committee encouraged and guided collaboration of Israeli scholars and agencies with the specific work of the Kaplan School of The Hebrew University, the Bank of Israel, and an Israeli government organization, the Central Bureau of Statistics. The basic system of national accounts, under the guidance of the researchers on the Project had been established during the first five years. Now the Falk Project could shift to more complex studies, continue the training of scholars, and prepare the way to leave to the educational forces of Israel itself the task of continuing research which could realize and even reach beyond, perhaps, the goals which the grants had aimed to support.

As the second five years of the Project were drawing to a close, the Falk Foundation administrators, pleased with the results, began to consider how the Foundation might assure the Project's future in a way most suitable for independent action inside Israel. Dr. Kuznets went to Israel in January 1961 to discuss with leading Israeli citizens in business, government, and education what they might favor for the future. As a result of his report to the Advisory Committee in New York in March, it was the Committee's unanimous opinion that the Falk Project should become a part of The Hebrew University in Jerusalem and operate under a Board of its own to be appointed by the University trustees and to consist in part of business and civic leaders not otherwise associated with the University. The Advisory Committee suggested, also, that the Israeli Board be given authority to decide what research should be made, determine the budget, and approve staff appointments. Their recommendation concerning financing of this continuing project was a Falk Foundation endowment grant of $500,000 to be matched by $500,000 by The Hebrew University.

❧ ❧ ❧ ❧ ❧

In October 1961 Director and Mrs. Gow visited Israel. Mr. Gow talked with fifteen outstanding citizens occupying high places in government, industry, agriculture, trade, finance, and education, and met scores of citizens at dinners, receptions, teas, and other social gatherings. He visited kibbutzim, desert country, and populous cities and towns. His report to the Board when he returned was most comprehensive and deeply interesting. In part, as background for his own recommendations and the Board's final action, he outlined some of the difficulties within the country thus:

Israel is striving heroicly to become self-sustaining. The country is not rich in natural resources. She is surrounded by hostile neighbors and so must maintain an expensive defense. Her population has grown rapidly through mass immigration, which strains her economy. And although nine-tenths of the population is Jewish it is far from homogeneous—for the people are of various nationalities and cultural and educational backgrounds—Western Europe, North and South America, Eastern Europe, and Africa. Most of them want

55

to live in cities, although there is great need to make an uncultivated soil productive, with irrigation and hard skilled work. The older settlers and the later ones sometimes have different ideas of what they want for Israel.

To counterbalance these, the greatest strengths of Israel, as I have seen them, are:

1. The dedicated spirit of its Jewish population. A visitor is deeply impressed by the determination of these people to make Israel a modern and progressive state that will have a position of dignity and influence in the family of nations. It is a thrilling experience to see the determination with which the Jewish people go about their work and to sense the strength of their conviction that they will make Israel not only a haven for the oppressed but also a dynamic and enlightened country to which many oppressed people will come from other lands.

2. In summary, a visit to Israel is a rich experience. It is a place of great contrasts. One finds there people of greatly diverse cultural, educational, and religious backgrounds who have had to be assimilated in such large numbers and so quickly that Israel has been called not a melting pot but a "pressure cooker." The contrast between antiquity and modernity is perhaps to be found in more vivid form in Israel than almost anywhere else in the world. The contrast between such elements of the population as the energetic and purposeful business leaders among the Jews in Haifa and Tel Aviv on the one hand, and the nomad Bedouins wandering on the sands of the Negev Desert and the listless Arabs slumbering in the sun in Jaffa on the other hand, is a sharp reminder that here is truly a complex country worth visiting again and again.

After I retire, Mrs. Gow and I hope to go back in the confident expectation that we shall see Israel still stronger than we found it in 1961.

The people with whom Mr. Gow conferred wanted the work of the Project to continue and were high in praise of its worth to Israel. This list of their names and titles suggests how important their opinions were to any plan of continuation: Mr. Hans Moller, managing director of ATA Textile Company, Ltd., Kfar Ata; Mr. Joseph Ami, general manager of Fertilizers and Chemicals in Israel, Ltd., Haifa; Mr. D. Horowitz, governor of the Bank of Israel, Jerusalem; Dr. J. E. Nebenzahl, chairman of the advisory committee and advisory council, Bank of Israel, Jerusalem; Mr. David Kohav, head of the research department, Bank of Israel, Jerusalem; Professor A. D. Bergman, president of the Ministry of Defense, Tel Aviv and Jerusalem; Mr. Levi Eshkol, minister of finance, Jerusalem (later prime minister); Mr. Abba Eban, minister of education, Jerusalem (later deputy prime minister); Mr. Aharon Becker, secretary-general of the Histadrut, Tel Aviv; Mr. John Shaw, first secretary for economic affairs, The American Embassy, Tel Aviv (with Mr. John Button of the U. S. Embassy's staff); Dr. Feurst, Union Bank, Tel Aviv; Dr. E. Lehmann, Bank Leumi Le'Israel, Tel Aviv; the late Professor G. Racah, rector and acting president of The Hebrew University, Jerusalem; Mr. H. Smith, Central Bureau of Statistics, Jerusalem; Mr. Theodore Kollek, director general, Office of the Prime Minister, Jerusalem. They were proud of the Israeli young men trained in the Project.

In a talk with Steele Gow, Mr. Eshkol, who was to become Prime Minister of Israel, expressed his hope that the Project would become a part of The Hebrew University and that it would be authorized to do research that would relate Israel's economy to the other countries of the Middle East and give Israel a chance to share what her economists learned with these neighboring states. When Mr. Gow reported this hope of Mr. Eshkol to the Advisory Committee and to his Board of Managers they agreed that to continue the Project was vital.

※ ※ ※ ※ ※

Those who wanted the Project to become part of another institution or organization, rather than continue to have independent status, without exception suggested The Hebrew University of Jerusalem as the institution to which the Project should be linked. Israel was proud of its University and—as Mr. Gow and others had found—justly so.

For two thousand years, ever since their dispersion, the Jewish people had cherished the hope of reestablishing a great center of learning in Jerusalem. Thirty years before the State of Israel was founded, in 1918, atop Mt. Scopus the foundations were laid on twelve cornerstones symbolic of the Twelve Tribes of Israel—and in April 1925 the doors were opened for teaching and research. In spite of the cutting off of Mt. Scopus during the War of Independence in 1948, classes and work had continued in makeshift quarters elsewhere in Jerusalem until in 1954 the new campus in Jerusalem was created

Mrs. Hosida Nitzan, secretary of the Falk Project in Israel—view of the southern Jerusalem hills in background, 1960.

to unify the faculties and gather in the great National Library of the Jewish people. The distinguished faculty today includes men and women with degrees and reputations earned at European and American universities and at The Hebrew University itself. The University has been affectionately and proudly supported by Jews throughout the world, especially by a group known as American Friends of The Hebrew University. By all standards and measurements it is deemed equal to universities anywhere.

It was clear that the University would give the Falk Project a permanency of highest standards and support within and without the University, with the freedom to develop accorded to scholarship and learning. Mr. Gow, by reason of his own background of educational administration, was eminently fitted to measure the University's educational stature, and his conclusions were respected by the Foundation Board:

In academic circles throughout the world The Hebrew University's standards are regarded as comparing favorably with those of the leading institutions of higher education.

Judging from the members of the faculty whom I was privileged to meet, I should say that the University has a truly distinguished staff of teachers and scholars. This is notably so in the fields of archeology, Jewish studies, and medicine, and is well on the way to being so in the fields of both the modern physical and social sciences. The men I met from the faculty of the Department of Economics would compare very favorably with men from the departments of economics of the best universities in our own country.

All in all, I regard The Hebrew University as a first-rate and dynamic institution that is destined to play a larger and larger role in the progress of Israel.

The Director's confidence for the future of the Project agreed with a consensus of the Advisory Committee and with individuals in the United States and in Israel who were competent to evaluate the Project's past and to plan its future.

Mr. Gow made his report to the Board at a dinner meeting, March 28, 1962, and they came promptly to the following decision, as reported in the official minutes:

In response to the report by the Executive Director it was moved, seconded, and unanimously voted that it be recorded as the consensus of this meeting that the Foundation is prepared (1) to receive and take action on a specific plan to effect a jointure between the Falk Project for Economic Research in Israel and The Hebrew University of Jerusalem and (2) subject to its approval of a jointure plan, to vote an endowment grant of $500,000 for the Project conditional on the raising of an additional endowment of not less than $500,000 for the Project by The Hebrew University or by American Friends of The Hebrew University.

Dr. Guilio Racah, at the time of the Gows's visit, was rector (equivalent to American *provost*) and acting president at The Hebrew University. He was born in Italy, and had been a nuclear physicist associated with the late Enrico Fermi, who played a leading role in the splitting of the atom during World War II. The Gows found him a friendly and charming host.

Mr. Gow's letter of April 2, 1962, to Professor Racah, explained to him the Board's decision as follows:

As a result of this motion the Foundation is now prepared to receive your reaction to the memorandum entitled "Proposed Relationship between the Falk Project for Economic Research in Israel and The Hebrew University of Jerusalem" which Dr. Simon Kuznets, chairman of the U. S. Advisory Committee for the Falk Project, sent to you with a covering letter dated March 19, 1962. If the Hebrew University gives this Proposal its approval the document can come before the Board of the Foundation at an early meeting for the Board's action.

[Word has just reached the Foundation of the death of Professor Racah as a result of an accident in Italy. "His death," Mr. Gow said immediately, "marks a great loss to the University and to Israel."]

The matching funds were guaranteed by the University through the American Friends of The Hebrew University. And in June 1962 the news media announced the establishment of The Maurice Falk Institute for Economic Research in Israel as a division of The Hebrew University of Jerusalem. A Foundation dinner in Pittsburgh honoring Eliahu Elath, who had recently been named president of the University, was attended by all the members of the United States Advisory Committee for the Project; officers of the Falk Foundation; the heads of Pittsburgh colleges and universities and foundations;

Publications in both Hebrew and English supply essential data on Israeli economy.

representatives of American Friends of The Hebrew University; and business and cultural leaders of Pittsburgh. Dr. Elath accepted the Falk grant, formally, and reported that he had received the matching funds. He expressed the confidence shared by those familiar with the economic studies in Israel that the stout support of the Foundation would continue to attract other aid to the educational and research programs of the University. He congratulated those who had worked and advised during the ten-year Project for the realization of the twofold aim—to publish in both Hebrew and English the results of sound research over a broad field of economic concern for the nation, and to train Israeli scholars to participate in the Maurice Falk Institute for Economic Research in Israel.

And so the work which began with two Falk grants-in-aid, totaling $814,575 over a ten-year period, continued under a Falk endowment grant of $500,000, matched by $500,000 gathered by the American Friends of The Hebrew University.

The United States Advisory Committee was replaced by an Israeli Board of Trustees. Guilio Racah, rector of The Hebrew University of Jerusalem, a post which continues through changes of presidency, became chairman of the Board and *ex officio* a member, along with David Horowitz, chairman of the executive committee of the University's Eliezer Kaplan School of Economics and Social Sciences; Jacob Katz, dean of the School; Michael Michaely, chairman of the Department of Economics; and Don Patinkin, director of research. The representatives of the University faculty on the Board are Roberto Bachi, professor of statistics and demography; Shmuel N. Eisenstadt, professor of sociology; and Haim Halperin, professor of agricultural economics. The public is represented on the Board by Yaakov Arnon, director general, Ministry of Finance; Yitshak Elam, general manager,

Koor Industries and Crafts Company, Ltd.; David Kochav, head, Economic Planning Authority, Office of the Prime Minister; Ernst Lehmann, joint general manager, Bank Leumi Le'Israel (vice chairman of the executive committee of the Institute); Dan Tolkowsky, executive manager, Discount Bank Investment Corp., Ltd.; and Simon Kuznets, professor of economics, Harvard University. (Professor Kuznets is a liaison with the earlier Project.)

On firm foundations, with careful selection of personnel, and the eager, dedicated spirit that pervades the business, governmental, and cultural life of Israel, study and publication go forward—seeking a healthy economy for Israel and for her neighbors whose welfare and progress depend on the welfare and progress of Israel. Experts and casual visitors have recognized what sound economic planning has meant to the young nation. Many observers and students have said that the pattern fashioned under the Falk Project can be helpful in working out the economic structure of other young emerging nations in Africa and Asia.

Certainly, Israel can say as did its forebears long ago, "The lines are fallen unto me in pleasant places; yea I have a goodly heritage." And it certainly may be that the wisdom and generosity of Maurice Falk and the cooperation of his friends and of the officers of his Foundation have helped make this so.

CHAPTER SIX

Economic Research in Colleges and Universities

When the Falk Foundation decided to concentrate its resources for a time on grants to economic research, the Managers and the Director were under no illusion that they had entered upon an easy task. To be sure there was growing recognition that economic study was necessary and fundamental—that the economic health of a nation as of an individual was a strong factor in determining a wholesome way of life. But the social sciences enter controversial areas, and the Foundation recognized that it was unlikely the findings or recommendations of any economic study would please everybody.

The Foundation policy was to make as sure as possible that grants were made to expert and reliable researchers and that financial support would never mean control of methods or conclusions. Neither did the Foundation expect that appropriations of funds for any study, however fundamental, would magically produce a panacea for economic ills. Rather its officers had faith that research institutions and personnel meriting the respect of specialists and the public would provide knowledge that could be used intelligently for the free choice and development of national and human welfare.

Following its initial grant to Brookings Institution in 1932 the Foundation made grants for economic research to educational institutions as well as to agencies of research set up for immediate or long-term projects.

❧ ❧ ❧ ❧ ❧

The first grant to an educational institution was to the University of Pittsburgh for a study, "Economics of the Iron and Steel Industry."

The Bureau of Business Research had been functioning at the University since 1924. An eight-year grant-in-aid from The Buhl Foundation of Pittsburgh in 1929 had made possible a staff and a program of regional economic research and analysis which the University still continues as a service to business and education in the Pittsburgh area. The Falk grant, which the University applied for in February 1934, was to supplement an initial smaller grant to the Bureau from the Brookings Institution for this special iron and steel industrial study.

Brookings, under a grant from the Rockefeller Foundation, was studying the effects on American business of the National Industrial Recovery Act—a code adopted in the depth of the depression and functioning for four years. The Brookings policy was to have specific industry studies made, as far as possible, where the industry was concentrated. And so Brookings commissioned the University of Pittsburgh's Bureau of Business Research to study specifically the effects of the Recovery Act and the Recovery Administration on the iron and steel industry.

The Falk Foundation honored the University's request for a grant of $26,000, which eventually was increased by two smaller grants to a total of $33,500. The University matched the two smaller grants and supplied other support to the study.

The project was under the personal supervision of Dr. Ralph J. Watkins, director of the Bureau, an economist with a wide background in teaching and research at other important educational institutions, and who later became director of economic research for Brookings Institution. His staff, chosen for this study, was composed of Dr. Melvin de Chazeau of the University of Virginia, Dr. Samuel S. Stratton of the Harvard School of Business Administration, and Dr. Carroll Daugherty of the University of Pittsburgh—all outstanding economists who have followed their careers to pinnacles of success in subsequent years. They were assisted by other senior and junior members of the Bureau staff.

The study was in progress when the Recovery Act was declared unconstitutional by the United States Supreme Court in May 1935. The Bureau staff decided to broaden the study to analyze long-run tendencies in the iron and steel industry, and the Foundation and the University approved expending the grant for the larger purpose.

The results of the investigations and the conclusions of the individual scholars were reported publicly in a paper read by Dr. Watkins at a Foundation dinner meeting, February 15, 1937. The dinner was attended by board and staff members of the Falk Foundation, of Brookings Institution, and of the University; by officials of the iron and steel industries, local and national; by other foundations' officials; by editors and publishers of the three Pittsburgh newspapers and of national business and general public media of communication. The substance of the report was—for 1937 at least—revolutionary and controversial. Many who heard it and many who reported it expressed severe criticism of its recommendations, which they said fitted facts to a social philosophy which challenged private enterprise. Others considered its provocative recommendations timely and useful. Most of the adverse criticism arose from the conclusions reached in the labor section of the study which recommended that the existing steel craft unions be broadened to become an industry-wide union.

66

The study was published in two volumes, 1,200 pages, by McGraw-Hill Book Company. Even among those who took issue with the conclusions there was wide approval for the sponsors, who demonstrated by their grants respect for the right of research to be free of interference or control—allowing the results to stand or fall on their own merits.

    ℳ   ℳ   ℳ   ℳ   ℳ

A later grant was made to the University of Pittsburgh in 1953 to "strengthen economic education in public, private, and parochial secondary schools"—a small grant to supplement other support for a summer workshop.

A workshop in economic education had been organized by the University, sponsored by the Tri-State Area School Study Council and the National Council on Economic Education—councils fostered by administrators and teachers in secondary education for whom the University's School of Education was a secretariate. Contributions from business firms and from other foundations raised the total support of the Workshop to $20,000. Fifty selected teachers and administrators from schools in the tri-state area of Pennsylvania, Ohio, and West Virginia attended the Workshop housed at Shady Side Academy from June 22 through July 10, 1953. The program of the work sessions summarized their importance to economic education. It includes the names of leaders in education, business management, and labor, outlines the topics studied and discussed, and describes the purpose of the Workshop thus:

The main objective of the workshop was to give public school teachers and administrators a clear overall view of the structure and functional operation of the American economy through direct contact with professional economists from the academic world and practical men of affairs from business, labor organizations, government, and research organizations. A second objective of the workshop was to help teachers devise instructional materials which would be of practical value in improving economic education in their classrooms in the public schools of the region. The third purpose of the workshop was to provide the opportunity for school and community leaders to work together and to develop a practicable plan for a continuing study of the problems of curricular improvement generally and economic education in particular.

࿓ ࿓ ࿓ ࿓ ࿓

In June 1951 Professor William T. Hogan, S. J. of Fordham University asked the Falk Foundation for a grant of $15,000 to organize and distribute for teaching in economics courses in college classrooms materials on the interdependence throughout American industries. The grant was made conditional on Fordham's gathering additional funds which together with the Falk grant would provide an annual budget of not less than $10,000.

The course, with text and illustrations, showed how growth in one industry stimulates and conditions growth in other industries. In the beginning five industries were selected to teach how their interdependence had formed an economic fabric over the years: steel, automobiles, railroads, petroleum, and electricity.

Stimulated by the Falk grant, which constituted an endorsement of the objectivity of the research, grants came from other foundations and from industries. When the fourth and final payment of the Falk grant was made in 1954, continued support for research and distribution was assured and seventy-seven colleges and universities had adopted the course and were using the publications and text developed by the Rev. J. Franklin Ewing at Fordham University.

࿓ ࿓ ࿓ ࿓ ࿓

In 1958 a Foundation grant of $76,500 and in 1961 another grant of $70,000 were made to The American Assembly, an independent organization affiliated with Columbia University.

The Assembly had been established in 1950 by Dwight D. Eisenhower when he was president of Columbia, to analyze, discuss, and report the vital public issues of the day. It met at Arden House, Harriman, New York, for its principal conference, which was followed by regional sessions around the country. The conferees were selected from leadership of industry, banking, labor, government, agriculture, education, communications, and other professions and occupations from all parts of the nation, and they represented varying points of view. From 1951 to 1958 the Assembly had published reports on state government, agriculture, the Far East, economic security, atomic energy, United Nations, Africa, foreign aid, and other topics of the discussions.

The Fifteenth Assembly of 1958, which discussed the subject "Wages, Prices, Profits, and Productivity," was financed by the Falk grant. The Arden House conferences for three days discussed the working papers which had been prepared before the conference and sent to subsections of the conferees in ample time for their study and reflection. The papers covered the subjects "Productivity and Wages: The Concepts and the Data"; "Patterns of Behavior of Wages, Prices, and Productivity"; Government Policy and Economic Environment"; "The Impact of Management Policy, Collective Bargaining, and Labor Movements"; "Experience of Other Countries with Wage-Price-Productivity Relationships"; "Choices for Policy in the United States." On the fourth day a synthesis which was the result of panel discussion was adopted. The background papers were published and sent to regional assemblies in the South,

Midwest, and Far West, which followed the plan set at Arden House for discussion and adoption.

The second grant, made to the Assembly in 1961, was for meetings to consider the present and future effects of automation on the lives of people in the United States and on the institutions that compose society. Besides financing the sessions of the Assembly at Arden House, the grant covered the cost of publication and of the regional assemblies following the united sessions. Contributions to the report published were those of Robert L. Heilbroner, author of *The Worldly Philosophers, The Future as History,* and other important books and articles; Lee A. DuBridge, president of the California Institute of Technology; Richard N. Cooper of the staff of the President's Council of Economic Advisors; Henry M. Wriston, chairman of the Board of The American Assembly; and others. The report, "Automation and Technological Change," was edited by John T. Dunlop, professor of economics at Harvard University.

These grants were made in the hope that they would stimulate further explorations on equally important economic problems by leaders in diversified professions and endeavors vital to American economic progress— and they did.

᪐ ᪐ ᪐ ᪐ ᪐

In October 1959 a Falk grant of $15,000 was made to the School of Advanced International Studies (Washington, D. C.) of The Johns Hopkins University to support studies of the economic status and development of foreign countries. The School offered training and research in international affairs under the direction of its dean, Francis O. Wilcox, an assistant secretary of state and for many years a leader of wide experience in international affairs. A branch of the School at

Bologna, Italy, was a center for immediate study of European economics.

Director Gow's *1959-1960 Biennial Report* thus describes the work financed by the Foundation:

> The studies are designed to serve the multiple objective of devising a more meaningful method of evaluating and comparing national economies, providing data on optimum rates of economic growth, producing guidelines for a more effective orientation of the American program of aid to foreign countries, and comparing the advantages of Western economies with those of the Soviet-system economies as a means toward economic development.

Other foundations, including Ford, Rockefeller, W. K. Kellogg, and Carnegie Corporation, contributed to a financing of the program for ten years. The Falk Foundation, pleased with the project and the use made of its grant, and confident that the program was assured future support, explained in a letter to Milton Eisenhower, president of The Johns Hopkins University, why the Falk Foundation could make no further grants. Mr. Gow explained the Foundation's decision to prepare for winding up its affairs in the next four years, as its Charter provided, and to concentrate in this final period on cultural and educational projects at home, in Pittsburgh.

᪥   ᪥   ᪥   ᪥   ᪥

Another grant complementary to studies of the economic structure in a foreign country had been made by the Foundation in February 1954.

In response to a request from Erwin N. Griswold, dean of the Law School, Harvard University, the Foundation granted $10,000 to support the Harvard Law School-Israel Cooperation Research Project for Israel's Legal Development. The project had been set up at

Harvard to cooperate with the Ministry of Justice in the State of Israel. Recognizing that research in the legal field would enhance the beneficial results of the Falk Foundation's larger commitment to support economic research in Israel, the Board made the grant to a study at Harvard which won larger support from other sources and resulted in important publications.

*   *   *   *   *

Other grants made to educational institutions for professorships, classroom buildings, and other facilities for the teaching of the social relationships and their problems will be described in subsequent chapters. The grants discussed here to five educational institutions in support of economic study and teaching helped promote grants from other philanthropic sources and so were instrumental in bringing substantial encouragement to the free inquiry which is the lifeblood of the truly democratic way of life.

CHAPTER SEVEN

Economic Research by
Independent Agencies

In September 1933, about twenty months after the Falk Foundation made its initial grant to the Brookings Institution, the Foundation Board of Managers authorized the first of four grants to the National Bureau of Economic Research, Inc., New York—grants which eventually totaled $496,700.

The National Bureau, a nonprofit corporation for study in economics and social sciences, since its establishment in 1920 had committed its resources to the scientific collection and appraisal of basic facts and theories relating to specific economic problems, without attempting to recommend actions for solving the problems the study brought to light. Its research had provided important source material for public administrators and businessmen in trade and industry, and for professional students of economics.

The first Falk Foundation grant to the National Bureau ($15,000) was made without assignment to any specific project. But the grant enabled the National Bureau to receive $75,000 a year from the Rockefeller Foundation—granted if $25,000 could be raised from other sources. Thus a Falk grant helped to stimulate other support.

Shortly after payment of the Falk Foundation grant was made the National Bureau asked permission to use it for bringing to the research staff a German economist displaced from a German institution by political crises in Germany. The Foundation Board was especially favorable to having Falk funds make possible the appointment.

Dr. Eugen Altschul, privat-dozent at the University of Frankfort and head of the Frankfurter Gesellschaft fur Konundtur forshung, was appointed to the National Bureau staff. He had organized a team of young investigators who under his supervision had made distinguished contributions to the study of economic fluctuations.

At the National Bureau Dr. Altschul was to study the relations between agricultural production and business cycles. Shortly after he arrived the Bureau arranged for him to direct, part time, a graduate seminar at the University of Minnesota. This post gave Professor Altschul a chance to study at close range the Middle West —a significant sector of American agriculture.

The University of Minnesota underwrote part of Dr. Altschul's salary—and so some of the Falk grant could be used to bring a second displaced German economist to the National Bureau. Dr. Fritz Strauss, also from the University of Frankfort, joined the Bureau staff. And the Foundation *Minutes* record a double use of the grant: important research and sponsorship of refugee scholars.

The National Bureau published the results of the Altschul-Strauss study in a 1937 Bulletin with the title, "Agriculture and the Business Cycle." The Falk Foundation, as was its practice, helped with the distribution of this and subsequent National Bureau books and pamphlets published from research made possible by Falk grants to the National Bureau. Frequently, books were summarized in pamphlets which the Foundation, in accord with its usual policy, purchased for free distribution to individuals and to educational institutions and organizations "provided they did not engage in efforts to influence legislation."

The same year, 1937, under a Falk grant of $30,000,

which in the next few years, as the scope of the study widened, was increased to a total of $217,500, the National Bureau published the first in a series of volumes reporting research studies of output, employment, and productivity of American industry, agriculture, and services. The first, *The Output of Manufacturing Industries,*

Publications of the National Bureau of Economic Research, Inc., New York, to which Falk Foundation grants contributed funds for research.

1899-1937, was followed in the next two decades with publications of studies of mining, agriculture, public service, education, and others. A few were published by the Princeton University Press; the majority, by the National Bureau itself. All those which were the fruit of research under Falk Foundation grants are listed in the Appendix of this history.

The author of the first book in the series was Solomon Fabricant, a Columbia University Doctor of Philosophy, who had been a member of the National Bureau staff since 1935 and was the author of earlier and subsequent economic studies, both books and articles in the *Occasional Papers,* a brochure published by the Bureau. The National Bureau research staff was composed of about twenty outstanding economists. When Dr. Fabricant became director of research in 1953, he succeeded Dr. Arthur F. Burns, another Columbia Doctor of Philosophy who had taught on the campuses of several institutions which are leaders in economic education: Lehigh, Dartmouth, Brown, Swarthmore, Chicago. Dr. Burns and his predecessor as director of research, Wesley C. Mitchell, also a Columbia Doctor of Philosophy, worked with Dr. Leo Wolman, Dr. Frederick C. Mills, and Dr. N. I. Stone in direction of the studies. Prominent economists—Dr. Harold Barger from Cambridge University and the London School of Economics; Dr. Hans H. Landsberg, who had studied economics at Freiburg, Berlin, Heidelburg, the London School of Economics, and Columbia; Sam H. Schurr, who had studied economics at Rutgers and Columbia; Jacob M. Gould, Columbia Doctor of Philosophy; and George J. Stigler, Chicago Doctor of Philosophy—were among the distinguished authors of studies in the series. And in the course of their careers they later served as economic advisors in government agencies and published widely in their special fields of knowledge.

The third grant to the National Bureau ($164,200) was made in 1957 to finance an investigation of the effects of public and private pension systems on savings and investments in the United States. Mr. Gow's *Biennial Report 1957-1958* presents the problem clearly:

Pension plans are not all of a piece. Taking account of the objectives set for their investment programs and the legal and institutional conditions under which the programs are carried out, one can distinguish at least four types: (1) The pension funds set up by the federal government are required by law to invest only in federal obligations or bonds guaranteed by the federal government; (2) The reserves of insured private pension plans, maintained by insurance companies for group annuities and individual policy pension trusts, are invested along with other reserves in the total pool of insurance company assets which consist very largely of fixed-income securities including mortgages; (3) Self-administered private pension plans, which have grown very rapidly, have been heavy purchasers of corporate securities, including equities (About 27 per cent of the new money obtained through the issuance of common stock in 1954 was made available by these pension funds.); (4) The funds set up in connection with the retirement programs established for the employees of state and local governments concentrate very largely on bonds, governmental and corporate.

To understand what difference in financial operations is made by the growth of pension funds it is essential to consider not only how pension funds invest but also how their practices compare with the investment patterns of other financial institutions through which savings are channeled. Even the most thorough investigation could not, on the basis of existing data, answer with precision and confidence all of the complex questions involved, but it is believed that substantial progress can be made.

The pension study was conducted by Professor Robert F. Murray and his associates, Professor David M. Holland of the School of Industrial Management of Massachusetts Institute of Technology and Professor Philip D. Cogan of Brown University. After six years of intensive research and painstaking checking with many other authorities, the Bureau hopes to publish the pension study in two volumes in 1965 or 1966. Meantime a draft summary featured in the *National Bureau Annual Report of 1964* has been subjected to the usual careful scrutiny and possible revisions of the text for the volumes.

In all Foundation records—*Biennial Reports, Minutes,* correspondence with economists inside and outside the Bureau, and other pertinent files—a unity prevails. Again and again are emphasized the confidence held by the Foundation and professional economists in the ability of the Bureau staff, individually and as a team, and the widening influence of their research on the application of economic information to national problems in business and public affairs.

Among the terminal grants anticipating the liquidation of the Foundation a grant of $100,000 was made to the National Bureau of Economic Research in December 1963 for general support of the Bureau's programs.

    🙠   🙠   🙠   🙠   🙠

The amounts expended by the Falk Foundation for grants to economic research and to distribute resulting publications increased during the 1940's as the problems of postwar economy and costs of military defense multiplied. The total program of economic research for which the Foundation concentrated its grants in the 1930's consistently reflected the care and thought which those directing Foundation affairs applied to the selection of projects to support, and to selection of the agencies to plan and carry through the research. The grants had a unity of purpose which made each grant a logical supplement of the ones preceding and following, in a scheme which kept research up-to-date as new needs and fresh problems arose.

    🙠   🙠   🙠   🙠   🙠

The Brookings Institution and the National Bureau of Economic Research, Inc. were well into their Falk-supported economic studies when requests for research funds came to the Foundation from two *ad hoc* organizations, the Committee on Postwar Tax (later renamed the Committee on Federal Tax Policy) and the Committee on Public Debt Policy.

Early in 1944, under the leadership of Dr. Henry M.

Tax and debt studies were made with Falk Foundation grants by independent bodies of experts. They discussed major problems facing the American people.

Wriston, president of Brown University, an independent body of lawyers, tax accountants, and professors of economics and of finance organized the Committee on Postwar Tax Policy to accomplish five objectives which they outlined thus:

To develop a simple, productive and reasonably equitable tax system, having in mind primarily the federal government, but having due regard, also, to the needs and the fiscal independence of the states. Changes in the tax system of the federal government may in turn require changes in the pattern of state and local taxes. The primary concern of the project should be the tax program of the federal government. A comprehensive attack on the problem of federal-state-tax coordination is an undertaking too great to be included within the time and financial limits here contemplated. Adequate treatment of the federal tax problem will necessarily involve, however, some consideration of state and local taxation.

To formulate and recommend methods of taxation that will, so far as possible, assure stability of revenues under varying business conditions.

To recommend taxes that will meet all reasonable and necessary federal budgetary requirements, including provision for systematic reduction of the federal debt.

To propose such changes and improvements of definitions and procedures as will promote, in the greatest degree possible, simplicity and clarity in the tax laws, and as will enable the average citizen to determine his tax liability without the need of spending for costly books and expert services.

To seek such distribution of the tax burden as will most effectively preserve and promote the vigor and vitality of the private enterprise system. In this connection the tax problems of little business should receive special attention.

The committee was composed of the late Roswell Magill, chairman, one of the great tax scholars of this generation, professor of law at Columbia University, former under-secretary of the Treasury, and member of the Board of Trustees of the Tax Foundation; Walter A. Cooper, past chairman of the Committee on Federal

Taxation of the American Institute of Accountants, officer and director of the New York State Society of Accountants, and member of the Advisory Committee to United States Treasury on Corporate Income Taxes; Fred R. Fairchild, Knox Professor of Economics at Yale University, former president of the National Tax Association, and former vice-president of the American Economic Association; Rowland R. Hughes, comptroller of the National City Bank of New York, member of the Tax Committee of the National Foreign Trade Council, and vice chairman of the Tax Committee of the New York Clearing House Association; Thomas N. Tarleau, formerly tax legislative counsel of the United States Treasury and legal assistant to the under-secretary of the Treasury, and member of the Income Tax Committee and Committee on International and Double Taxation of the American Bar Association. Dr. Harley L. Lutz, professor of public finance at Princeton University, served as director of the Committee's research; he had been director or advisor for a number of public tax commissions and was president of the National Tax Association. Alfred Parker served as associate director. These men were to supervise the study and recommend a program. The Committee was to disband as soon as its project was finished.

At the Committee's request the Falk Foundation in 1944 appropriated $100,000 for the project. And the report, *A Tax Program for a Solvent America,* was published in 1945 by the Ronald Press Company.

In December 1946 the Foundation Board voted an additional grant of $19,300 to allow the Committee to give attention to "basic structural changes of a technical nature in the tax laws which had not been treated in the original report." This supplementary report, the final work, was published February 1947.

The Committee's conclusions were that the best hope

for the future of the country lies in the maintenance and growth of the free enterprise system, and that for this reason taxes, even burdensome ones, are necessary to maintain public service and help retire debt. The Committee recommended structural improvements in the tax laws, especially as they relate to gifts and wills and the like. And it recommended improvements in the Internal Revenue Code to improve its operation and make the laws and the Code more understandable to the general public.

In 1950 the same committee with a new title, Committee on Federal Tax Policy, was granted $63,240 to bring its proposals up-to-date again. The title of their report, *Financing Defense: The Tax Program,* explains why the *ad hoc* study of 1944-1945 had to be reactivated. For the third time in a generation the nation was forced to assume the burden of a costly military program, and the dangers of deficit financing demonstrated during and following the two World Wars showed the need for careful consideration of broader-based federal taxes from individuals and corporations and for careful planning by government personnel.

ᴊ   ᴊ   ᴊ   ᴊ   ᴊ

At the November 1945 meeting of the Foundation Board, Director Gow recommended that the Foundation interest itself in financing a study of managing the public debt, and he requested authority to explore the possibilities of encouraging the organization of a committee similar in structure to the Committee on Postwar Tax Policy, whose initial studies had just been published. Director Gow also suggested W. Randolph Burgess, vice chairman of the Board of the National City Bank of New York, as probably the best man to chair such a committee. The Foundation Board unanimously approved the exploration, and E. T. Weir expressed enthusiasm toward the idea of persuading Randolph Burgess to organize a study of the public debt.

Mr. Burgess' distinguished career had won him the confidence of leaders in many walks of American life—industry and business, banking, public affairs, scholarship. He was a graduate of Brown University with a Doctor of Philosophy degree from Columbia University. He had served in executive positions at the Russell Sage Foundation, the New York Federal Reserve Bank, the American Academy of Political Science, and the leading banking associations, local and national. He was a member of the boards of the Mutual Life Insurance Company, the National City Bank, Brown University, Columbia University, the Carnegie Corporation, the American Academy of Political Science, and the American Historical Association—and the author of treatises on American fiscal affairs, both scholarly and popular.

Dr. Burgess recruited a group of men qualified for membership on the Committee, which promptly elected him chairman.

The Foundation Board of Managers agreed unanimously, in February 1946, to grant $100,000 to the *ad hoc* Committee on Public Debt Policy for a series of studies which it was expected could be published at intervals within the next two years.

John S. Sinclair, executive vice president of the New York Life Insurance Company, served as vice chairman of the Committee, and Donald B. Woodward, research assistant to the president of the Mutual Life Insurance Company of New York, served as secretary.

Other members of the Committee were General Leonard P. Ayres, Cleveland Trust Company, Cleveland, Ohio; Daniel W. Bell, president of The American Security Trust Company of Washington, D. C. and former under-secretary of the Treasury; E. E. Brown, president of the First National Bank of Chicago; Lewis W. Douglas, president of the Mutual Life Insurance Company of New York; Marion B. Folsom, treasurer of the Eastman Kodak Company, Rochester, New York; Robert L. Garner, treasurer of the General Foods Corporation, New York City; Harold M. Groves, professor of economics, University of Wisconsin; B. U. Ratchford, professor of economics, Duke University; Earl B. Schulst, executive vice president of The Bowery Savings Bank; G. Willard Smith, president of the Burlington Savings Bank, Burlington, Vermont; and Lee Wiggins, businessman and banker of Hartsville, South Carolina.

Consultants to the committee included Professor C. C. Abbott, Graduate School of Business Administration, Harvard University; Sherwin Badger, financial secretary of the New England Mutual Life Insurance Company; Professor B. H. Beckhart, Columbia University, director of research of the Chase National Bank; Dr. Jules Bogen, New York University, editor of the *New York Journal of Commerce;* S. M. Foster, economic advisor of the New York Life Insurance Company; Dr. Marcus Nadler, Graduate School of Business Administration, New York University; Roy L. Reierson, assistant vice president, Bankers Trust Company; George B. Roberts, vice president of The National City Bank of New York; and Murray Shields, vice president of The Bank of Manhattan Company.

The director of research was Professor James J. O'Leary, Wesleyan University, Middletown, Connecticut.

During the time of the separate phases of the study, five members were replaced: Messrs. Wiggins, Douglas, and Garner resigned to accept important public offices; Professor Groves resigned because of the pressure of his university duties; and Brigadier General Ayres died soon after writing a section of the study.

Seven phases of the complete study were first distributed as separate pamphlets—twelve thousand of each by the Foundation, as was its usual policy concerning studies made under Falk grants—and many more thousands were sold by the Committee's agency at nominal cost. Finally, all seven were gathered and published in a book, in 1949, by Harcourt Brace and Company, Inc. The titles of the separate pamphlets and their authors were: "Our National Debt after Great Wars," Leonard P. Ayres; "The Debt and the Budget," Dr. Benjamin U. Ratchford; "The Debt and the Banks," Dr. Roy L. Reierson; "The Debt and Interest Rates," Dr. James J. O'Leary; "The Debt and our Savings," Mrs. Eleanor S. Bagley, Stephen M. Foster, and Dr. O'Leary; "The Debt and Life Insurance," Sherwin C. Badger; and "The Debt and the National Welfare," W. Randolph Burgess and George B. Roberts. The entire committee and its advisors assumed responsibility for the conclusions, and the technical language was edited by Messrs. John W. Love, Samuel T. Williamson, and George B. Roberts to make the book readable for the public.

In the final chapter the Committee summarized the five basic steps which it considered essential to successful management of the debt—control the budget, reduce the debt, distribute the debt more widely, restore flexible interest rates, nourish a dynamic economy.

The reports following distribution of the book included favorable reviews and comments from competent professional sources. The Committee thanked Director Gow and the Foundation Board for "hearty, vigorous, and prompt support" to the study of a "major problem facing the American people during the next generation." They reported also that the individual pamphlets and the book had "run the gauntlet of professional opinion" and that queries from government officials, especially in the Treasury department, showed that the study was influencing people in the government councils.

❧　❧　❧　❧　❧

Another study, crucial in this time of rapid economic change, was started in October 1947 and published in November 1948 under a Falk Foundation grant of $10,500 to the Foundation for Economic Education, Inc. at Irvington-on-Hudson, New York. Dr. Leo Wolman, a member of the staff of the National Bureau of Economic Research, made the study and wrote the booklet, "Industry-Wide Bargaining."

Dr. Wolman was eminently suited for an objective research on this subject because of his wide experience in scholarly study and teaching at the universities of Johns Hopkins and Michigan and at the School of Social Research, and because of studies he made for the Amalgamated Clothing Workers of America, 1920-1931.

In substance the booklet was a detailed description of the issues raised by the position of unionism, which had changed radically in a decade from a system of bargaining with a single employer to dealing with an entire industry acting as a unit. Along with change had arisen many problems of costs and prices and other matters affecting the general public interest. It brought up the question, which the study explored, whether uniting of labor dealing with an industry which was widely located, although its labor problems were primarily local concerns, might force uniting of employers and in time break down the antimonopoly policy and thus be a step toward a regulated or planned economy. It gave a clear exposition of the problems which up to this time had been written about considerably, but treated only casually and moderately and without a thoroughly rounded discussion of the issues raised by collective bargaining and its critical consequences if not dealt with thoughtfully.

Twenty thousand copies of the booklet circulated

widely, and the publication was reviewed in editorials and news stories and consulted by legislators and economists and by many interested in labor relations and labor policies and their effect on the public welfare.

* * * * *

The Foundation *Minutes* of October 8, 1959, record a grant of $250,000 to the American Jewish Committee to endow a research program to be known as the *Maurice Falk Studies*. This was the first of a series of grants to this program, which extended through the remaining years of the Foundation's life.

The American Jewish Committee, which had requested the grant through its executive vice president, Dr. John Slawson, was one of the oldest organizations in America, as its purpose stated, "devoted to eliminating the obstacles to full participation in the life of America which confront minority groups." Although its primary concern was to secure equal educational, economic, and social opportunity for Jews, it was also concerned with the freedoms and opportunities of all Americans, whatever their race or religion. Its resources were in the larger part devoted to education and research and the dissemination of publications resulting from the study among opinion moulders in education, industry, and professional organizations, such as the National Education Association and the writers and readers of business and industrial publications. Financial support came from diversified sources: foundations, individuals, and philanthropic organizations, Jewish and non-Jewish.

The American Jewish Committee had long been widely respected for the objectivity, thoroughness, and competence of its research, most of which was conducted on college campuses such as those of Columbia and Harvard. Its leaders and officers were men of eminence in various professions and businesses—such men as Louis Marshall, Julius Rosenwald, and Oscar Strauss.

The Maurice Falk Studies were to gather and distribute data on the effects of prejudice and discrimination on the American economy. Cases of prejudice had long been gathered and understood, but a study of the economic consequences of prejudicial attitudes and practices entered a new field of inquiry. The Foundation Board of Managers, however, told the Committee that although the Foundation's primary interest was on economic studies the use of the funds "need not be confined to the economic field."

The initial inquiries fostered by the Falk grant were conducted at Harvard, Michigan, California, and Cornell under the direction of highly competent research

Publications resulting from The Maurice Falk Studies, a research program of the American Jewish Committee: studies at Harvard, Michigan, California, Cornell, answering the question, "How do prejudices affect the American economy?"

scholars in economics, industrial management, political science, education, sociology, and psychology. There was also an excellent group of advisors for the studies. Publication of the results appeared from time to time in newspapers, magazines, and business journals such as the *Wall Street Journal* and the *Harvard Business Review*, and in popular publications such as *Time, Business Week*, and others.

The main question answered by the studies was "How do prejudices affect the American economy?" Emphasis was consistently on the point that aside from ethical implications, prejudices, whether acknowledged or merely of long-standing habit, were economic loss to the nation. Pools of highly trained and skilled graduates of the best colleges and technical schools were untapped resources to fill vacancies in management and executive positions.

The earliest Maurice Falk Studies of prejudice at the managerial level have become known as the "Executive Suite Studies," because they have revealed that many management heads have failed to hire or promote personnel from a minority group which they regard as unacceptable socially for the "executive suite," even when well-qualified for the elevation. The loss to the economic life of the nation was demonstrated objectively by the college and university scholars who made the studies. The list of studies by titles in the Appendix show their wide range and variety.

"The Ethnics of Executive Selection" by Lewis B. Ward in the *Harvard Business Review*, March-April 1965, is one illustration of the kind of article that in reprint and digest in the public press, circulating among corporation and business offices could influence wider understanding of the problem and its solution. In footnotes or otherwise the Falk Foundation was acknowledged in these publications as a donor for the study.

In December 1963, on Mr. Gow's recommendation, the Board of Managers unanimously voted two additional grants to the American Jewish Committee. The original grant of October 1959 allowed spending of the principal when necessary. A 1963 grant of $40,000 was "to restore the principal of the endowment of the Maurice Falk Studies to its full level of $250,000," with the understanding that hereafter only the income on the endowment would be drawn upon. And a non-endowment grant of $55,000 was added to support the Maurice Falk Studies to date.

Finally, in February 1965, in response to a proposal from Dr. John Slawson, executive vice president of the American Jewish Committee, the Falk Foundation granted $15,000 for preparation and publication of a special volume. This book is to report in a readable style that might "hold the interest of business leaders and the public at large" the essence of each "Executive Suite" study.

The Foundation has expressed approval of the Studies as a fitting memorial to Maurice Falk, whose deepest interests, as one of his friends has said, were with people "who daily strive to earn a living and a life of comfort, peace, and good will."

CHAPTER EIGHT

Appraisal of Program and
Distribution of Publications

The Maurice and Laura Falk Foundation celebrated its tenth anniversary on September 24, 1940, at a special dinner in the historic Hotel Schenley which is now the University of Pittsburgh Student Union. Maurice Falk, the founder, all members of the original Board of Managers, and the director of the Foundation entertained about four hundred guests: business and civic leaders; heads of other foundations; scholars from research institutions and colleges and universities; heads of local colleges and universities; journalists and authors, local and national; and many other friends of the Foundation. As chairman of the Board of Managers, Leon Falk, Jr. thanked all who had cooperated in the work of the Foundation and had encouraged and guided its program. Director J. Steele Gow reviewed briefly Falk Foundation policies and the activities of the first ten years, and said the Foundation anticipated that competent economic research necessary for the national well-being would continue to be supported by Falk grants. He said in part:

For ten years now we have been at work through grants to competent economic research organizations to finance definitive studies of specific problems affecting the development of American industry, trade, and finance. From the outset we have worked through existing research facilities. We have refrained from duplicating these facilities by establishing new organizations or by creating a research setup within our own organization. What was most needed, we believed, was the sharpening of existing facilities and not additions to their number.

I assured you that I would not this evening attempt an appraisal of our performance. The public must be the judge, ultimately, of whether we are serving it well. . . .

What studies we shall attempt in the future I can not say, because the picture of what problems are ahead for America is blurred and confused. Will our economy move ahead along established lines, or will the impact of the war require us to face in new directions and plot a future for America fitted to new conditions? Of one thing we can be sure. America's future will depend in no small measure on her economic soundness and the Falk Foundation's opportunity for service will be in proportion to the extent America's economy is beset by problems.

The Foundation this evening rededicates its resources and its energy to the promotion of progress in the American standard of living, and to the American people we shall hold ourselves constantly accountable for the trust we have accepted.

The program at the dinner featured the speeches of three economic leaders—men high in the esteem of their

Board of Managers and the Director, The Maurice and Laura Falk Foundation, on the Tenth Anniversary, September 24, 1940. Seated, left to right: Arthur E. Braun, Ernest T. Weir, Maurice Falk, Frank B. Bell. Standing, left to right: J. Steele Gow, Eugene B. Strassburger, Leon Falk, Jr., Nathan B. Jacobs, Israel A. Simon.

peers, authors of books and articles contributing to the public understanding of the economy of a democratic way of life. Two were eminent scholar-economists: Harold Moulton, president of Brookings Institution, Washington, D. C., and Leo Wolman, member of the research staff, National Bureau of Economic Research, New York City. Their institutions were recipients of Falk Foundation grants which have been discussed in earlier chapters. The third was Alfred P. Sloan, Jr., prominent industrialist and founder of the Alfred P. Sloan Foundation.

Dr. Moulton reported on the findings of a study made at the request of the United States War Department by Brookings scholar Charles O. Hardy under a grant from the Falk Foundation. Dr. Moulton's subject was "Wartime Price Control," and he reviewed and appraised the price controls during the First World War, analyzed the problems of these controls in relation to private enterprise, and recommended coordination of method and a unified program as most important for the present need. He had written many authoritative articles and pamphlets under Falk Foundation grants. He had an unusual capacity to interpret scientific research so that the average man could understand. And yet, he never popularized to the level of mediocrity. His speech bore out the promise of his writings.

Dr. Leo Wolman reported on the findings of a study by Solomon Fabricant of the National Bureau of Economic Research made and written under a Falk grant, *Output of Manufacturing Industries, 1899-1937.* His talk, "Physical Output and Efficiency of American Manufacturers," demonstrated that the four decades analyzed in the Fabricant book revealed a steady and accelerated increase of government activity touching business and industry which, he warned, if not consciously favorable to private enterprise might slow down industrial energy and multiply government obligations of support and of control, even in periods of advance and expansion for industry.

Alfred P. Sloan, Jr. had been chairman of General Motors Corporation and was a man of broad experience in the practical aspects of industry. His speech, direct and quotable in style, attracted the attention of the nation-wide press at a time when our country's gearing itself to supply war materials seemed to have opened up an era of prosperity. His subject was "The Economic State of the Nation." Most often the commentators in the public press and in business reviews quoted his warning, "Every dollar of defense orders means less for some of our people, somewhere and at some time . . . debts paid for partly today and partly passed on as a liability to the future generations."

Mr. Sloan's speech and the other speeches of that evening emphasized the need for objective economic study, and more than that, the need for economic education of the American people.

The anniversary dinner celebrated much more than a ten-year birthday. The many congratulations from the guests for Maurice Falk and the Board and the Foundation staff, and the editorials and news stories which reported the evening, were assurance that the ten years had been fruitful years and that the future, headed toward the twenty-five years remaining to the Foundation, held increased opportunity and increased responsibility for public service.

❧   ❧   ❧   ❧   ❧

About a year later Dr. Leo Wolman of the National Bureau of Economic Research, who had been one of the speakers at the Tenth Anniversary celebration, was invited to the Foundation Board Meeting of November

1941 to discuss with the Board the value of the program to which the Foundation had concentrated a major part of its resources for a decade.

Mr. Gow stated the problem which concerned the members of the Board and suggested the alternatives to be considered. Some, he said, were wondering whether in view of the wartime emergency and its attendant needs the Foundation should postpone making new grants for research until a return to more usual conditions. He summarized the time and money already invested in economic research by the Falk Foundation and suggested that to postpone might be unwise because "the Foundation might lose the momentum of the established program if economic research could be really helpful under the apparently discouraging conditions of the day."

Dr. Wolman said that the emergency was forcing too many issues to be settled on the basis of political considerations and that unless reliable economic study and dissemination of the knowledge gained continued somewhere, national catastrophe was ahead. He cited specific instances where tested research was helping effective government decision. And he stressed especially the need for continuous production of research to "feed reliable economic information to colleges, universities, and other institutions engaged in training future generations of leaders." It was important, he said, that teachers be supplied with sound information based on scientific research such as that the Foundation was supporting at the Brookings Institution and at the National Bureau of Economic Research. He stated frankly that a policy which deprived economic research of its tools would be short-sighted, no matter what the immediate emergency might demand in energy and cost.

The Foundation Board decided to meet the challenge and continue to invest in the long run. Grants continued during the war years to studies underway, and more were initiated which have been described in earlier chapters. The resulting publications served a teaching purpose immediately and in the long run. Economics and other social science departments in colleges and universities were finding textbooks out-of-date and were glad to have this new material. But the teaching, as was intended, reached a much broader audience than that bounded by a school campus. The publications were distributed to reach libraries, corporations, professional offices, and others of the reading public through newspaper and magazine reviews and digests.

⚜   ⚜   ⚜   ⚜   ⚜

Education is more, much more, than the training of an individual or a group of individuals in the formal setting of a school or within the planned body of courses of a specializing institution. It is the preparation for complete living—for the individual as he lives with himself, intellectually, morally, and spiritually—for the individual as he earns his daily bread, as he works and plays and gets along with others, within horizons that are stretched by widening demands and deeper satisfactions. Education begins with the beginning of life and continues until its end.

The grants which the Falk Foundation made to writing and publication of economic research were often made to inform and teach young people and their teachers on college or university campuses, but they were more often made to prepare and disseminate sound and tested information important to men and women beyond school years—those who were responsible for the business, professional, governmental, and social well-being of a people committed to a democratic way of life. Behind the dissemination of information in books and pamphlets and reports which the Foundation grants helped the experts to prepare and distribute were the several grants outlined in this section of the history. They were made for economic research by reliable institutions staffed with scholars and writers—men with the training and experience to make the study needed and the skill to communicate the findings to other specialists and, more important, to the average citizen.

The teaching value of the research consistently was held as important by the Foundation as the soundness of the research itself. Well over one-half million dollars financed the preparation of pamphlet-digests of studies in economics and other social sciences and the distribution of these pamphlets to specialized and general libraries and to organizations and individuals who could use them for the analyses, conclusions, and recommendations affecting the public welfare.

Beginning with 1935 and continuing throughout several years grants totaling $65,000 were made to the Public Affairs Committee, Inc. of New York City, at the request of its chairman Raymond Leslie Buell and its executive secretary Francis P. Miller, to prepare pamphlet-digests of economic and social science research studies which had been fostered by Falk Foundation grants and by grants from others.

In 1938 (to cite one instance of the Falk Foundation's way of making sure the educational value of the research was not overlooked) the Foundation bought and helped to distribute to industrial and educational personnel and the general public 125,000 copies of the pamphlet, "Industrial Price Politics and Economic Progress," which before digest in popular style under a Falk grant had been prepared for more technical users by the Brookings Institution.

The pamphlets published by the Public Affairs Committee for which Falk grants had helped pay the initial

97

costs eventually circulated in large enough quantities to pay their own way.

   ❧   ❧   ❧   ❧   ❧

The Alfred P. Sloan Foundation, much larger in resources than the Falk Foundation, was established in 1936 "to engage in general economic education as well as research."

On more than one occasion the Sloan Foundation matched Falk Foundation grants to the Public Affairs Committee for distribution of economic information. Both foundations shared an interest in communicating to as wide a reading public as possible the recommendations of sound economic research.

In 1947 the Falk Foundation cooperated with the

The value of research was emphasized by the Foundation's support to wide public distribution. These are *ad hoc* studies from Brookings Institution scholars with acknowledgment of Foundation grants in their colophons or their introductions.

Sloan Foundation by making an experimental grant to support a newer medium for even wider possible popular distribution of educational material than the printed page could offer.

For several years the Alfred P. Sloan Foundation had been experimenting with live-action motion pictures to disseminate an understanding of economics to the general public. They had not found the medium satisfactory. Now they were exploring the Disney-type animated cartoon and finding it better for the purpose. The films of the cartoons were made by a Hollywood producer to illustrate a script drafted by educational advisers in the Sloan Foundation. The Sloan Foundation then arranged with a distributor to have the films included in the repertoire of thousands of theaters throughout the country.

At the request of the Sloan Foundation the Falk Foundation agreed to share in the financing of films on technology, on profits, on the relationship of wages to prices—as factors in economic progress. The public reception of the films was to determine whether further support would be given.

Eventually, between 1947 and 1951, the Falk Foundation Board of Managers, pleased with the reception of the films, voted a total of $230,000 in grants to their support.

The films were always privately previewed for approval by the Falk Foundation Board and the Foundation Director, and individual members reported their good reception by theater audiences when they appeared as "shorts" among long film features and news reels. The titles and the cartoons were often amusing, always attractive, and appealing to patriotic and real life situations. Between 1947 and 1951 there appeared from time to time for public education through entertainment *Albert in Blunderland* (a regimented economy), *Dear Uncle* (taxes), *The Devil and John Q* (inflation), *Fresh-Laid Plans* (how one economic control leads to another), *Going Places* (the profit motive in American economy), *Inside Cackle Corners* (fruition of the profit motive), *It's Only the Beginning* (industrial research), *Make Mine Freedom* (creative role of freedom in economic enterprise), *Meet King Joe* (technology as a factor in economic progress), and *Why Play Leapfrog?* (relation of wages to prices).

❧   ❧   ❧   ❧   ❧

When in the Foundation's early years the Board of Managers agreed to support economic research it was understood that it would not always be possible to estimate completely the final results. After all, one value of foundations is that their funds can be spent for risk-taking experimental projects for which governmental or educational budgets do not provide. But the critical review which the Falk Foundation applied from time to time by outside experts asked to appraise the projects showed that the program was sound and the results useful. Objective always moved forward in pace with accomplishment. Each grant added another stone on the base established by earlier grants. The research was entrusted to experts and so was the preparation of written material to be distributed. The importance of the long run was never forgotten and the faith that preceded the grant sustained the project as firmly as the results have justified it.

THE MAURICE

AND LAURA FALK

FOUNDATION

Part Three

GRANTS TO

POLITICAL EDUCATION

Politics is the practical exercise of the art of self-government, and somebody must attend to it if we are to have self-government; somebody must study it, and learn the art, and exercise patience and sympathy and skill to bring the multitude of opinions and wishes of self-governing people into such order that some prevailing opinion may be expressed and peaceably accepted. Otherwise, confusion will result either in dictatorship or anarchy. The principal ground of reproach against any American citizen should be that he is not a politician. Everyone ought to be, as Lincoln was.—ELIHU ROOT
July 28, 1920. Speech presenting statue of Lincoln to the British people.

CHAPTER NINE

A New Program

The charter under which The Maurice and Laura Falk Foundation operated required that both capital and income be expended in thirty-five years. And so, in the last months of 1948 and in the early months of 1949 J. Steele Gow discussed with the Board of Managers plans for scheduling the grants in the remaining fifteen years.

During the past two decades substantial grants had been made for economic research and education, the Foundation's first field of concentration. These have been discussed in previous chapters. There were also in these decades grants to projects outside the economic program which will be discussed in later chapters.

❧ ❧ ❧ ❧ ❧

There were still commitments to the economic program when the following several questions were raised by the Director as to future programs for Foundation support: "Should the Foundation expand the economic program beyond present commitments? Should it select another area of concentration? Should it leave opportunity open to fill requests for support to constructive programs in a variety of fields? If a new field of concentration were adopted, should it focus on Pittsburgh area programs?"

Any of these questions answered affirmatively brought other questions, until they all resolved into one question: "On what could the funds be spent to contribute most effectively to the welfare of the largest number of people?"

The economic research supported by the Foundation had centered increasingly on matters of governmental policy as they affected the national economy. During the twenty years of Foundation activity the role of government in economic affairs had become a dominant influence upon American business, and the trend of Foundation grants had followed the national trend. This is shown concretely by the publications resulting from the research which are listed in the Appendix.

At the Board meeting in December 1949 E. T. Weir, who had assumed responsibilities to his political party, said he thought Americans ought to be more sophisticated in politics. American society, he said, was dependent on the party system; to protect society every American, man or woman, should understand the value of politics and take an active part in political life. Nathan Jacobs submitted a newspaper editorial criticizing the many citizens who did not bother even to vote. All members of the Board were enthusiastic about exploring political education as a possible field for support, and they asked Steele Gow to investigate and suggest a specific project.

Soon after this and quite by chance a leaflet came to the Foundation in the mail—a condensation of an article which had appeared in the *New York Times Magazine* of March 9, 1947 and had been reprinted later in *Tax Outlet* for April 1947. It was *Better Minds for Better Politics* by Arthur T. Vanderbilt, dean of the Law School of New York University.

Dean Vanderbilt had been judge of the Circuit Court of New Jersey and was chief justice of the Supreme Court of New Jersey. He had been a president of the American Bar Association; he was a life member of the American Law Institute and had been its chairman for many important legal commissions and conferences. His academic career was notable, too, as a professor, dean,

104

trustee, and recipient of many honorary degrees. He was a man of more than one career and distinguished in all.

The leaflet told of a meeting in Montclair, New Jersey, where Dean Vanderbilt, who had been counsel for Essex County for twenty-five years, was asked to hold an audience pending the arrival of the scheduled speaker. Dean Vanderbilt passed the time quizzing the audience, made up largely, as the leaflet told, of "county committee men and women, election board members, officers of political clubs—all actively interested in politics." He learned that too few knew the names of elected public officers and that very few wanted their sons or daughters to "go into politics" because, as they said, it had a connotation of dishonesty. In short, the results of the quiz corroborated what he already knew—that there was a dangerous lack of knowledge and a shrinking from active service extremely important to a democratic government.

Judge Vanderbilt said in the article that he felt colleges and universities ought to educate youth for active participation in good citizenship. Young men and women needed to know the intelligent leaders in the party of their choice, to discuss constructively among themselves the political issues, and to know how to take an intelligent and effective part in politics: to vote, and to understand and help to preserve the political structure upon which the freedom and welfare of American democracy have been built.

Mr. Gow brought to the Board in 1950 Judge Vanderbilt's leaflet and a report of his own exploration into the problem of education in practical politics. He had interviewed personally and by exchange of letters more than a score of persons: college presidents, educators, chairmen of municipal and urban political leagues, and many others. The list included Former President Herbert Hoover; Chief Justice Arthur T. Vanderbilt, New

Jersey Supreme Court; President Henry M. Wriston, Brown University; President Arthur S. Flemming, Ohio Wesleyan University; President William F. Russell, Teachers College, Columbia University; Former United States Commissioner of Education John W. Studebaker; Dean Emeritus Henry W. Holmes, Harvard Graduate School of Education; Professor of Education Emeritus John J. Mahoney, Boston University; Mr. Richard S. Childs, chairman of the Executive Committee of the National Municipal League; Mr. Alfred Willoughby, executive director of the National Municipal League; Professor O. Garfield Jones, political science, University of Toledo; Assistant Professor Arthur L. Thexton, political science, Bridgeport University; Professor Dayton McKean, political science, Dartmouth; Mr. George H. Williams, executive secretary of The Citizenship Clearing House of New York University; Professor Roy A. Price, social sciences, Maxwell School of Citizenship and Public Affairs, Syracuse University; Professor Emeritus Thomas H. Reed, political science, University of Michigan; Dr. A. D. H. Kaplan, former coordinator of the Government Management Program, Denver University.

Mr. Gow had found in his investigations that all these men and many others recognized the need for education in practical politics, and that a few of them had been associated with concrete efforts to fill the need. They agreed with Judge Vanderbilt that something dynamic should be added to the education program on different levels to excite young people to do their part in keeping alive and preserving the structure of democracy. And they also approved the idea that some plan should be promoted to give young people practical experience in politics while they were being educated for their chosen careers in life beyond graduation.

※　※　※　※　※

In the school curriculum education for political participation was new. The Carnegie Corporation was financing an effort in Teachers College, Columbia University, in cooperation with public school systems in eight towns and cities of the Eastern United States, to find a program of citizenship training that could be used generally. And there were plans being tried out in political science departments of colleges, here and there.

The first real need was to find out what was being done, and where; and how to coordinate a plan that would give clinical experience as well as theory to students, to teachers, and to adult community groups. After much discussion, in which everyone on the Board took an enthusiastic part, the Foundation decided to find out what was in fact being done to educate youth politically in colleges and universities.

To help gather information for a report on what was already being done throughout the country was the first step in a program which became the Falk Foundation's second field of concentrated support.

    ❧   ❧   ❧   ❧   ❧

The education of citizens for politics was the broad substance of the program which the Foundation supported with more than $3,000,000 through the decade beginning in 1952. And although there were diverse projects included in the program they had a unity of aim and purpose: to encourage colleges and universities in undergraduate and graduate study of politics; to give young men and women opportunities to learn in a practical way their responsibilities to the political life of the nation; to support workshops and courses for teachers needed to fill posts in teaching practical politics at the college level; to support summer internships in field experience for advanced students to work with the political party of their choice or with mayors, legislators, or other political officials as supplement to classroom study; to support programs and publications which could give the citizen generally an understanding of the worth of political education and the importance of intelligent citizen-wide participation in politics.

These diverse programs, united in their aim, will be discussed in the chapters immediately following.

CHAPTER TEN

The Citizenship Clearing House and the Reed Survey

The Falk Foundation program of grants to education in practical politics followed the same policy as its program of grants to research and education in economics. The planning and evaluating of the program in political education were carried out by competent experts in existing independent agencies and on college and university campuses. The Foundation role was to find persons of both political and educational experience qualified to explore ways and means of making political education practical both for students and for citizens generally; to select institutions with personnel capable of carrying through the project; and to make the grants needed to realize satisfactory programs and publications for teaching and for wide usefulness.

❧   ❧   ❧   ❧   ❧

In September 1950 the Director arranged a dinner meeting with the Board of Managers and four men whom he had selected to report their own successful experiments in political education and to suggest the kind of program and support that could mean most. Dean Arthur Vanderbilt and Professors Arthur L. Thexton, Thomas H. Reed, and O. Garfield Jones attended the dinner and discussed with the members of the Board ideas from which the Foundation program was developed.

Judge Vanderbilt in 1948 had organized The Citizenship Clearing House at the New York University Law School. His varied academic, political, and legal experience, which has been delineated in the preceding chapter, had given him firsthand awareness of many aspects of the need for political education.

Professor Thexton, after his graduation from Williams College, had a successful career in business, from which he retired to enter professionally the teaching of political science because he believed political knowledge to be essential to the development of the best in American life. Further graduate study at Columbia University prompted him to seek an opportunity to teach political science where he could develop a college course in practical politics. He had been developing such a course at the University of Bridgeport in Connecticut. While he taught politics in a dynamic way to students there he had been a promotion manager for the Democratic Party in Connecticut, and had urged his students themselves to seek practical experience working for the party of their choice.

Professor O. Garfield Jones was a graduate of Ohio Wesleyan University and a Doctor of Philosophy of the University of California. He had studied, too, in graduate courses at the universities of Cornell, Ohio State, Chicago, and Wisconsin, thus gaining political knowledge in different regions of the country. As a professor at Toledo University he had developed a strong course in politics which made him a pioneer in a new field of college teaching.

Professor Thomas H. Reed was a graduate of Harvard College and held a doctorate from the University of Brussels. He had been admitted to the Bar in New York and in California. His academic career was outstanding, in professorships of government and of political science at the universities of California and of Michigan. He had held important commissions and consultancies with national and municipal governments and had known other experience in practical politics on the staff of Hiram

110

Johnson and, later, on the Program Committee of the Republican Party. He was not unknown in Pittsburgh: in 1929-39 he had directed the research in the Metropolitan Pittsburgh Plan. In 1950 The Citizenship Clearing House had published "Evaluation of Citizenship Training and Incentive in American Colleges and Universities," which reported a survey made through correspondence with the colleges by Dr. Reed and his wife Doris D. Reed for The Citizenship Clearing House and the Association of American Colleges. The Reeds were eager for a chance to follow this preliminary questionnaire survey with more direct and intimate field study.

Questions followed each dinner guest's presentation of his conviction that political education was needed on every educational level and in every community.

        ❧   ❧   ❧   ❧   ❧

Two months later, November 20, 1950, the Board adopted Mr. Gow's suggestion that a grant be made to support at least the first part of a proposal received from Judge Vanderbilt and Col. George H. Williams, who was director of The Citizenship Clearing House. The plan had six parts: to investigate and evaluate the relatively few courses now given on college campuses; to prepare a syllabus in which laboratory, clinical, and field methods would be used along with texts and collateral readings, suitable for different kinds of institutions —large and small, public and private, nondenominational and sectarian; to develop a seminar in the summer vacation, with lectures by outstanding political leaders, which could prepare teachers for the new course and for ways of interesting college administrators and trustees in adding the course to the college curriculum; to set up state or regional conferences of political science teachers and political leaders for frank discussion of citizenship education; to develop a citizenship clearing house at colleges in important regions of the country for exchange of information, having as objective introducing young graduates recommended by their college professors to honest and intelligent political leaders in the party of their selection, so the beginner in politics might start his active political experience with favorable and helpful guidance.

Support to the first recommendation, to explore what was being offered in political education on the college level, was undertaken by the Foundation with a grant of $50,000 in November 7, 1950 to The Citizenship Clearing House of New York to commission Dr. and Mrs. Thomas H. Reed to make a year's field study of courses offered at colleges and universities over the United States and report their findings to the Foundation.

❧ ❧ ❧ ❧ ❧

The Reed report was published by The Citizenship Clearing House in 1952, and with the aid of a supplemental grant from the Falk Foundation was widely distributed among colleges and universities, practicing politicians, and other groups and individuals interested in education for the responsibilities of citizenship and in solving the problems of making this kind of education available.

Preparing College Men and Women for Politics by Thomas H. Reed and Doris D. Reed presented some interesting conclusions concerning the training being given college students for active participation in politics. They found many schools which recognized the need, but only a few with effective programs. They found faculties in many colleges believing that political science should be philosophical, historical, theoretical in character and that training for participation in politics lacked academic respectability. Some trustees and administrators feared

112

the controversial aspects of the training, the objections of parents, and the attitude of professional politicians who would consider such training invasion of their domain by "idealistic reformers."

But they found some colleges attempting practical

Preparing College Men and Women for Politics by Thomas H. Reed and Doris D. Reed (1952), the report of the status of teaching in colleges and universities to prepare youth for responsibilities of citizenship and *Going Into Politics* by Robert E. Merriam and Rachel Goetz (1957, Harper and Brothers) were the result of research financed by Falk Foundation grants to The Citizenship Clearing House.

programs and willing to develop them to greater length.

The Reeds recommended a five-point program of action which echoed the plan proposed by Judge Vanderbilt: "A systematic program of grants to selected colleges and universities to establish political education courses and projects aimed directly at training for politics; a vigorous campaign among college and university trustees, administrative officials, faculties, and professional politicians, stressing the need and obligation to train our youth to assume their responsibilities as the citizens of a free representative democracy; the establishment of teacher-training programs to demonstrate to young teachers how to teach politics in realistic and practical terms; the establishment of a strong national organization to serve as a clearing house for the continuous promotion of college efforts to train for politics, for the publication of a periodical reporting the progress made in that direction, and for the exchange of course syllabi and the like; and the establishment of state or regional clearing houses through which college students might be directed to suitable opportunities for participation in local political activities."

The next chapter will show how the Falk Foundation adopted the Reeds's first suggestion, to support programs on college campuses where administrative and teaching leadership seemed to justify support.

❦ ❦ ❦ ❦ ❦

Meantime, beginning in 1952 grants were made to The Citizenship Clearing House in a series of payments which eventually totaled more than half a million dollars.

Affiliate clearing houses were set up in regions which covered twenty-seven states from New England to Florida and through the Midwest to the Pacific Coast and Hawaii. The headquarters and the areas they served were:

114

Amherst College	New England
Florida State University	Florida
Hunter College	Southern New York
Lewis and Clark College	Oregon
Ohio Wesleyan University	Ohio
Principia College	Illinois
Rutgers University	New Jersey
Stanford University	Northern California
State University of Iowa	Iowa
Syracuse University	Upstate New York
University of Colorado	Rocky Mountains
University of Hawaii	Hawaii
University of Kansas	Kansas-Missouri
University of Michigan	Michigan
University of Minnesota	Minnesota
University of Pennsylvania	Eastern Pennsylvania
University of Pittsburgh	Western Pennsylvania
University of Southern California	Southern California-Arizona
University of Washington	Washington-Northern Idaho
University of Wisconsin	Wisconsin
Wabash College	Indiana

San Francisco Seminar (1954), one of many diverse activities of The Citizenship Clearing House (since 1962, National Center for Education in Politics). The Clearing House was designed to encourage participation in activities of the individual's chosen party— training of teachers; workshops; seminars; conferences; publications.

The activities of these affiliate clearing houses varied, according to local conditions and needs. But they all worked with area schools and their programs of classroom courses, conferences, workshops, internship programs, publications, and the like. And the activities were on three levels: state and regional (teacher workshops and student conferences); cooperative institutional (where two or more neighboring institutions cooperate in research and fieldwork); and individual institutional (courses plus fieldwork of internships for students). Through these affiliate clearing houses a realistic teaching of politics was encouraged in more than 500 colleges and universities and a climate of mutual interest and cooperation was created among students, faculties, college administrators, and political and civic leaders.

❧   ❧   ❧   ❧   ❧

In 1953 the Foundation granted The Citizenship Clearing House $15,000 to commission an author "to state the case for citizen participation in politics." The result was a very successful book, *Going into Politics—A Guide for Citizens,* by Robert E. Merriam and Rachel M. Goetz, published in 1957 by Harper & Brothers, New York.

Mr. Merriam had been a professional politician in Chicago, where he had been drafted as a candidate for mayor and had conducted a reform campaign. He was a Republican, and in the Eisenhower administration became, after his defeat in Chicago, an assistant director of the Bureau of the Budget. Mrs. Goetz was a Democrat. She had recently been a writer with the editorial and research division of the Adlai Stevenson campaign. Thus, the book was written out of two authors' backgrounds: the experience of both political parties and the deep conviction that good government requires more devoted citizens to take part in the day-by-day opera-

116

tions of political parties and the volunteer work needed.

The book stresses the opportunities the individual has as a citizen to work for the political party of his choice. It deals with such practical matters as how candidates are selected and elected, or fail to be elected; how campaigns are organized and managed; how to use mass communication techniques; and how politics can operate if intelligence and hard work are brought to bear on political programs needed to guarantee national welfare.

       ꙮ   ꙮ   ꙮ   ꙮ   ꙮ

Besides the two books already mentioned—the report on political education in colleges and universities by Thomas H. Reed and Doris D. Reed and *Going Into Politics* by Robert E. Merriam and Rachel M. Goetz— The Citizenship Clearing House published monthly a *Bulletin* for the exchange of ideas between the central Clearing House and its affiliates; state guides to politics which gave basic facts about political organizations, nominating procedures, and electors; a bibliography of selected books and pamphlets in politics; and various pamphlets and brochures which described the aims of the Clearing House and reported its progress.

       ꙮ   ꙮ   ꙮ   ꙮ   ꙮ

In 1959 the Foundation granted The Citizenship Clearing House $139,550 to support an undergraduate political internship program. This program annually gave 200 undergraduates a full or part-time supervised practical experience in some aspect of American politics for periods varying from four to eight weeks. Support to the internship program enriched the programs of teaching, research, and learning in undergraduate and graduate political education. It reached beyond the textbook and the lecture into living politics.

In his *Biennial Report 1959-1960* Director Gow thus describes the internship:

> The internship is one of the most effective methods yet found to give the student practical political experience within an educational framework. It provides the essential summit experience for the student who has developed through his course work a high degree of political knowledge and enthusiasm for political participation. It differs from the usual fieldwork assignment in that the student is required to perform—under academic supervision or in connection with theoretical academic study—in an actual working situation, substantially full-time over a relatively extensive period. The intern may be assigned to a political party headquarters or a candidate's office, to the office of a congressman or legislator, to the staff of a political official or executive such as a governor, a mayor, a policy-shaping administrator, or perhaps to the office of a pressure group.

ﻼ　ﻼ　ﻼ　ﻼ　ﻼ

The central Citizenship Clearing House and its affiliate clearing houses made a unique contribution to the development of political education. Leaders in education and in party and government activities and students in more than five hundred colleges and universities used the services. On January 26, 1962, the name was changed to National Center for Education in Politics, which more accurately describes the maturity and the national recognition The Citizenship Clearing House had won itself.

The Falk Foundation, through the years, contributed nearly $800,000 in subventions to the Clearing House for its affiliates and their workshops, conferences, internships, and publications.

Many week-end conferences of college teachers, administrators, trustees, and civic leaders were conducted throughout the country. Short-term workshops informed many college teachers of the materials and methods for teaching practical and realistic politics. Summer workshops were conducted in many places—two of them at the widely separated centers of San Francisco and Harvard. Falk grants contributed to all these educational programs.

The teacher-training workshops of the Clearing House affiliates were maintained until graduate fellowship programs in selected colleges and universities were well established. These will be described in the next chapter. As the Foundation drew near its end and as support from other sources increased, Falk Foundation support went to the clearing houses on a descending scale, until a terminal grant ($140,000) was made in 1964.

Made originally because of determination to do something concrete to encourage citizens to be responsible through their own efforts for maintaining a government "of the people and by the people," these grants supported an important phase of the Falk Foundation program in political education.

Intelligent political leaders where politics is a career or where politics is a good citizen's avocation; first-rate teachers of political science; political reporters, commentators, and editorial writers; and authors of important works have been educated in their college years to become more responsible citizens as a result of the concentrated effort in political education supported by the Falk Foundation.

Director Bernard C. Hennessy of the National Center for Education in Politics (professor, New York University School of Law) expressed thus in his report 1964-1965 his appreciation of Falk Foundation grants: "Appreciation to the officers and staffs of the Ford and the Falk Foundations—and most of all to Dr. J. Steele Gow for his confidence in NCEP and in the thousands of young men and women whom he has aided, in the Falk internships, to the knowledge and the fun and the satisfactions of political life."

CHAPTER ELEVEN

College and University Programs

When the Reed survey was reviewed by the Board of Managers at the meeting of April 30, 1952 the discussion culminated in unanimous approval of three grants which initiated Foundation support to programs encouraging citizens to take a responsible part in politics.

Underlying the decision to establish these grants and the many which were made to political education in the next decade was the conviction that a democracy cannot realize full potential without citizens ready for constructive and public-spirited participation in political affairs. The place to begin education for this important role, the Board agreed, was with young people while they are in school.

It would have been impossible for Foundation resources to cover political education on all school levels—elementary, secondary, college—so the Board had decided to focus support on programs in colleges and universities. This decision had prompted the Reed survey, which corroborated what was already suspected—that there were very few college campuses where attempts were being made to offer practical training in politics. There were a few where recognition was growing that something should be done to offer students more than theory, and in political science departments and among college administrators there was genuine hope that resources could be found to prepare teachers and provide materials for effective political education.

The first grant approved at the April meeting was to The Law Center at New York University for the use of The Citizenship Clearing House. This first grant and subsequent grants to the Clearing House have been explained in the preceding chapter.

The second grant was to Pennsylvania College for Women in Pittsburgh (now Chatham College). It was the first in a series of grants for political education on the campuses of colleges and universities, nation-wide. These will be discussed in this chapter.

The third, also discussed in this chapter, made available $3,000 to the Pennsylvania Association of Colleges and Universities toward the expenses of a summer conference for college and university teachers and administrators to consider what the recommendations of the Reed survey might mean for the Association's member institutions.

꙼   ꙼   ꙼   ꙼   ꙼

The conference was held at Franklin and Marshall College in Lancaster, Pennsylvania, June 1952. Judge Vanderbilt sounded the keynote and the Reeds presented their critical appraisal of citizenship training in colleges and universities throughout the nation. There were group discussions on how to improve political science teaching and the preparation of teachers and what the obligations of the Association's members were for encouraging students to take part in political activities in their own neighborhoods and with the political party of their choice. There was, too, an address by a leader from each of the two main political parties.

Two members from each institution had been invited to the conference—one a teacher, the other an administrator who was usually the college president or a dean or a trustee. Forty-six out of the sixty-three institutional members were represented—as reported by Dr. Carl E. Seifert, executive secretary of the Association. State colleges which were not members had also been invited to attend, and many of them came.

There was much discussion in groups large and small. Some were reluctant to introduce the new program. But the final consensus was recognition of college and university responsibility to train young people to take a part in maintaining good government, local and national, and resolution to persuade trustees and administrative officers to initiate and strengthen political education on college campuses in the undergraduate and graduate programs. In short, this conference, because of the wide publicity it received inside and outside Pennsylvania, proved to be a firm step in a wide-spread program of training in practical politics at the college level. Similar conferences were held elsewhere, as time went on, by similar associations and for the same purpose.

*   *   *   *   *

The next phase in the program, as the Foundation had planned it, was to select colleges in large cities and in smaller towns to develop programs in diverse geographical areas which might serve as pilot programs for the political education venture. Following the grant to Chatham College in Pittsburgh (then Pennsylvania College for Women) made in April 1952, the Foundation made grants in June to Boston University (Massachusetts); Hamline University (Minnesota); Ohio Wesleyan (Delaware, Ohio); Allegheny College (Meadville, Pennsylvania); and, in October, to Washington Square College of Arts and Science (New York University).

These were granted support for three years to a program which each described in a proposal submitted to the Foundation. There were interesting differences in the activities of the colleges, adapted to the individual campus and environmental conditions and local community encouragement. All were carried on with enthusiasm and all resulted in new interest in the political science courses of the college curricula, in the communities and among the practising politicians of the different parties in the area in which the college was centered. And the Foundation made available additional three-year grants to the colleges pioneering the program as the growth of their programs justified increased support.

During the decade 1953-1963 more colleges and universities asked for grants and received them to initiate and sustain the substantial programs described in their requests for support. But eventually, as the grants were expended, the respective colleges assumed responsibility either by absorbing the costs in their own budgets or by seeking support elsewhere.

A list below of those receiving grants illustrates the broad national scope of the stimulus the Falk Foundation brought to political education in colleges and universities.

Undergraduate Programs

Allegheny College	Meadville, Pennsylvania
Amherst College	Amherst, Massachusetts
*Bethany College	Bethany, West Virginia
Boston University	Boston, Massachusetts
Chatham College	Pittsburgh, Pennsylvania
College of Wooster	Wooster, Ohio
Goucher College	Baltimore, Maryland
Grinnell College	Grinnell, Iowa
Hamline University	Saint Paul, Minnesota
Howard University	Washington, D. C.
Knox College	Galesburg, Illinois
Massachusetts Institute of Technology	Cambridge, Massachusetts
Mount Holyoke College	South Hadley, Massachusetts
Ohio Wesleyan University	Delaware, Ohio
Pomona College	Claremont, California
Rollins College	Winter Park, Florida

*A pilot program in practical politics for adults has been added to programs offered at Bethany College. (See Chapter Fourteen)

123

University of North Carolina	Chapel Hill, North Carolina
University of Oregon	Eugene, Oregon
University of Pittsburgh	Pittsburgh, Pennsylvania
Vanderbilt University	Nashville, Tennessee
Wabash College	Crawfordsville, Indiana
Washington Square College of Arts and Science, N. Y. U.	New York, New York
Wesleyan University	Middletown, Connecticut

Graduate Programs

Michigan State University	East Lansing, Michigan
University of California	Berkeley and Los Angeles, California
University of Chicago	Chicago, Illinois
**University of North Carolina	Chapel Hill, North Carolina
**University of Pittsburgh	Pittsburgh, Pennsylvania
University of Washington	Seattle, Washington
**Vanderbilt University	Nashville, Tennessee
Yale University	New Haven, Connecticut

**Programs at Vanderbilt University, University of North Carolina, and University of Pittsburgh are at both the undergraduate and graduate levels.

⚜ ⚜ ⚜ ⚜ ⚜

The grants enabled colleges to develop teaching and library materials and teaching methods that benefited even students not majoring in political science, and they provided the student specializing in political science necessary funds for fieldwork in party politics as a laboratory experience. Upper-class students in intensive study of politics, by reason of the careful planning of their instructors, were enabled to work under supervision at the headquarters of the party of their choice or with a candidate of their selection. The grants made possible the special scheduling and expert direction required.

One of the colleges, Ohio Wesleyan University, used part of the grant to develop tests for measuring student interest and knowledge in the field before and after taking the courses and participating in the fieldwork, and for measuring the effect of training on participation in politics after graduation. The results showed substantial and increased interest in politics by those who had participated in the student programs, and it showed, too, a need to refine tests to measure continued interest following graduation.

Washington Square College of Arts and Science at New York University developed various materials and methods that could be used where only limited attention could be given to politics in a course more general in its content and in the social sciences as a whole.

Each school stressed a continuation of classroom instruction and supervised fieldwork. And each used its resources strengthened by Falk grants to coordinate the work of classroom, laboratory, and library to provoke dynamic opportunities for students and faculty. Avocational participation beyond college was the main objective, although some students pursued their interest in politics after graduation to a vocational end—running for office in their hometown or state, or working in city, state, and national political and governmental offices.

ᴈ   ᴈ   ᴈ   ᴈ   ᴈ

The pattern for undergraduate study was essentially similar in each of the colleges and universities receiving grants. A basic course, *American Government,* was the nucleus for freshmen and sophomores, and *Political Parties* was the course for the juniors and seniors. Everywhere the conventional classroom study was enlivened with whatever practical experience was possible in the particular location of the college. Supervised work in political campaigns, elections, and other activities in the party of the student's choice, sometimes a survey of the politi-

125

cal geography of the region, or other research activity made politics take on new and lasting significance for the student. Students not majoring in political science, too, were often attracted to lectures by practical politicians and to other collateral activities of the specialized course.

Political education, which had become the second program for concentrated support by the Foundation was a creative program, objective, and of course without favor to any particular political party, but with recognition that, in the best sense, party politics is the core of modern free government. Each grantee followed a local pattern of opportunity and need. Students, teachers, administrators, politicians—all contributed vitally. The program won academic endorsement and approval and the enthusiastic support of politicians in both political parties.

There are many letters in the Foundation files from college administrators and civic leaders expressing enthusiasm and approval. Perhaps most of those with academic approval can be summarized in a comment made by Dr. Louis T. Benezet, president of Allegheny College in Pennsylvania. In 1953 he called the program "the most significant innovation in the curriculum in the past decade."

Two evaluations of the programs were financed by Falk grants. Professor James W. Miller of Michigan State University was commissioned late in 1953 to appraise the work in progress under Falk grants at colleges and universities. And in 1958 Professor Rhoten A. Smith of the University of Kansas was commissioned by the Foundation to appraise the work again.

Both scholars approved the work being done on the several campuses to realize the important goal set by each institution and hoped for by the Foundation. Most schools, the surveys showed, were accumulating political libraries on their campuses—books, tape recordings of election speeches, newspaper clippings, voting statistics, campaign materials. Centers and institutes were developing on several campuses to sponsor invitations to professional politicians to speak to students and faculty in their areas—a hitherto unheard of event in the lives of many educational institutions.

Dr. William J. Keefe of Chatham College and Dr. Ivan Hinderaker of the University of California at Los Angeles, who had assisted in the investigation, on September 19, 1958 reported so favorably on the impact of the political education program of The Maurice and Laura Falk Foundation that Director Gow proposed that the Board not only continue grants for college and university undergraduate and graduate programs but consider new grants for summer political internships for college students and, in some instances, for research investigations of political subjects about which more needed to be known if the teaching of politics at the college level was to be a feature of the graduate curriculum. It was the consensus of the Board that the Foundation should continue to serve the field of education in politics and also to consider the broader program.

❧   ❧   ❧   ❧   ❧

While the Falk Foundation was supporting political education in the undergraduate schools in the 1950's, the Foundation and the colleges had become increasingly aware of the need for teachers trained specifically for the program, if the program was to thrive and become a national movement in higher education—the ultimate hope and purpose of the grants.

And so, under Falk grants teacher-education programs were established at universities scattered geographically from coast to coast: at Yale, Michigan State, North

127

Carolina, Vanderbilt, Washington, Chicago, California (both at Berkeley and at Los Angeles), and Pittsburgh.

Much of the success of the undergraduate program as it continues today and promises to continue in the future can be credited to the teachers whose graduate training included sound sequences of courses in politics and allied subjects along with opportunities for field studies and research into political organizations as they actually function.

❧ ❧ ❧ ❧ ❧

The Falk Foundation grants for graduate schools were in the form of stipends for fellowships to outstanding students selected by the faculties of the schools (not by the Foundation) to study politics as a major interest of their work for the degree, Doctor of Philosophy. Also, the grants provided for travel, field investigation, and research. And they provided for guest lecturers on political subjects, and for other related projects assisting in the education of teachers.

The first Falk Fellowships were established at Yale University in 1953 (where the Fellowships were later endowed) under a grant which eventually totaled $174,500, and at Michigan State University in 1954 under a total grant of $124,800. These universities accepted the challenge to demonstrate how funds for training teachers to fill the important and specific need could be used most effectively. The Falk Fellows engaged in field projects, some with course credits and some not. They also were given teaching assignments under supervision in political science courses to give them at least elementary experience as teachers before they were elected to faculty posts. This became essentially the pattern on the other six campuses, and the masters and doctoral graduates of all eight were a source of supply for political science

128

teachers in many American colleges.

The University of North Carolina ($139,500) and Vanderbilt University ($84,400), both receiving initial grants for graduate programs in 1957, had programs both undergraduate and graduate. And here the Falk Fellows spent a third of their time as teaching fellows or laboratory assistants for the undergraduate political science majors.

In 1958 the University of Washington initiated its teacher-training program, with agreement to continue support after the Falk grant of $59,232 should expire. California ($132,000 for two campuses) and Chicago ($56,000) began their graduate programs in 1959, both were centers of population growth creating many political problems. Thus the Falk-sponsored graduate program extended into the West and the Far West.

The reports which came in regularly to the Foundation from every campus showed the variety and different environmental influences on the program. But all were enthusiastic about the results, the liveliness of interest, and the excitement generated on the campus.

Chicago reported the encouragement the grants had given students to continue beyond the masters degree to the doctorate. This had been a crucial period in academic growth. Along with others in the program on other campuses the Chicago faculty emphasized the value it was to a teacher to have the chance for research in living politics, city, state, and national.

And they all reported development in the quality of written reports which were the fruit of research into the political structure of the party system and its value to American well-being. Delivering the reports to a class, they said, gave students the best kind of teaching experience, the crown of which, for the individual and for the broad program of responsible citizenship, was that a student-teacher eventually become a teacher of teachers. General articles and books sometimes resulted from these reports. But, above all, living daily in an atmosphere which emphasized the importance of politics and the importance of active participation in a chosen party was a guarantee of continuing lifetime interest and action.

At California two campuses, Berkeley and Los Angeles, exchanged professors and library materials and held joint conferences. As at all the universities given grants, Falk Fellows were selected from the very best of candidates. Research was promoted and political literature developed which made the program at California rank with the best of those in older universities of the East. And always at California as elsewhere the primary aim was to turn out teachers with up-to-date programs, the resourcefulness to carry them to wider areas and fresher emphasis, and greater awareness of the need to improve the quality of politics in our democracy.

The Foundation hoped that these successful projects would call forth support from other donors with the larger resources which this program of national magnitude and importance required. To insure that the teaching fellowships would continue, the Falk Foundation in 1962 granted an endowment of $500,000 to Yale, which had been the first university to receive a graduate program grant, and to the University of Pittsburgh the Foundation in 1964 made an endowment grant of $500,000 to establish a Maurice Falk Professorship of Politics for the education of teachers of political science at the college level.

Thus two important Falk projects in political education are assured of continuance.

.⸴   .⸴   .⸴   .⸴   .⸴

In the *Biennial Report for 1961-62,* Steele Gow summarized the value of political education, the Foundation's second field of concentration, in this way:

Among the 1961-1962 grants for education in politics were several which brought to completion the Foundation's financing of programs in politics at the level of the undergraduate college. Since 1953 the Foundation has made fifty-one grants to twenty-three colleges and universities, spread from Connecticut to California and from Oregon to Florida, to support the establishment, and operation over six-year periods, of undergraduate programs of classroom instruction in politics combined with supervised practical experience in political campaigns, elections, and other activities of the regular political parties and also of special-interest political groups . . . Without a single exception, the schools involved have agreed to continue the financing of their programs within their own budgets or by means of funds secured from sources other than the Falk Foundation. This result gives strong evidence that the programs are favorably regarded by their host institutions. With the completion of the Foundation's financing of this segment of its activity in political education, there has been established a basis for hope, even for confidence, that education in practical politics has made a successful entry into the world of the undergraduate college and can reasonably expect to find a hospitable climate in an increasing number of institutions as the years pass.

Besides stimulating colleges themselves to continue support to both undergraduate and graduate programs, the Falk grants stimulated other kinds of support, and programs developed in more places and at greater depth. When time and increased support from other sources brought an end to Falk Foundation commitments, the Foundation withdrew. However, before this happened, other special programs in political education—not all campus centered—had received Falk Foundation grants. They will be described in the next chapter. They have given to more and more people generally a chance to keep alert and knowledgable about political affairs and to be aware of the importance of each individual's part in preserving the American way of life.

131

❧ ❧ ❧ ❧ ❧

Political education developing out of Falk Foundation grants embraced a broad series of activity for students and their teachers. Surveys of political attitudes; workshops in which on campuses in smaller communities the public took part; special radio programs presenting the panel discussions of students and candidates for office of both parties, or those already serving in office; research papers exchanged for critical appraisal; visits to government units of all kinds; publications offering information to encourage the vote and an understanding of issues and candidates; participation of party officials of both parties in class seminars, where sometimes whole communities shared information and special talents (for instance, at Grinnell in 1964 Former President Truman helped conduct a seminar); and in the graduate programs, internships, not only in the offices of national, state, and local politicians, but with veteran political reporters for newspapers, the Associated Press, and other wire services; doctoral dissertations; and published books. All these, with the strong undergirding of classroom instruction, appropriate readings, and advice from experts, helped to lift politics for many citizens out of the slough of indifference, or at best of casual interest; helped to place political education firmly in the teaching and research of colleges and universities; and assured the Foundation that its grants were well spent in this second major concentration of Falk funds.

COLLEGE AND UNIVERSITY PROGRAMS

The programs pictured here and on the next two pages have been supported by Falk Foundation grants to colleges and universities from coast to coast to educate youth for citizenship in a democracy.

Falk graduate fellows, University of North Carolina.

Falk graduate fellows, Yale University.

Young Democrats, Knox College, with Senator Paul Douglas.

Learning political techniques, Rollins College

Mock political convention, 1952, Ohio Wesleyan.

Students of Howard University visit the House of Delegates of Maryland.

Falk graduate fellows, Michigan State, at lunch with a Michigan congressman.

Conference of computer analysis of election statistics, Rollins College.

CHAPTER TWELVE

Related Programs in Political Education

Between 1952 and 1964 the Falk Foundation made grants of more than $200,000 to programs related to education for politics. These grants supplemented or contributed in some important way to the education programs preparing undergraduate college students for avocational participation in politics after graduation and to those providing young political scientists working for graduate degrees with realistic and sound academic preparation for teaching.

The Foundation supported the overall program in colleges and universities and the related educational programs by about $4,000,000.

*   *   *   *   *

One of the largest of the related grants (total $43,050) was made to Pittsburgh's Metropolitan Educational Television Station WQED.

The initial grant to the Station was made in 1954 to meet the costs of ten half-hour telecasts on the role of political parties in campaigns, elections, and legislation. Five in the fall of 1954 dealt with local and national campaigns and elections; five in the spring dealt with local and national legislative processes. Each telecast presented four panelists—two moderators and two local or national politicians. Kinescopes were made available to colleges and public schools.

Organizations of Local Campaigns out of National Campaigns; Importance of Party Organization; Analysis of National Election Results and of State Election Results; Legislative Process on State Level and on National Level; Public Policy Issues in the Pennsylvania Legislature; Election Process; and the Pennsylvania Plan to answer the question "Should we take our judges out of politics?" were discussed in one series called *It's Your Politics.*

The Foundation granted $30,000 to support eight telecasts on the presidential nominating process, made available by the Station to schools requesting the kinescopes. This series called *Prelude to the Presidency* included these programs: Office of the President, Preconvention Strategy of the Candidates, Organization and Operation of the National Conventions, Nomination of Candidates for President and Vice President, Evaluation of the National Convention as a Nominating Device, Evaluation of the National Convention as a Means for Settling Party Pol-

Pittsburgh's educational television station WQED televising a program supported by a Falk Foundation grant. Two professors and two United States Representatives took part.

icy, and A Preview of Democratic and Republican Conventions.

And in December 1961 WQED was granted $10,000 toward a city-wide campaign soliciting $200,000 to help meet operating requirements and to restore the Station's technical equipment to standards befitting the nation's pioneer educational television station.

᪣ ᪣ ᪣ ᪣ ᪣

The American Heritage Foundation in 1955 requested and received from the Falk Foundation $10,000 in support of the *American Heritage Register-and-Vote Campaign.*

The American Heritage Foundation had been founded in 1947 with a board of trustees of leaders in education, industry, and labor, and with a purpose which harmonized with the Falk Foundation's purpose as it fostered political education: "Only by active participation in the affairs of our nation can we safeguard our freedoms. . . ."

The public press had acknowledged the success of American Heritage educational campaigns in the 1952 election, supported by larger foundations and organizations, notably the Ford Foundation, the labor unions, and several corporations.

The Falk grant to the American Heritage Foundation, although outside the formal program of grants to educational institutions, to the Board of Managers seemed justified because it was used in a widely supported cause to stir citizens generally throughout the nation to political responsibility. And Falk Foundation's participation dramatized nationally its own broad program of support to colleges and universities for political education.

᪣ ᪣ ᪣ ᪣ ᪣

An allocation of $15,000 was authorized by the Foundation's Board of Managers in June 1960 to be used at the discretion of the Executive Director to finance research which promised to produce useful teaching materials for the college and university political programs.

And with this authority, in December 1960 a total of $15,308 was allocated to five projects of the Eagleton Institute of Politics at Rutgers University in New Jersey: a study of voter perception of issues and politics in metropolitan area reform; a study of county political party organization in Ohio; a study of the Wisconsin presidential primary of 1960; a study of the National Committee for an Effective Congress; and a study of leadership in a small community.

These studies, important to the understanding and teaching of American politics, resulted in articles and monographs in the series, *Cases in Practical Politics,* which was published by McGraw-Hill Book Company, Inc. in collaboration with the Eagleton Institute. The *Cases* were prepared under the general editorship of Paul Tillett of the Eagleton staff, with assistance from a Case Advisory Committee, who were administrators of Rutgers University. The Wells Phillips and Florence Peshine Eagleton Institute of Politics held the conviction consonant with the objective and philosophy of the Falk Foundation, which the Eagleton Institute expressed in this way: "The cultivation of civic responsibility and leadership among the American people in the field of practical political affairs is of vital and increasing importance to our state and nation."

❧   ❧   ❧   ❧   ❧

Appended to the Falk Foundation *Minutes of the Board Meeting, May 17, 1954* are suggestions which always guided the Falk Foundation in making grants to political education. This policy statement had been carefully written and circulated before the meeting for the approval of the Board by Director J. Steele Gow. At that time, under Falk grants, political education for undergraduates was underway on nine campuses and for graduate majors who were candidates for doctorates in political science at Yale University. Professor James W. Miller of Michigan State University had recently submitted his appraisal approving these programs. The policy suggestions stand in the *Minutes* firm and permanent evidence of the Director's talent to sift the relevant from the irrelevant in a plan reaching ahead on a steady and consistent way to conclusion. From the beginning of the program in 1952 until the final grant was made in 1965, the five points of policy were followed to successful realization.

–POLITICAL EDUCATION POLICY SUGGESTIONS–

Undergraduate Education:

1. Make grants to establish a limited number of political education programs where they do not now exist.

2. Make grants to strengthen a few carefully selected existing programs in the interest of sharpening their influence as demonstrations.

Graduate Education:

3. Make grants for graduate fellowship programs (like the Yale-Falk fellowships) to a few outstanding graduate schools in strategic parts of the country.

Teaching Materials:

4. Make an occasional grant for a carefully devised research project to develop materials for use in both undergraduate colleges and graduate schools (in some cases, such research projects should also yield findings which have important worth to political party organizations).

Promotion:

5. Finance for another year or so The Citizenship Clearing House at its present level of operation in the expectation that thereafter this support can be on a declining scale with support from other sources on an ascending scale.

The first three of the policy suggestions and the fifth were carried out in the programs described in Chapters Eleven, Twelve, and Thirteen.

The fourth suggestion, to make an occasional grant to develop materials for use in the undergraduate and graduate schools for the encouragement of research—which in turn might yield findings important to political party organizations—was realized in the grants to WQED and to the Eagleton Institute of Politics at Rutgers. The teaching use of their programs has already been discussed in this chapter. The folders, pamphlets, articles, and books published as the result of research in colleges and universities by students, fellows, and professors were certainly realization of the hope written into point four.

     .c.   .c.   .c.   .c.   .c.

Two grants made in the 1950's also carried out the interest expressed in point four: $4,500 to Wesleyan University at Middletown, Connecticut, made possible publication of research on a college campus *(Local Political Surveys.* Holt, Rinehart and Winston, Inc., 1962), and $47,500 to the Governmental Affairs Institute in Washington, D. C. made possible publication of material of the greatest importance to scholars and professionals in every facet of political life *(America at the Polls.* University of Pittsburgh Press, 1966).

     .c.   .c.   .c.   .c.   .c.

A dynamic professor at Wesleyan University in Connecticut and his professor colleague at the University of California in Berkeley collaborated in production of a handbook for local political surveys to be used by teachers and students.

Professor of Government E. E. Schattschneider was

chairman of the Public Affairs Center at Wesleyan University. In 1956-1957 he was president of the American Political Science Association and in 1958-1959 chairman of the Board of Directors of The Citizenship Clearing House. He was the author of outstanding books in the political field. His colleague Professor Victor Jones was a political scientist of equal stature. He had been a staff member of the International City Managers Association in 1942, assistant chairman of the Regional War Labor Board, San Francisco, in 1943, was director of the University of California Center at Bologna, Italy, 1959-1961, and had written and published articles and books important in his field.

The authors described the book supported by the Falk grant this way:

> This is a book for teachers and students, especially those who enjoy working together in the fabulous social complex known as American local government and politics. It can be used by individual students working independently on projects of their own, or by whole classes or groups, in or out of college, that want to make cooperative surveys . . .
>
> A glance through this guide should convince the reader that the purpose of the authors has not been to encourage anyone to suppose that fieldwork is a substitute for the more conventional kinds of learning. The bibliographies and book notes throughout this volume emphasize the need for heroic reading and hard library research as integral parts of any good survey. We believe that the combination of hard book work and hard fieldwork will produce miracles of scholarship.

Other Falk grants to Wesleyan University had made it possible for Professor Schattschneider to organize a course to start in February to prepare students for fieldwork in the following summer. Each student engaged in a community political survey in his own county of his native state, under supervision of his teacher, and as a result learned to use the tools and methods of scientific survey and of party politics in the party of his choice. In the fall he reported orally and in a written paper the results of his survey. Academically sound standards were observed—summer was not a holiday, either for student or teacher. Professor Jones had directed similar work in the University of California—and out of their joint experiences and that of their students came this useful handbook in which the Falk Foundation was pleased to have had its part.

.st   .st   .st   .st   .st

The grant to the Governmental Affairs Institute contributed to the costs of compiling and publishing voting statistics for United States elections between 1920 and 1964. The volume *America at the Polls,* published by the University of Pittsburgh Press in the fall of 1965, brings together in one volume the basic facts of electoral behavior for each of twelve Presidential elections, from Warren Harding to Lyndon Johnson—actual voting figures for every county in every state. For writer, researcher, student, and teacher this volume has important value.

The elections research staff of the Governmental Affairs Institute prepared the material for the book under direction of Richard D. Scammon, whose articles have appeared in political science journals and popular magazines. From 1961 to 1965 he was director of the Bureau of the Census. He is also the editor of the five-volume *America Votes,* University of Pittsburgh Press, an excellent series for the use of political scholars, students, and practising politicians.

.st   .st   .st   .st   .st

Growing out of the major classwork and fieldwork in the colleges and universities to which the Falk Foundation granted aid were several subsidiary projects. To these, when the proposals presented demonstrated they played a part in the overall purpose of the program worthy of support, the Foundation made specific *ad hoc* grants. One of these, a $5,000 grant to Ohio Wesleyan University to finance the development of tests to measure student interest in politics before and after taking the course and the field trips, has been mentioned in the preceding chapter. There were others related in the same way to the main project, varied in character, and complementary or growing out of interests developed in the pursuit of education for politics.

❧ ❧ ❧ ❧ ❧

To the University of Pittsburgh, in 1954, the Foundation granted $75,000, a five-year grant for the expansion of an Institute of Local Government.

The Institute was founded by Professor Elmer D. Graper and he was its director until his retirement from the University of Pittsburgh in 1955, when he was succeeded by Professor William G. Willis, author of *The Pittsburgh Manual* (1950) a survey of the organization and functions of the government of the City of Pittsburgh. The purpose of the Institute was to help local officials do the best possible job. It worked closely with the Allegheny Conference on Community Development, the Pittsburgh Regional Planning Association, and the Pennsylvania Economy League—leading political and business leaders devoted to promoting the best political and economic life for Pittsburgh. The officials of several hundred local government units were clients of the Institute and contributed of their collective knowledge. To find help in solving some of the practical problems of local government was their reason for attending seminars, reading in the library, and consulting the director and his staff. More than 1,000 local officials had enrolled in the Institute's noncredit courses and conferences. A local *News-Letter* and several bulletins and research memoranda were made available (one copy free and additional copies at a minimum cost). The Institute also maintained a valuable library and served as a secretariat for local government agencies.

The Falk grant made possible much greater service and released professors for more time to spend on the work of the Institute (instruction, information, and assistance to local officials) and moved other organizations to support the work. The Wherrett Memorial Fund of the Pittsburgh Foundation provided a capital grant of $17,000 for an annual lecture series.

᪾ ᪾ ᪾ ᪾ ᪾

Two other *ad hoc* grants important to the growth of political education in Western Pennsylvania were made to the University of Pittsburgh.

The Foundation gave $7,000 to help defray the expenses of the 1957 meeting in Pittsburgh of the Executive Committee of the International Political Science Association, the first held in the United States. The Committee devoted its sessions to considering pressure groups in politics as they operate in countries throughout the world. The University of Pittsburgh Press published these essays on pressure groups (each essay by a leader in each of the countries attending) in a book which was widely purchased by students of political science and others interested in the international picture of the function and organization of politics.

᪾ ᪾ ᪾ ᪾ ᪾

In 1961 the Foundation made a one-time grant of

$6,588 for establishing at the University of Pittsburgh the Pitt Center for Politics, for increasing its library collections ($3,850), and for one-half the cost of a Conference on the Administration of Elections.

The Conference was held jointly by the Pitt Center for Politics and the Chatham College Center for the Study of American Politics. Chatham College, a women's college in Pittsburgh, at its request was given a Foundation grant of $7,238: $3,500 to establish a Chatham center and pay administration expenses over four years; $1,000 for books and other literature in the field of politics; $2,738 for one-half the cost of the Conference held jointly with the University.

About thirty election officials and political scientists attending the Conference heard papers and discussed them, on five major topics: Problems of Citizen Participation in Elections; Problems in the Administration of Elections; Problems of Innovation in Election Administration; and Communication Among Election Officials. Among the related topics of discussion were registration systems, absentee voting, obstacles to voter participation, federal court rights-legislation and the right to vote; training of election personnel; new developments in the field; model election law; modernization of election administration. Both Pitt and Chatham expressed satisfaction with the Conference and acknowledged the value of the Foundation help which had made possible cooperation of two Pittsburgh colleges in an attempt to formulate suggestions for improvement of election procedures. The working together of the two colleges had resulted in an effective pooling of student talents and teaching and library resources.

 ❧ ❧ ❧ ❧ ❧

Another cooperative project between two colleges had

146

been supported with success the previous year, June 1960. The Amherst-Mount Holyoke Political Studies Center was granted $8,550 to organize, catalog, file, and promote the use of political campaign materials and other literature on politics for which the Center had been named a depositary by the Republican National Committee and the Democratic National Committee. These colleges were among those which had received grants earlier for their political education programs.

Dr. Victoria Schuck of Mount Holyoke College and Dr. Earl Latham of Amherst College submitted the joint proposal, and the Foundation Board expressed enthusiastic approval for the undertaking by the two leading colleges to help give practical experience to undergraduate students in collecting and organizing political literature of both parties. Designation of the Amherst-Mount Holyoke Political Studies Center as a depositary by the two major political parties, the Foundation was gratified to observe, was a recognition of the national standing which the cooperative Center had won for itself.

꙳   ꙳   ꙳   ꙳   ꙳

Two other interesting special programs related to the major programs of political education on college campuses were those at the College of Wooster in Ohio and Grinnell College in Iowa.

To The College of Wooster the Foundation made a grant in 1961 of $6,300 for a program which the College called *Dialogues in Politics*. This grant was to supplement the overall educational program already supported by the Foundation. Under this special program the scholar of politics and the practising politician were brought together in a new way. Governor of New Hampshire Sherman Adams, who had once been Speaker of the New Hampshire House of Representatives, a member of the United States Congress, and assistant to President Eisenhower brought the perspective of public service. Professor Earl Latham of Amherst College, followed by Professor Ralph K. Huitt of the University of Wisconsin, brought the scholar's perspective. They had both been active in the offices of the American Political Science Association, the National Center for Education in Politics, and other similar organizations. The program served the campus community fivefold:

1. A one-credit course, presenting fifteen fifty-minute discussions on a theme or themes carefully prepared in advance. These programs eventually were divided between lecture and dialogue; but for some of the time, at any rate, both men engaged in conversation on the topic at hand: such themes as Ethics and Politics, Ethnic Groups in American Politics, The Problem of Effective Party Organization, and The Question of Party Responsibility.

2. Several addresses and/or dialogues to the students assembled in chapel.

3. At least one dialogue in a public meeting.

4. Occasional extra-curricular activities.

5. Interviews with students preparing special papers and independent study projects. The program was of great value indeed to the Juniors and Seniors preparing theses in politics.

* * * * *

And to Grinnell College in Iowa the Foundation in 1963 granted $4,500 for political newsgathering internships which made possible $1,500 a year for three students, carefully selected, to serve as interns in the Des Moines, Iowa, Bureaus of Associated Press and United Press. The two Bureaus cooperated well with the College in an important program which helped initiate a new field for political internships.

These programs supplementing the major educational ventures supported by the Foundation encouraged other colleges to establish and support other original supplementary programs suitable for their campuses.

❧ ❧ ❧ ❧ ❧

It would be difficult to overestimate the contribution of Executive-Director J. Steele Gow to this second major interest of the Foundation. Much thoughtful planning before the program was launched; care and discrimination in selecting colleges and universities with faculty and students devoted to the integration of classroom, fieldwork, and internship; many trips back and forth across the country for personal firsthand observation of the various aspects of the program; consultation with authorities and those able to appraise progress and achievement; hours of examining reports of evaluation

Grinnell student mock national political convention, 1960, with a United States congressman and senator presiding. Both political parties are represented.

and of realization of aims and goals; encouragement and enthusiasm and faith in the value of political education for national welfare and freedom—all these efforts and much more characterized the dedicated and creative spirit which Mr. Gow gave to help make this program vital and successful in its ramifications, great and small.

It is fitting, indeed, that in celebration of Steele Gow's seventieth birthday, January 3, 1965, he was honored unanimously by the Board of Managers when they established a trust in the Mellon National Bank and Trust Company, Pittsburgh, as an open-end endowment ($60,000) in support of the J. Steele Gow Political Internship Fund of the Pittsburgh Foundation. The income from this is to be used "for awards to undergraduate college students, preferably residents of Western Pennsylvania, who wish to serve as interns in political and governmental offices or organizations as part of their training for avocational participation after graduation in the activities of the political party of their choice." The Pittsburgh Foundation, a community trust for which Dr. Stanton Belfour is the director, will administer the Fund.

ᴥ   ᴥ   ᴥ   ᴥ   ᴥ

Also in 1965, among the final grants made possible at the time of the liquidation of the Foundation, was a grant to political education of $46,000 to Bethany College, West Virginia, "to initiate a pilot program in practical politics for adults of post-college age." Request for support to the program came from Perry E. Gresham, president of Bethany College, and to his proposal he attached a detailed plan, a policy, and a purpose.

Bethany will use the grant for a two-year pilot program to be known as "The Bethany College Institute for Responsible Citizenship." The College and its friends will supply $600,000 needed to construct a building to house the Institute on the campus and "provide a center from which the program can be carried to other parts of the country."

The Institute will plan to reach mature men and women from business, industry, trade, and finance, and from the professions and other vocations. It will conduct seminars, conferences, workshops, and offer courses and field trips for training adults in methods of party politics at local, state, and national levels and for making them understand political issues in their own communities. Fiscal problems, business interests, legislation, taxes, civil rights are among the political issues that will be presented and discussed from time to time. It is another field of pioneer support by the Falk Foundation—making it possible for the first time for an institution of higher education to offer noncredit work in political education beyond the undergraduate and graduate level which assures soundness of substance and objectivity of approach.

To assure broad representation for the future and to preserve the objectivity of performance the National Board of Fellows for Bethany College will serve as the governing body. This Board of Fellows is distinct from the Bethany College Board of Trustees. The Board of Fellows serves as an advisory board for the College programs of liberal arts and sciences. This new responsibility for the Board of Fellows to govern the affairs of the pilot program in practical politics, President Gresham says, will "insure close cooperation with the college in terms of standards of excellence and charter control while preserving the relative autonomy of the Institute for Responsible Citizenship."

The present Board of Fellows is balanced between Republicans and Democrats, and it is planned to keep to this policy.

152

This terminal grant to Bethany College of $46,000 for adult education brings the total Falk Foundation support to Bethany programs in political education to $102,050 (including $56,050 to undergraduate education for politics in 1958).

❧ ❧ ❧ ❧ ❧

As the Falk Foundation Board and Staff had hoped, others continue to spend their greater resources for this vital cause, "education for politics." In every phase of the program supported by Falk grants—students in the classroom and in the field, undergraduate and graduate; teachers preparing to qualify in their profession or studying to enrich it; the citizen working for his party in support of worthy candidates and issues; the practical politician seeking intelligent support for reaching goals important to the common welfare—there were victories for the Foundation. The program, as Judge Arthur Vanderbilt had described his Clearing House plan, has indeed proved itself to be "a very necessary instrumentality for bringing into active politics young men and women equipped and willing to dedicate themselves to the vital task of making the American form of government work . . . for encouraging young men and women of foresight and integrity to contribute to the future welfare of our nation."

THE MAURICE
AND LAURA FALK
FOUNDATION

Part Four

GRANTS TO PITTSBURGH

*Seek ye the welfare of the city . . . for
in its welfare shall ye fare well.—*
JEREMIAH

CHAPTER THIRTEEN

Grants to Education

The grants recorded in these final chapters of Falk Foundation history unify in a third major program called *Pittsburgh*. They are grants made outside the Foundation's two other major programs, *Economics* and *Politics,* and they are with few exceptions *ad hoc* and terminal, in contrast to the integrated series of grants seeking cumulative results in economic research and political education. These *Pittsburgh* grants are grants to education, to medicine, to culture, and to organized charities. Many of them have been established in honor of Maurice Falk or Laura Falk.

The Falk Foundation's *Pittsburgh* grants cover the years from 1937 to 1964; the majority of them fall within the decade specified by the Articles of Agreement as final in the life of the Foundation; and they increased when the long-term programs in the first two fields of concentrated support had developed far enough and well enough to be fulfilled in purpose or to gain other support.

ꗸ   ꗸ   ꗸ   ꗸ   ꗸ

This chapter records twenty-four grants made to education—twenty-two to Pittsburgh schools, totaling more than $3,000,000, and two to national educational projects calling upon Pittsburgh leadership and support and totaling $60,000.

Between 1937 and 1964 Falk *Pittsburgh* grants went to three colleges and two universities; to three independent preparatory schools; to two schools for children, the handicapped and the retarded; and to two nation-wide educational projects.

157

❧   ❧   ❧   ❧   ❧

Late in 1937 the largest single grant made by the Foundation up to that time, the first to be initiated entirely from principal funds, endowed a chair of social relations in Pittsburgh's Carnegie Institute of Technology.

In recognition of Maurice Falk's lifelong service to industrial development in Pittsburgh and of his deep sense of social responsibility, the Carnegie Tech trustees and President Robert E. Doherty named the professorship The Maurice Falk Professorship of Social Relations (later "of Economics and Social Sciences"). Maurice Falk was living at the time and was pleased to be thus honored.

This grant and the professorship led the way into what President Doherty called The Carnegie Plan of Professional Education. The Plan, affecting all areas of Carnegie Tech, was to develop, as part of technical and scientific education, a larger program relating science and technology to society in a democracy, and to give the student while he was building a technical foundation for graduate work and a career the "basic elements of a liberal education from which might grow an understanding of social and economic organization, humane appreciation, and the capacity for clear thought and expression."

The Falk grant had especial significance for Carnegie Tech's College of Engineering and Science. It supported, besides the professorial salary, efforts necessary to modify the curriculum and teaching methods and to reorient faculty and student outlook.

The Falk Professorship grants at Carnegie Tech, which eventually totaled $765,000, are illustrations of grants that have grown beyond their own dimensions. The Carnegie Corporation of New York, in 1946, contributed another $600,000 for the Carnegie Plan. Similar schools of engineering and science have developed throughout the nation. Other professorships for Carnegie Tech have

158

followed the pioneering Falk grant, based on gifts from other Pittsburgh foundations, from leading corporations, and from alumni and friends. The library, the faculty, and the students have benefited. Research and teaching have been enriched. The physical plant and the financial structure have developed to accommodate the Plan, which continued to grow with added support and good will under Dr. J. C. Warner, a great teacher on the Carnegie Tech faculty who succeeded to the presidency of Carnegie Tech when Dr. Doherty retired. And it still continues to grow, since Dr. Warner's retirement, under President Horton Guyford Stever, a California Tech Ph.D., recently from the staff of Massachusetts Institute of Technology.

Dr. Willard E. Hotchkiss, who brought from teaching and industry strong background experience for the post, was first to occupy the Falk Chair. He was a graduate of Cornell University, had received a doctorate there, and had taught at the universities, Pennsylvania, North-western, Stanford, and Minnesota. His experience in industry was equally broad—in labor arbitration, consultancies to government, and management problems. Dr. Hotchkiss was subsequently succeeded by others prepared well to strengthen the skills and morale of our industrial free and liberal society: Eliot Dunlap Smith, with degrees from Harvard and Yale, held the Falk Chair 1946-1958; and the present occupant of the Falk Chair, George Leland Bach, formerly head of Carnegie Tech's department of economics and dean of the Graduate School of Industrial Administration. These have all been men of superior academic background and practical experience.

The philosophy behind the training of engineers and the purpose for which the Falk grants were made recognizes that the scientist and the engineer are shaping industrial society and so must be educated in responsibility for the social consequences of technological progress.

159

One-fourth time in the Carnegie Tech curriculum is given to understanding the history of man; to learning how to read purposefully and write effectively; to awakening a desire to learn and function as a citizen; to cultivating a capacity for appreciating the creations of the artist and the realization of the "good life."

In his retirement report of 1950, President Doherty recognized the Falk grants thus: "The Falk Foundation was first to give financial support to Carnegie's nontechnical curriculum in 1937 . . . The Maurice Falk Professorship not only initiated the Social Relations Program; it has been a primary factor in its development and in making it an integral part of professional education at C.I.T."

⚜ ⚜ ⚜ ⚜ ⚜

A modest grant important to popular education on current problems was made to Carnegie Tech in 1952. A letter signed by George H. Love, chairman of the Board of Consolidation Coal Company, and by Roger M. Blough, chairman of the Board of the United States Steel Corporation, came to Leon Falk, Jr. as chairman of the Falk Foundation Board of Managers requesting a grant to help establish a series of lectures at Carnegie Tech in memory of the late Benjamin F. Fairless. Mr. Fairless had served on the Board of Trustees at Carnegie Tech for fifteen years and had given much to education at Tech and other institutions.

The endowment to be raised for the lectures was $150,000. The Falk Foundation granted $5,000. More than $200,000 was gathered from many sources before plans were complete for the first lecture given under the auspices of Carnegie Tech's Graduate School of Industrial Administration.

The lectures, three a year, were to treat of "aspects of

business or public administration; the relationships between business and government, management and labor; or with a subject related to the theme of preserving economic freedom, human liberty, and the strengthening of individual enterprise—all of which were matters of deep concern to Mr. Fairless throughout his career."

Gabriel Hauge, president of Manufacturers Hanover Trust Company, New York, gave the 1963 lectures; Theodore O. Yntema, vice president of the Ford Motor Company, gave the 1964 lectures; and Arthur F. Burns, president of the National Bureau of Economic Research and 1953-1956 chairman of economic advisers to President Eisenhower, gave the 1965 lectures.

    🙚 🙚 🙚 🙚 🙚

In June 1964 a Falk grant of $125,000 was made to Carnegie Institute of Technology—the Maurice Falk Endowment for Research in the Humanities. The income from this endowment is to be used for small research grants to selected Carnegie Tech scholars in the humanities. The primary purpose of the grants will be to aid the humanities faculty to help Carnegie Tech reach toward excellence in teaching and research as a part of the professional education of scientists, engineers, and artists.

    🙚 🙚 🙚 🙚 🙚

Each of these grants to education at Pittsburgh's Carnegie Institute of Technology has strengthened the program begun in 1937 of a more liberal education for specialists. They total $895,000.

    🙚 🙚 🙚 🙚 🙚

161

In the Foundation's last years, 1956-1964, four Falk Foundation grants to the University of Pittsburgh totaling $722,500, like the grants to Carnegie Tech and to the other Pittsburgh schools, have pushed forward Western Pennsylvania's educational growth.

These four grants to the University of Pittsburgh are in addition to those already recorded as part of the grants to *Economics* and *Politics,* and they are in addition to larger grants made by the Foundation for the development of the University's Medical Center and its programs, which total more than $1,500,000 and are summarized in the next chapter.

Altogether Falk Foundation grants to the University of Pittsburgh total more than $3,600,000. Added to special Falk family grants made before and after the Foundation was organized, Falk gifts to the University total more than $5,000,000.

* * * * *

In 1955 a new chancellor came to the University charged by the Board of Trustees to make the University "one of the best in the country." Dr. Edward Harold Litchfield came from a professorship in administration and a deanship of the Graduate School of Business Administration at Cornell University. Before that he had had a distinguished career, in education, administrative science, government service, and in business. He holds a Bachelor of Arts and a Doctor of Philosophy from the University of Michigan and has been honored with many advanced degrees and other academic awards. Besides dynamic teaching and research at Brown and at Cornell he had lectured widely on administrative problems and contributed articles and other publications in political science. He also had had an outstanding career as assistant to the United States Chief of Mission to Germany for the U. S. State Department, in 1945-46, and as director of civil administration in Berlin, Germany. Dr. Litchfield had been and is now no less successful in the business world, as chairman of the board of Smith-Corona Marchant, Inc. and in other ventures of his own.

Chancellor Litchfield brought fresh energy to the community and new dimensions of learning to Western Pennsylvania and the University, where education and the tradition of learning have been respected for nearly two hundred years.

Part of Chancellor Litchfield's inauguration ceremony was a series of seventeen seminars where guest authorities, University faculty, and invited community leaders examined current concepts in various fields of knowledge with the idea of finding those of value for the future educational programs of the University of Pittsburgh. These were attended by large groups of alumni, citizens of Pittsburgh, and guests from other educational institutions. The Falk Foundation granted $22,500 to cover the costs of three seminars and other ceremonies inaugurating Edward H. Litchfield as the twelfth chancellor of the University.

✄   ✄   ✄   ✄   ✄

In the same year $100,000 was granted the University of Pittsburgh toward establishing and meeting the first year's expenses of an integrated Student Counseling Center and Placement Service. This was a great contribution toward the goals for which the University planned to strive. It made possible the hiring of a capable professional staff to help students choose programs which could develop as broadly as possible their own capabilities and talents, and to help them adjust their educational experience effectively to life beyond graduation. The Foundation made the grant because the Board supported

163

wholeheartedly the concept of what such a service could mean for conserving and developing the capabilities of youth, which Director Gow called "the community's most important resource."

❧   ❧   ❧   ❧   ❧

The following year, 1957, the Board of Managers of the Foundation granted the University of Pittsburgh $100,000 to recruit faculty, develop curricula, and plan generally for a Graduate School of Public and International Affairs.

The University's Institute of Local Government, to which the Foundation had made a grant of $75,000 in 1954, was to become a part of the new School, and the Administrative Science unit recently established by the University was to be a research affiliate to help develop theories in administration and their application. The proposal for the grant made clear that courses to train selected students for government and for community and civic agencies were to be offered in administration, in community affairs, in city planning and urban development, and in international affairs.

Appointed as dean of the new School was Donald C. Stone, graduate of Colgate University, Master of Science from Syracuse University, a former president of Springfield College, the recipient of doctoral degrees and other honors recognizing his accomplishments. He was skilled in professional service to governmental management— city, county, state, and nation—and the author of books and articles on education, government, and international affairs. He has recruited an able faculty and consultant staff. Graduate students and officials from over the United States and from many foreign countries come to Pittsburgh to benefit from the instruction and research in many kinds of governmental management—from the broad experience offered by the professional staff, the association with scholars, and the resources of the new School within the University. The community has welcomed the School and its library and consultant services with increasing interest.

⚜ ⚜ ⚜ ⚜ ⚜

In February 1964 the Falk Foundation educational grants to the University of Pittsburgh terminated with an endowment grant of $500,000 from Foundation principal funds to establish and support a Maurice Falk Professorship of Politics. This grant has also been mentioned in Chapter Thirteen with college and university programs in political education.

The Board of Managers had discussed the possibility of such a grant at several meetings in 1963 when plans were being considered for using the Foundation's remaining resources in Pittsburgh institutions. Chancellor Litchfield's proposal of December 1963 for a professorship in politics at the graduate level met with approval by the Board.

The University had a vigorous and dedicated political science faculty with an able head, Professor Holbert Carroll, a Doctor of Philosophy from Harvard, and the author of significant writings in political science. With earlier Falk grants and with an earlier able head of the department, Professor Elmer Graper, the University's undergraduate program of political education had developed in effectiveness and had made students and the community aware of the obligation to seek and to support political knowledge in a free society.

Announcement of the grant for the Maurice Falk Professorship was followed promptly by announcement of the first professor to occupy the chair, Dr. Peter H. Odegard, Doctor of Philosophy, Doctor of Laws, Doctor

165

of Letters. Dr. Odegard had the title Visiting Maurice Falk Professor of Politics, and his appointment covered the winter trimester of 1965. Dr. Odegard was eminently qualified to initiate the graduate professorship and to aid in the recruitment of a longterm appointee as his successor. He has an imposing array of degrees and of titles he has held on the faculties of Columbia, Williams, Ohio State, Amherst, Stanford, and California and as president for three years of Reed College, Oregon. A list of publications both scholarly and popular attest his ability to organize ideas into clear communication.

Both the University and the Foundation are pleased to have in so vital a field of education and in one of the Foundation's major fields of interest this Pittsburgh honor to Maurice Falk.

￼ ￼ ￼ ￼ ￼

Duquesne, another strong Pittsburgh university, received two important Falk grants totaling $300,000—one in 1954, the other in 1964.

Duquesne is a coeducational university with an urban campus stretching over more than thirty acres of plateau land, high on a bluff above the Monongahela River, adjacent to Pittsburgh's industrial and cultural Golden Triangle. Although it operates under the auspices of the Roman Catholic Church it serves the whole community, for more than one-fourth of the student body and an even larger percentage of the faculty are non-Catholic and four-fifths of the alumni live and work in the Pittsburgh area. Many alumni hold positions of leadership throughout the community, in the law courts as attorneys and judges, in the hospitals as pharmacists and nurses, in the schools as teachers, in the banks, newspapers, and business houses.

Duquesne responded early to the challenge of the

166

Allegheny Conference on Community Development to help remove areas of urban blight and cultivate Pittsburgh's natural beauty. And it accepted enthusiastically its logical role of serving the urban need, physically and academically. The curriculum has been revamped to strengthen teaching and promote courses and divisions of study to keep American life strong to meet the challenge of the future.

In response to a proposal from the Duquesne Board of Trustees and the president, The Very Reverend Vernon F. Gallagher, the Falk Foundation was pleased to make available to Duquesne in 1954 the $100,000 required to provide moot court rooms for the Law School in the new building with a seven-story front on Forbes Avenue which houses Duquesne's Schools of Business Administration and Law. The Duquesne Law School is important to Pittsburgh and Allegheny County. It is the only evening law school in Western Pennsylvania. Its faculty and courses

The Maurice Falk Moot Court at Duquesne University, Pittsburgh.

rate high in the field of legal education. The rooms which the Falk grant have provided comprise a Moot Court: a model courtroom complete with judge's bench, jury box, counsel tables, spectators' section of 100 seats, reception room, judges' retiring rooms, and a lounge library. They are practical facilities for teaching law and are used for special meetings of Pittsburgh attorneys and businessmen to keep them abreast of new legislation.

The check for the grant arrived on Christmas Eve, and many graduates of Duquesne wrote personal letters to the Foundation Board and the Director commenting on the appropriate date. Judge Hugh Boyle of the Orphans' Court of Allegheny County wrote, "No private gift in years has caused so much favorable comment in the community."

The building itself, which cost over $4,000,000, has been dedicated to Colonel Willard F. Rockwell, good friend of Duquesne University, and for him called Rockwell Hall. The Moot Court is marked with a plate which reads:

The Maurice Falk Moot Court
Gift of
The Maurice and Laura Falk Foundation

⚜ ⚜ ⚜ ⚜ ⚜

In 1964 Duquesne University as part of its Master Plan (physically, a complex of handsome dormitories and classroom and recreational structures) was asking the community for funds to build a stone science building on the bluff, behind the familiar old administration building, which stands against the skyline opposite Mt. Washington across the Monongahela, high on the embankment rising from the Liberty Bridge extension. The science building will house the classrooms and labora-

168

tories of pharmacy, biology, chemistry, physics—graduate and undergraduate.

The Falk grant ($200,000) transmitted to Duquesne University through its president, The Very Reverend Henry J. McAnulty, has provided for twin lecture halls on the ground floor, flanking the main lobby of the Science Center Building. Each will seat approximately 245 people. In the main lobby, facing the campus Academic Walk and visible through the glass wall of the building, a bronze tablet will record the names of the halls—one, The Laura Falk Lecture Hall, the other, The Maurice Falk Lecture Hall.

꙼   ꙼   ꙼   ꙼   ꙼

Two grants were made, one in 1952 and one in 1964, to Chatham College, and these are in addition to two grants to Chatham made in 1955 and 1961, explained in earlier chapters as part of the Foundation's program of support to political education. The total of all grants to Chatham College from the Falk Foundation is $655,688 —$55,688 to political education, $350,000 to a memorial building, and $250,000 to a memorial endowment.

Chatham College, among the top liberal arts colleges for women, is situated in a beautiful wooded park-like area of Pittsburgh, the neighborhood for homes of distinguished and prominent citizens. It was known as Pennsylvania College for Women until the name was changed in 1955 to Chatham, the title of the earldom of William Pitt whose name the city shares. The enrollment is about 600 young women, not merely local but nation-wide and from other countries. For support it depends on income from student tuition and from private gifts. In recognition of the quality of its service to a special kind of education the College has received support from many.

Chatham College buildings dedicated May 2, 1955. The Laura Falk Hall of Social Studies is in the center.

Left to right; Franklin and Marshall College President Theodore Distler; Falk Foundation Director J. Steele Gow; Laura Falk's niece, Mrs. Nathan B. Jacobs; Mr. A. E. Braun's daughter, Mrs. Paul Ernst; Chatham Alumna Mrs. Robert D. Campbell; Buhl Foundation Director Charles F. Lewis; Chatham College President Paul Anderson at the dedication.

In the documents coming to the Falk Foundation from President Paul Anderson with the 1952 proposal is a statement of the ideas and ideals of learning to which the College and its excellent faculty are committed (here somewhat condensed and paraphrased): a recognition of the importance to modern society of the liberal arts; the special abilities of women to contribute to society; the need for freedom to explore relationships among the traditional disciplines of learning; the need for imagination, and substance in teaching, research, government service, arts, and management; the need to rear the new generations to think without prejudice and without being satisfied with the mediocre and the expedient; and the need for sensible, articulate, and sensitive understanding and communication.

The Falk Foundation grant of $350,000 helped to meet the costs of constructing and equipping the social studies unit of a three-unit building. A wing to house the humanities was financed by a grant from Pittsburgh's Buhl Foundation and named for Cora Helen Coolidge, a former president of the College. An administrative wing was given by Arthur E. Braun, chairman of the Board of the College, and named for him. The social studies unit, providing classrooms, laboratories, offices, and other facilities for teaching economics, history, political science, psychology, and sociology, was named the Laura Falk Hall of Social Studies. A physical education building, given anonymously, was dedicated the same day as this beautiful triple-unit building.

※　※　※　※　※

At the request of its recently appointed president, Edward D. Eddy, Jr., a Falk Foundation grant of $250,000, known as The Maurice Falk Endowment for the Enrichment of Undergraduate Teaching, was made in 1964 to

171

Chatham College. The income will be used for periodic review of selected areas of the curriculum, for research to seek new and special teaching materials and methods to enrich undergraduate teaching at the College.

❧   ❧   ❧   ❧   ❧

Another excellent undergraduate liberal arts women's college in Pittsburgh, Mt. Mercy College, received a grant of $50,000 from the Falk Foundation in 1964 toward a goal to raise $1,750,000 for a new science building, as part of an overall program to cost $17,200,000, a total to be completed in 1980. Sister M. Thomas Aquinas (Carroll), a University of Pittsburgh graduate and a Doctor of Philosophy from Catholic University in Washington, is president of Mt. Mercy College, which has an enrollment of approximately 1,400 full time students, about 400 of them in residence. Although Roman Catholic in sponsorship Mt. Mercy is nonsectarian in enrollment. Besides the liberal arts programs the College has fully approved and accredited programs for educating nurses and teachers for elementary and secondary schools.

Mt. Mercy's request to the Falk Foundation marked the first time the College had asked for any public support. Sister M. Thomas Aquinas, the president, and Sister M. Camillus, the librarian and development officer, came first to the Falk Foundation because, as they said, they knew that the Foundation made only "carefully weighed and intelligently allocated contributions to higher education in Western Pennsylvania." They recognized, they said, that a Falk Foundation grant would be worth more than just money; it would create in others confidence in the College and so bring more support. And so it has.

With support which has followed the Falk Foundation grant, on its high Oakland campus not far from the University of Pittsburgh, Mt. Mercy is erecting handsome new buildings for dormitories and classrooms.

      ✤   ✤   ✤   ✤   ✤

In the Falk Foundation's *Biennial Report 1957-1958* there is recorded, to meet a special kind of education need in Pittsburgh, a grant to the Pittsburgh Foundation as fiscal agent of the Pittsburgh Board of Public Education "for the construction of a school building to meet the needs of physically handicapped children." The Report says, in part:

> Pittsburgh had long needed a public school building designed and equipped to meet the special requirements of physically handicapped children. For this purpose, the Sarah Mellon Scaife Foundation had voted a grant of $375,000 on condition that a matching amount be raised from other sources. In 1957 a group of citizens of Pittsburgh undertook to raise the matching $375,000 from local foundations, business firms and other groups, and individuals. The Falk Foundation voted a contribution of $15,000 toward this matching fund.

The new school, named Pioneer School, has been constructed on a thirteen-acre tract in the Brookline area of Pittsburgh. It provides facilities for 180 children from nursery school through high school. The site permits the construction later of additional facilities if they are needed.

      ✤   ✤   ✤   ✤   ✤

During the same biennium, 1957-1958, the Falk Foundation granted St. Anthony's School of Oakmont (a suburb of Pittsburgh on the Allegheny River) $35,000 toward the cost of constructing shops and classrooms for vocational training of the mentally retarded child. St. Anthony's School is a unit of the Roman Catholic Diocese

The Pioneer School in Pittsburgh for physically handicapped children, support of which was shared with others by the Falk Foundation.

St. Anthony's School for Exceptional Children, vocational training for the mentally retarded child, supported by a Falk Foundation grant and gifts from other sources.

of Pittsburgh. Entrants are tested to determine their individual requirements and capabilities. The teachers are specialists in this kind of education. The children live at home, and the school and home cooperate. No tuition is charged. Since 1953 St. Anthony's has trained and educated mentally retarded children, ages six to sixteen, from families of various racial and religious backgrounds.

꙳ ꙳ ꙳ ꙳ ꙳

Two grants included in this chapter were made to cover a wider area than Pittsburgh, although they were, of course, of benefit to Pittsburgh, too, and many Pittsburgh leaders in education contributed to them their talents and other support. One was a grant made to the 1960 White House Conference on Children and Youth; the other, a grant made in 1964, the year of terminal grants, was to the United Negro College Fund.

꙳ ꙳ ꙳ ꙳ ꙳

The White House Conference has been held every ten years during this century. The particular focus of this, the 1960 "Golden Anniversary Conference," was to study the factors which influence individual fulfillment—family, religion, education, health, and community life. Citizens, private and public agencies—local, state, national—were represented. The 1960 Conference covered five days of meetings and included, besides those in the usual categories, 700 young people, leaders in the United States youth organizations, and 500 international guests.

The purpose of the 1960 White House Conference, called by President Dwight D. Eisenhower, like similar earlier conferences was to find ways and means to promote for children and youth realization of their "full

175

potential for a creative life in freedom and dignity." To this cause the Foundation granted $10,000.

    ♪   ♪   ♪   ♪   ♪

The purpose of the United Negro College Fund, Inc. in 1964 was to raise $50,000,000 for capital, plant, and program improvements in thiry-two private educational institutions in the South. The Falk Foundation *Minutes* record the grant and its purpose thus: "realizing the basic importance and special significance of higher education for negroes under current conditions, as one of its terminal grants, the Falk Foundation Board votes unanimously to make payable to the United Negro College Fund, Inc., a grant of $50,000."

    ♪   ♪   ♪   ♪   ♪

In the late 1950's and the early 1960's the Falk Foundation made substantial grants to three independent preparatory schools in Pittsburgh. In the *Biennial Report of 1959-1960* Director Gow explained the philosophy which prompted the grants:

The grants of $90,000 to Shady Side Academy for a scholarship and for faculty salaries, $50,000 to The Ellis School for faculty salaries, and $50,000 to Winchester-Thurston School for land acquisition deserve special mention because they are this Foundation's first grants to independent, or private, secondary schools, a field not often served by the foundations of this country but well worth their careful consideration in the future if these important institutions are to survive in full vigor for the leadership they can give to improving the quality of education. Public schools, of course, have much to contribute to the pioneering of new educational methods and materials and to the advancement of academic standards, but the independent schools have special advantages for leading in these respects because each is pretty much the master of its own destiny and thus enjoys a freedom and a flexibility not always given to the individual institution in the organizational network of our public school systems. Fortunately, there are indications that foundations are preparing to give more attention to the independent secondary school as a key institution in the nation's total education effort.

The three private schools received substantial terminal grants in 1964 which the Board considered also a contribution to the "Pittsburgh Renaissance," discussed in Chapter Fifteen. The Renaissance sought as one aim to strengthen cultural institutions which would hold and attract more skilled and intelligent men and women to work and make their homes in Pittsburgh.

    ❦   ❦   ❦   ❦   ❦

Shady Side is the largest and most widely recognized nonsectarian independent boys' school in the Pittsburgh community. Most of its alumni after college graduation return to Pittsburgh to live and work. In 1959, when Shady Side's request for support came to the Foundation, George L. Follansbee was president. The Board of Trustees of Shady Side had embarked on a Capital Fund Campaign to raise $3,591,500 for the school's three levels of education—senior, middle, and junior. This was the first time since its founding in 1883 that Shady Side had felt it needed a public campaign. The aim was to raise scholarship funds to make possible a democratic cross section of enrollment; to augment faculty salaries and benefits; to improve the old plant; build new buildings; and provide generally for educational improvements.

The Falk Foundation endowment grant of $90,000 provided $40,000 for a Maurice Falk Scholarship in the Senior School and $50,000 to increase the salaries of faculty in the Senior School.

A terminal grant to Shady Side in 1964 provided an endowment of $50,000 toward increases in salaries in the Junior and Middle Schools, bringing the total grants to Shady Side to $140,000.

᙭ ᙭ ᙭ ᙭ ᙭

The Ellis School is a Pittsburgh independent day school for girls from kindergarten through elementary and secondary education. Charles C. Arensberg, president of the Board, and Marion Hope Hamilton, head mistress, presented a request in 1960 for $50,000 as an endowment to benefit faculty salaries, which the Falk Foundation Board unanimously granted. In 1964, as a terminal grant, the School received from the Foundation $50,000 more. The Ellis School chose to use the total $100,000 as a memorial endowment for the Maurice Falk Chair of History.

᙭ ᙭ ᙭ ᙭ ᙭

Winchester-Thurston is also a Pittsburgh independent school for the education of girls from kindergarten to college. It accommodates both day- and boarding-students.

The Winchester-Thurston School, a Pittsburgh independent school educating girls in the elementary and secondary fields of learning, contains The Maurice Falk Auditorium.

178

It represents the unity of two Pittsburgh schools for girls —Thurston, founded in 1887, and Winchester, founded in 1902. The rapid rate of its growth and the needs for future development in 1960 required relocation on a larger campus and buildings to meet the needs of modern education. The new campus is a plot of ground in Oakland once occupied by Shady Side Academy and later by the Ellsworth Center of the University of Pittsburgh.

The Falk grant to Winchester-Thurston in 1960 ($150,000) was to help acquire land and aid in the construction of the new buildings. The second and terminal Falk grant of 1964 added $50,000 more. The school chose to spend the total $200,000 to construct an auditorium, which is a handsome feature of the main building. The auditorium is marked with a plaque which reads:

The Maurice Falk Auditorium
Given in Memory of Maurice Falk
By
The Maurice and Laura Falk Foundation

❧ ❧ ❧ ❧ ❧

It is good that these Pittsburgh schools have honored Maurice and Laura Falk. Men and their foundations do not lightly give away the fruit of their ingenuity and labor. Perhaps, however, they never give to anything more happily than when they give to learning. There is so much of courage and hope and the joy of reaching for excellence in the world of learning. The Maurice and Laura Falk Foundation, like many other foundations and individuals, is pleased to be a part of that world and to be remembered in it.

179

CHAPTER FOURTEEN

Grants to Medicine

Always the Board of Managers remembered the earnest wish of Maurice Falk to use the resources of the Foundation "for the welfare of mankind." And so the Falk Foundation consistently assigned grants to research and educational institutions staffed and geared to seek solutions for the problems which interfere with human welfare and to communicate widely what they sought and what they found. Many of these grants, those to economic study and those to political education, especially, were made to institutions outside of Pittsburgh, and, of course, benefited Pittsburgh, too. But even early in 1931, when the Board of Managers agreed to concentrate support on economic research as a way to contribute basically to human welfare, they passed, unanimously, resolutions to regard the welfare of Pittsburgh a primary consideration. And many grants made directly to Pittsburgh institutions punctuate the record throughout Foundation tenure.

The preceding chapter records grants which have strengthened educational resources in Pittsburgh. This chapter records those which have strengthened medical resources in Pittsburgh. Both, of course, are basic to the welfare of mankind.

꙾ ꙾ ꙾ ꙾ ꙾

In 1935 and year after year to the end of the Falk Foundation's life the Board of Managers assigned many grants to Pittsburgh institutions which promote health, another cause basic to "the welfare of mankind."

Among the first gifts Maurice Falk made to Pittsburgh, even before he gave his surplus to originate The Maurice and Laura Falk Foundation, was a gift he made to medical welfare in 1928 with his brother Leon Falk, Sr. The physical welfare of those who live and work in the Pittsburgh area prompted this family gift of nearly $1,000,000 to the University of Pittsburgh to establish the Falk Clinic. The doors of the Clinic opened in the depth of the depression which hit hard the people of industrial Pittsburgh, and the Clinic under its director, Dr. Joseph Barach, served well for many years those for whom medical care would otherwise have been impossible. The Falk Clinic, with subsequent Falk Foundation support, has matured as an important unit of the great Health Center in Pittsburgh for research, education, and care of the sick.

ࣲ ࣲ ࣲ ࣲ ࣲ

As a matter of fact, Falk Foundation grants in the medical field have been substantial enough to justify calling *Medicine* a major field of commitment alongside the fields of *Economics* and *Politics,* and although the Falk medical grants have in every instance been made to strengthen Pittsburgh institutions they benefit mankind everywhere. Falk Foundation grants to Pittsburgh health institutions have helped make possible buildings, research tools and facilities, a medical school library, physical and mental health aid for children and adults in hospitals and in special institutions, a medical fund with its own program of allocations—and they total nearly $17,000,000. Not counting the Maurice Falk Medical Fund, where assets are measured largely in stock values, Foundation grants to health total over $4,000,000.

❧ ❧ ❧ ❧ ❧

The Foundation's first gift for medical care was to Montefiore Hospital, where Maurice Falk had been a member of the Hospital Board.

In Maurice Falk's name $20,000 was given in 1935 to Montefiore Hospital to construct, equip, and experiment in the development of two oxygen-therapy rooms. When the grant was made, Mr. Abraham Oseroff, then superintendent of the Hospital, visited leading medical centers elsewhere and brought back ideas for equipping the rooms for use of patients with respiratory and heart ailments, and with flexibility to be adapted for the use of patients with other illnesses should the rooms not be required for their specific intent. The rooms served their specialized purpose well until 1949 when the rapid growth of medical knowledge developed even better and more economical facilities and rendered old methods obsolete. The rooms, now occupied continuously by patients with many kinds of illnesses, as Maurice Falk requested, are dedicated to the memory of his wife, Laura K. Falk.

❧ ❧ ❧ ❧ ❧

The Montefiore Hospital in the Oakland area of Pittsburgh is an affiliate and geographically a part of the University Health Center of Pittsburgh with major services in medicine, surgery, and their several specialties.

For many years the Hospital's ophthalmological department had been outstanding, under the able leadership of Dr. Harvey E. Thorpe and a staff of specialists. The Montefiore Hospital in November 1964 presented to the Falk Foundation over the signatures of Irwin Goldberg, executive director, and Stanley J. Kann, president of the Board of Trustees, a request for funds "to carry on research and investigation into the causes, diagnoses, and treatment of ocular diseases, to make findings known by publication and lectures . . . to carry on postgraduate courses for teaching and practicing ophthalmologists and to have fellowships."

The Falk Foundation granted $137,500 for the purposes outlined in the proposal. And the gift was announced in the public press December 1964 as a grant to establish at Montefiore Hospital The Maurice Falk Center for Research and Postgraduate Studies in Ophthalmology under the aegis of Dr. Harvey E. Thorpe, eminent international scholar and practitioner in the field he had served for many years.

꙳   ꙳   ꙳   ꙳   ꙳

Maurice Falk died in 1946, when the Foundation had been active over one-half the time designated as its duration. Out of respect for the gift Maurice Falk and his brother Leon Falk, Sr. had made to establish the Falk Clinic before the Foundation was organized, the Board of Managers granted $5,000 to the University of Pittsburgh in aid of the work of the Falk Clinic. And they agreed that $5,000 was to be an annual contribution to the work of the Clinic, payable in the sum of $2,500 semi-annually, until the Foundation should terminate the grant. The grant was terminated in April 1954 when it had totaled $42,500 and when a new grant was made to the University of Pittsburgh for the Falk Clinic.

This new grant to the Falk Clinic, made in July 1954, gave $100,000 toward the costs of remodeling certain parts of the interior of the building to provide office and laboratory facilities for teachers and research personnel of the University of Pittsburgh's School of Medicine. The request came directly from Dr. Robert A. Moore, then vice chancellor of the University for the Schools of the Health Professions. Vice Chancellor Moore, when the grant was made, acknowledged it as very material help for "an initial and necessary step in the development of the Medical School." It enabled the University to proceed with confidence in the appointment of top-level men and programs in the medical field. The plan was organized so that when the new University building to house schools and divisions of medicine was completed the remodeled rooms could be used for the specific services of the Falk Clinic.

❧ ❧ ❧ ❧ ❧

And in November 1964 the Falk Foundation granted $1,000,000 to the University of Pittsburgh toward the construction of an above-ground covered passageway connecting the Falk Clinic building with the Presbyterian-University Hospital and the Nurses Residence, and toward renovations to the building which will make possible up-to-date service to ambulatory patients of the University Health Center, and help to raise the quality of medical education and research related to the treatment of patients.

The University and the Foundation Board of Managers and Director recognized that new requirements for service to patients, and the need to make the Clinic a closer integral part of the medical complex of hospitals and the other teaching and research units in the University Health Center made the grant important to Pittsburgh's medical advance. And they recognized, too, that the Clinic's history of service to the community under Dr. Joseph Barach, the first director of the Clinic, and his successors, and its memorial character justified a substantial grant toward its future development.

The large and terminal grant transferred certain

Foundation-owned securities to the University plus a check to complete the total $1,000,000 grant. And since the remodeling and renovation will date beyond the termination of the Foundation, the Board of Managers has stipulated that the University hold the Foundation grant in a special account and submit for approval to a designee of the Foundation expenditures made from it.

    ❦   ❦   ❦   ❦   ❦

The year 1949 was a busy year for the Foundation. It marked the Foundation's twentieth anniversary. Grants to Brookings Institution for economic studies and their publication had multiplied, extending into research surveying medical service in the United States, problems of social security, problems of pensions and income tax, and other matters either of immediate or long-term basic study. The field of political education received its first grant—a grant for exploratory purposes (the Reed Survey, discussed in Chapter Twelve). Pittsburgh cultural projects, feeling the pinch of increased costs, were helped to continue in the community, and the Pittsburgh organized charities supported privately by Maurice Falk before his death in 1946 were extended support by the Foundation. The year 1949 was also the year of the deaths of Frank Bell and Israel Simon, which brought about the first changes in the personnel of the Board of Managers since the Foundation's beginning in 1929. Davitt S. Bell succeeded his father on the Board and Attorney Louis Caplan succeeded Israel Simon, and so the high quality of trusteeship set by the appointees of Maurice Falk has been preserved.

    ❦   ❦   ❦   ❦   ❦

Perhaps the highlight among the grants made that

busy year, and among the finest and perhaps most lasting to honor Maurice and Laura Falk, was the gift which established a medical library in the University of Pittsburgh School of Medicine.

Rufus H. Fitzgerald was chancellor of the University, William S. McEllroy was dean of the School of Medicine, and Alan M. Scaife was chairman of the University Board of Trustees. Their request for a grant from the Foundation explained that the funds would contribute toward a goal to raise $12,700,000 from private gifts for the University's Building Fund Campaign, and would establish a worthy and lasting memorial to Maurice and Laura Falk.

As time passed in the development of the campaign and as the plans for the new medical building were enlarged by Vice Chancellor Robert A. Moore, the concept of service for the medical library expanded. And by July 1954 the Falk Foundation increased its initial grant of $300,000 to $800,000 to establish a greater library than the one originally planned in the new Health Center building which was designed to house the Schools of Medicine, Dentistry, Pharmacy, and Nursing. This increase in the grant by $500,000 made

Plaque outside the Maurice and Laura Falk Library for the Health Professions in Alan Magee Scaife Hall, University of Pittsburgh.

possible support to the combined libraries of these four schools. (Western Psychiatric Institute and Clinic and the Graduate School of Public Health have their own separate libraries.)

Under Librarian Carroll F. Reynolds this library in Alan Magee Scaife Hall is the heart of the work of the health services, in teaching and learning, in research, and in care and treatment and prevention of disease. The building houses the four professional health schools, their student laboratories, research units, clinical laboratories, and administrative offices; and it is in close proximity to the vital components of the University health complex of hospitals and clinics. And so the library is used by a large number of professional medical personnel (including the County Medical Society). This very important library is called The Maurice and Laura Falk Library for the Health Professions.

ぷ   ぷ   ぷ   ぷ   ぷ

The Falk Foundation in 1953 made a one-time grant to the National Fund for Medical Education. This was the only grant to medicine the Foundation made outside the Pittsburgh area.

A request for $5,000 to help defray a year's operating budget of $387,740, a fund to be sought in full from foundations, came to J. Steele Gow over the signature of S. Sloan Colt, president of the National Fund.

The Fund had been organized in 1949 at the suggestion of Dwight D. Eisenhower when he was president of Columbia University; Herbert Hoover was honorary chairman; and five other university presidents had joined in organizing the Fund.

The purpose was to raise $10,000,000 yearly from foundations, industries, corporations, medical associations, and individuals for the operation deficits of the

187

more than eighty accredited medical schools of the nation.

Recognizing that it is important to keep a high quality of teaching staff in the medical schools and to provide education at a reasonable cost to the student (including postgraduate and refresher education) and to avoid any large-scale government subsidization, the Board unanimously voted to grant its share, which was $5,000. Because they realized that their first responsibility was to preserve and advance the quality of medical education in Pittsburgh, the Board stipulated that the grant could not be extended to provide for future needs of the National Fund.

       ❦   ❦   ❦   ❦   ❦

In the late 1940's and the early 1950's the medical field was emphasizing that mental health was an outstanding and acute problem. Early in 1949 Leon Falk, Jr., chairman of the Board of Managers, had suggested that the director of the Falk Foundation explore this field of medicine and bring to the Board a report which might include recommendations for support to some Pittsburgh institutions staffed and equipped to contribute knowledge and skill to mental health. J. Steele Gow and his assistant Margaret Happel drafted a report and recommendations based on their research. The report included a canvass of what Pittsburgh institutions were doing in the field of mental health and what their needs were and how and where foundation grants might aid.

Later in 1949 (September) the University of Pittsburgh at the request of the Commonwealth of Pennsylvania assumed responsibility for the Western Psychiatric Institute and Clinic. The University's School of Medicine was confronted with the problem of staffing the Institute and Clinic and setting up an appropriate program throughout the health schools of the University for research, teaching, and patient care. The Foundation's Board of Managers received the report with enthusiasm for the recommendations it contained.

The recommendations favored attention to a request signed by William S. McEllroy, dean of the School of Medicine, and Rufus H. Fitzgerald, chancellor of the University, for a grant toward an annual sum of $150,000 needed to augment the commonwealth appropriations for Western Psychiatric Institute and Clinic. The grant was to help the University bring to the work of the Institute top flight psychiatrists, specialists in the up-to-date knowledge and skills of the profession.

The Falk Foundation, in November 1950, granted to the University for the Western Psychiatric Institute and Clinic $50,000 annually for five years ($250,000), with the stipulation that the grants be allocated to the phase of the program concerned directly with child psychiatry and child development.

Dean McEllroy and the Board of Trustees of the University recruited three outstanding practitioners and teachers: Dr. Henry Brosin from the University of Chicago, Dr. I. Arthur Mirsky from the University of Cincinnati, and Dr. Benjamin Spock from the Mayo Clinic. Their appointments resulted in a strong program and staff throughout the Health Center. Dr. Spock after five years at the University accepted a position at Western Reserve University in Cleveland, Ohio, but he has been succeeded by others prominent in the specialty of child welfare.

.⁙. .⁙. .⁙. .⁙. .⁙.

Three more grants were made by the Falk Foundation which combined with gifts from other Pittsburgh foundations, organizations, and individuals brought

189

further strength specifically to the treatment and prevention of mental illness in children.

❧ ❧ ❧ ❧ ❧

To the Pittsburgh Child Guidance Center, in 1955, the Falk Foundation granted $40,000 toward the funds required to expand professional staff and physical facilities for the Center. The Foundation recognized, as did others in the community who helped—professionals and laymen alike—that child psychiatry had special significance as the best hope for early detection of emotional and mental abnormalities and preventive treatment of them.

The Child Guidance Center had a history of excellence in both research and practice. But it was inade-

Mental health has been generously supported by the Falk Foundation. A child guidance center in the University Health Center of Pittsburgh—a complex of hospitals, laboratories, health schools, and medical libraries—has been a particular interest of the Foundation.

190

quately housed to meet the increased demands on its resources. Its ambitious role was to prevent and treat emotional disorders through parent and child therapy, to train specialists in psychiatry, psychology, and social work, to carry on research, and to promote mental health in the community. Had it not been for the high quality and dedicated work of the staff in the beginning years (Dr. George Mohr, Dr. Harry Little, Dr. Doris Phillips, Dr. William Finzer, Dr. Nettie Ledwith, Dr. Margaret Brennan and their co-workers) the inadequate quarters would have been even more of a handicap.

In 1955 Mrs. Herbert Byrne and Mrs. Leon Falk, Jr. (Josephine S.) between them raised $700,000 toward a fund to provide permanent housing for the Child Guidance Center in the University of Pittsburgh's Health Center. The University found space to fit the plans for a building in the heart of the health complex, close by the Children's Hospital and the Western Psychiatric Institute and Clinic. The new building through the generous cooperation of Pittsburgh foundations and individuals is equipped with up-to-date facilities for its work, and is staffed with specialists to cooperate with the University's other Schools and divisions in the health field. These resources make the Child Guidance Center one of the most effective of such institutions in the United States.

※　※　※　※　※

The Falk Foundation *Biennial Report for 1955-1956* records a grant of $120,000 to Children's Hospital of Pittsburgh to establish a psychiatric training and service program in the Hospital. The request for funds came over the signature of the medical director of the Hospital, Dr. E. R. McCluskey, and the executive director, Walter J. Rome. The grant was made in three annual payments, 1956, 1957, 1958, and during these years and

191

later it encouraged other support. For the program in the Children's Hospital, the Falk grants made possible a specialist in child psychiatry on the hospital staff. The grants gave medical and nursing students of the University of Pittsburgh opportunity for clinical experience in the field, and they provided service to parents and their children who suffered from chronic ailments which created unhappy emotional behavior. The work at Children's Hospital and the work at the Child Guidance Center were complementary in their service to mental health of children in Pittsburgh.

❧ ❧ ❧ ❧ ❧

A gift made in 1963 crowned the Falk Foundation's support to the Child Guidance Center. In 1957 Josephine Falk had suggested that the Center intensify the research phase of its program. She had continued to work with unflagging enthusiasm and energy for the Child Guidance Center, for its new building and for the expansion of its programs. And so, when after her death a request came to the Foundation, presented jointly by Director Meyer Sonis and the advisory committee—for funds to draw upon the talents of the top child psychiatry personnel of the University of Pittsburgh's Schools of Medicine, Social Work, Education, Public Health, and the departments of psychiatry, psychology, learning research and development, and preventive medicine—the Falk Foundation made a substantial terminal grant to the Center. In tribute to the memory of Josephine S. Falk (Mrs. Leon Falk, Jr.) and of her efforts in behalf of child mental health the Falk Foundation granted $400,000 for the research unit of the Child Guidance Center to be named in honor of Josephine S. Falk. This brought Falk Foundation grants to the Child Guidance Center to a total of $440,000.

❧   ❧   ❧   ❧   ❧

In the same year, 1963, another grant was made by the Falk Foundation in the chain of support to emotionally disturbed children. At the request of Mrs. Benjamin Fisher and the members of the Board of the Pressley House in Pittsburgh the Falk Foundation granted $35,000 to a campaign toward additional building facilities for the work of the House. This nonsectarian interracial House is the only resident center for disturbed children, boys and girls, in Western Pennsylvania. For over a century Pressley House had been a haven for children in the community. Its early residence in Old Allegheny, landmark as a retreat for mentally ill children, was no longer adequate. The new modern cottage dormitories on Marshall Avenue in Allegheny, surrounded by seventeen acres of fields and woods, commanding a view of the river valleys and the city below, guarantee a better setting and facilities for the future good work of the House.

❧   ❧   ❧   ❧   ❧

Grants from the Falk Foundation helped the University of Pittsburgh purchase two hospital buildings to provide additional teaching and research units in the Health Center.

The first was a $300,000 grant made by the Falk Foundation in 1957 to be applied to purchase from the City of Pittsburgh the building housing the Municipal Hospital.

Pittsburgh no longer needed a special hospital for treatment of contagious diseases. The University had been renting a portion of the building, where Dr. Jonas E. Salk and his colleagues had conducted their investigations isolating viruses, propagating them, and developing a safe virus as an effective innoculation against crippling poliomyelitis.

Other Pittsburgh foundations helped to buy the building, and the grants to the University for that purpose totaled $1,000,000. In recognition of Dr. Salk's great contribution to world health the building is called Jonas E. Salk Hall.

As further honor to Dr. Salk's work while a professor in the University of Pittsburgh School of Medicine the Commonwealth of Pennsylvania has established a Jonas E. Salk Professorship in Preventive Medicine at the university. Dr. Salk has won many awards, local, national, and international, in gratitude for his contributions to preventive medicine.

꙯   ꙯   ꙯   ꙯   ꙯

In the best interests of medical development for human welfare in the community the Falk Foundation contributed to the University of Pittsburgh a grant of $200,000, which combined with other gifts and grants from Pittsburgh foundations and individuals, made possible the purchase of building and equipment of the Woman's Hospital. This hospital was one unit of a triple-unit building in which another unit was the Eye and Ear Hospital and another, the central unit, was the Presbyterian Hospital. Purchase of Woman's Hospital made possible enlargement of space and services in patient care, teaching, and research for Presbyterian, the general hospital of the Health Center. The enlarged double unit is called Presbyterian-University Hospital. Woman's Hospital is moved to a separate Oakland location and merged with Magee Hospital (Magee-Woman's), which emphasizes obstetrical care and training. Both preserve their autonomy in name and in purpose.

194

ʒ   ʒ   ʒ   ʒ   ʒ

On December 21, 1960 the Board of Managers of the Falk Foundation voted a grant toward endowment of the Maurice Falk Medical Fund, which had recently been incorporated under the laws of the Commonwealth of Pennsylvania as a nonprofit philanthropic organization. Its Board of Trustees: Leon Falk, Jr., chairman; Henry L. Hillman, vice chairman; Julian Ruslander, secretary; John A. Mayer, treasurer; Harry M. Epstine; Nathan Katzen; and Thomas E. Millsop had petitioned the Falk Foundation for the grant to honor Maurice Falk by continued support of his concern for medical welfare.

The Maurice Falk Medical Fund had been chartered in honor of Maurice Falk and his life-long interest in health as a component of "the welfare of mankind," which he considered a personal and individual obligation. The purpose of the Fund was defined "to promote personal and public health, both physical and mental, and the relief, care, and prevention of ailments of men, women, and children regardless of race, color, or creed." The Falk grant, paid from Foundation principal, provided the Medical Fund with its initial capital.

Dr. John T. Cowles, graduate of Princeton and a Doctor of Philosophy of Yale, former teacher at California, Illinois, Princeton, and Pittsburgh, was announced by the trustees of the Medical Fund as the Fund president. He had been a member of the University of Pittsburgh faculty since 1954. In 1963 he resigned from his position with the Medical Fund to return to teaching. In September 1963 Philip B. Hallen, former planning associate at the Hospital Planning Association of Allegheny County, became president of the Maurice Falk Medical Fund.

In 1964 the Falk Foundation made additional grants

to the Maurice Falk Medical Fund, in the form of stock with a market value of $8,622,568.50.

Through the Maurice Falk Medical Fund the works of Maurice Falk for human welfare will continue. And through all the Falk Foundation grants to medical progress in Pittsburgh his sincere wish to contribute to the health of the community to which he had contributed much in industrial development abides, beyond measure.

CHAPTER FIFTEEN

Grants to Cultural Welfare and to Organized Charities

It is not easy to separate *culture* from *education* or *medicine* or *economics* or *politics*. Any of these can be *culture*. And the cultural institutions of man contribute as effectively to his whole welfare and well-being as the institutions with labels we more often recognize as basic and practical. Nor is philanthropy which is limited geographically less effective in time than that which covers wider territory —nor are larger gifts of greater significance than small ones. Grants to Pittsburgh institutions can be, in their fulfillment, of benefit not only locally, but regionally, nationally, or even world-wide.

Falk Foundation grants include all these in kind— local, national, even a few outside the United States— large gifts and small. They are the records which make up what we call the history of the Falk Foundation. Like the histories of other foundations, great and small, Falk Foundation history is woven of human values which at times and in diverse chapters cross each other or sharply separate but hold throughout a design which "shall maintain the fabric of the world."

Like other human institutions, foundations express and project the personality of one and of many. The Falk Foundation has extended into other lives the personality of the donor, of those who approved the grants and distributed the funds, and of those who have received and expended them. That part of the story is not easy to interpret with assurance that no one is missed or that all are fully honored.

197

⋇ ⋇ ⋇ ⋇ ⋇

This chapter records grants, large and small, to seven cultural institutions to which many besides the Falk Foundation have contributed. These are part of what the Foundation calls "out-of-program grants," which means all grants that were not made either to economic research or to political education. This chapter records, too, grants to organized charities which Maurice Falk had supported personally before his death in 1946, and for which he asked that Foundation support be continued until those accustomed to his own support could find other donors. It includes one-time grants to causes also fitting the policies of Falk Foundation philanthropy—made to fulfill the warmhearted purpose of Maurice Falk's "trust for the welfare of mankind."

⋇ ⋇ ⋇ ⋇ ⋇

The grants to cultural development in Pittsburgh are in character very diversified.

The first was made in 1945 to help toward the initial operating expenses of a new foundation in Pittsburgh.

At the Falk Foundation Board Meeting of March 27, 1945, Mr. Gow reported the establishment in Pittsburgh of a new foundation which was to be a multiple purpose community trust for Allegheny County similar to those in Cleveland, New York, and other places. It would gather the gifts and bequests intended for varied philanthropic uses, some earmarked for specified giving and some for which the use of principal or income was not limited to a particular interest. These gifts and bequests were to be distributed at the discretion of a distinguished committee of selected Pittsburgh leaders and with the advice of specialists in many kinds of local philanthropy. The distribution was to be made with the best development of the community in mind. A request had come to the Falk Foundation from the Distribution Committee of The Pittsburgh Foundation to join with other local foundations in short-term initial support for operating expenses of the new organization. The Falk Foundation Board approvingly voted its share for the purpose outlined in the request.

The Pittsburgh Foundation from its beginning has been administered by a director-secretary, Stanton Belfour. His able assistant for many years has been Mrs. Isabel H. Cooper. Dr. Belfour is a graduate of the University of Pittsburgh and has received honorary degrees from many colleges for his services to education, in several capacities at the University of Pittsburgh, and for his services to many institutions since beginning to direct the affairs of The Pittsburgh Foundation. He brought to the work of the new Foundation vision and common sense, a deep awareness of Pittsburgh's past strength, and a dedication to promoting sound and gracious living, now and in the future, for Western Pennsylvania. Under his direction The Pittsburgh Foundation has been successful in amassing funds for a constructive and substantial program of giving.

As one of the Falk Foundation's terminal grants, at the request of Stanton Belfour, the Falk Foundation gave a modest sum to meet The Pittsburgh Foundation's expenses as host for the sixteenth annual national conference of the Council on Foundations, held in Pittsburgh in May 1965, a date coinciding with the twentieth anniversary of The Pittsburgh Foundation. This was an event important to the city itself, for it was a chance to show leaders from many parts of the nation the physical and cultural improvements throughout Pittsburgh known as the "Pittsburgh Renaissance."

❧ ❧ ❧ ❧ ❧

Music from the beginning of settlement here on the frontier has been a major cultural interest in Pittsburgh. The public schools have for many decades featured musical performance and musical appreciation, and various forms of professional musical performance have attracted appreciative audiences.

The city is proud of its Symphony Orchestra, which under the baton of William Steinberg has won acclaim around the world. And the Symphony Society has worked diligently for many years to gain support for this cultural activity which cannot pay for itself—especially if it is to be enjoyed by any considerable number of people.

In December 1950 the Falk Foundation, when grants were concentrated on the programmed giving which is recorded in earlier chapters, gave $10,000 to help the Society with "unusual operation problems." The "problems" referred to were the effects of an unusually bitter winter; snow and ice made transportation so precarious that attendance for both performers and audience presented insurmountable difficulties.

And in 1964 and 1965, as one of its terminal grants, the Falk Foundation, supplementing larger grants from other sources, gave the Pittsburgh Symphony Endowment $150,000 toward a capital fund to provide income for the Symphony Society's operating expenses and to be a part of the community effort for support of this excellent orchestra.

❦   ❦   ❦   ❦   ❦

In 1951, with a special gift to the Falk Foundation from Leon Falk, Jr. and his sister, Marjorie Falk, the Falk Foundation gave $2,500 to the Metropolitan Opera Association of New York City. This was made in anticipation of later gifts to the Metropolitan which have gone directly from the Falk family.

✢ ✢ ✢ ✢ ✢

In September 1955 a request came to the Falk Foundation for a grant to help toward the rehabilitation of the Carnegie Institute building in the beautiful Oakland area of Pittsburgh. The revered old building was in dire need of repair and renovation. It houses a large public library, an excellent museum, music and lecture halls, a fine arts department, and galleries for displaying painting, sculpture, and other works of art. It is the center for the International Art Exhibit which brings artists and visitors to Pittsburgh from over the world. For many, many years the Institute has been a center of cultural enjoyment for Pittsburghers in all walks of life, children and adults. Its free service to the community through organ recitals, natural history and art exhibits, lectures, and library books is beyond measurement in terms of cultural value. The request for a grant in 1955 came from James M. Bovard, the farsighted president of the Institute.

Campaigners for the Institute were asking the community to raise $1,500,000 to make possible a matching grant from the Carnegie Corporation of New York. The City of Pittsburgh and the County of Allegheny each contributed $375,000. Falk Foundation's contribution to the portion assigned to Pittsburgh foundations was $25,000. And before the end of 1955, with the help of volunteer solicitors and the loyalty of Pittsburgh citizens, the money was raised and the Carnegie Corporation grant was matched.

✢ ✢ ✢ ✢ ✢

Beginning on Thanksgiving Day, November 27, 1958, and extending through 1959, the City of Pittsburgh celebrated the two hundredth anniversary of its founding.

The Educational Committee of the Bicentennial Association planned to feature as part of the celebration a number of special programs by the University of Pittsburgh, Duquesne University, Carnegie Institute of Technology, Mount Mercy College, and Chatham College. These five schools were to join in an academic convocation for the conferring of honorary degrees on distinguished persons, to hold conferences of scholars in various disciplines, to give public lectures, and to present historical and other displays. The cost of these events was budgeted at $25,000, and this amount the Falk Foundation granted.

There were many other features downtown at "The Point" and along the rivers to which other foundations and corporations contributed, but they are not a part of this history.

☙   ☙   ☙   ☙   ☙

Pittsburgh throughout its more than two centuries has always had visitors from other parts of the continent and from across the seas. The city is unique in its setting among many hills and in the valleys of three great rivers. The visitors have climbed on foot and by inclined planes to see and admire the panorama below and beyond the hilltops. They have visited Pittsburgh museums, art galleries, observatories, planetarium, aviary, industries, educational centers, and homes. Pittsburgh's urban redevelopment, praised in many magazines and books, has attracted increasing numbers of them. A committee of public-spirited citizens set a Pittsburgh Council for International Visitors to aid the planning and costs of entertaining the many visitors.

The Falk Foundation gave its share in the gifts estimated by the committee as needed from foundations, in response to a request from Alex Lowenthal who was chairman of the Council's Budget and Finance Committee. This was one of the Foundation's terminal grants.

The central office for planning and reception and allocation of hospitality for foreign visitors is part of the Office of Cultural and Educational Exchange on the campus of the University of Pittsburgh. Many hundreds have been met and assigned to guided tours of Pittsburgh corporations, river trips, educational institutions, museums, news media, city government offices, housing and other urban improvements, and the scenic views of the river valleys.

❧   ❧   ❧   ❧   ❧

Perhaps the most distinctive of the "out-of-program grants" contributing to the cultural welfare of the larger Pittsburgh region is the grant made in October 1962 to the Western Pennsylvania Conservancy.

The Conservancy's purpose, expressed in its charter, is to "preserve or aid in the preservation of areas of scenic, biologic, historic, or recreational importance in Western Pennsylvania in the public interest, and to establish or aid in the establishment of nature reserves or other protected areas for scientific, educational, or aesthetic purposes." The dues-paying membership is growing rapidly and Pittsburgh foundations, public-spirited leaders, botanical students, and many who realize the importance of preserving unspoiled lands against the encroachment of urban and industrial development contribute to Conservancy plans and activities.

The Board of Directors of the Conservancy represents the strength which makes the organization one of the most effective cultural forces in Western Pennsylvania. It is composed of business executives, jurists, artists, architects, housewives, writers—all dedicated to the preservation of natural beauty. Dr. Charles F. Lewis, president of the Board, was formerly a successful editor of one of

Two Falk Foundation grants to the Western Pennsylvania Conservancy in Pittsburgh helped develop physical facilities and an education program in the Raccoon Valley, Beaver County, Pennsylvania.

The Hungerford cabin, a center for Conservancy programs.

Max Henrici, well-known naturalist, among the famous ostrich ferns.

A leaf-carpeted trail in the Wild Flower Reserve in Raccoon Valley.

Pittsburgh's largest newspapers and more recently was the executive director of The Buhl Foundation, which under his leadership has made strong and lasting contributions to the best life in Pittsburgh, in research, education, medicine, housing, publishing, culture, and public welfare.

The Falk Foundation made two grants to Conservancy programs: $50,000 toward the costs of the physical development of the Conservancy-owned 300 acre wild flower preserve in the Raccoon Valley, Beaver County; and $16,000 to help finance the initial development of the Conservancy's education program in relation to the wild flower preserve. The land is within twenty-five miles of downtown Pittsburgh, strategically located to serve a large city population, in an area with hundreds of garden clubs and botanical groups and amateur botanists, and with twenty-five colleges and many other schools teaching botany. The region has for generations been a focal point of interest for professional and amateur botanists; no other region has greater variety of flora nor so many different species. And the Raccoon Valley itself is a kind of central borderline country for wild flowers typical of those farther north, farther south, and farther west.

The Falk Foundation grants to the Conservancy have made possible in the Raccoon Valley restoration of buildings and shelters, improvement of roads and trails, and the beginnings of an education program benefiting many sections of the Upper Ohio Valley (Pennsylvania, West Virginia, and Ohio) and beyond.

        ℐ   ℐ   ℐ   ℐ   ℐ

A letter to the Board of Managers, dated July 3, 1936, and filed with the *Minutes* of the Board along with Maurice Falk's *Will* shows that he did not forget his charitable and sectarian beneficiaries and that he also considered them his public trust.

Board of Managers
The Maurice and Laura Falk Foundation
Pittsburgh, Pennsylvania

Gentlemen:

My *Last Will and Testament* will provide according to my present intention that a certain part of my residuary estate will go to The Maurice and Laura Falk Foundation, Pittsburgh, Pennsylvania, for the general work of the Foundation. In accordance with traditional foundation policies, the program of the Falk Foundation, as formulated by its Board of Managers, has been primarily concerned with constructive philanthropy through contributions to nonsectarian organizations. Accordingly, the policy of the Foundation has not provided for grants to organizations which are engaged chiefly in charity and similar relief activities or which are sectarian in nature.

Although the primary purpose of this bequest in my *Last Will and Testament* is to put additional funds at the disposal of the Board of Managers of the Foundation for their use in promoting the Foundation's general program of activity as it may be formulated by the Board from time to time, I should like to suggest that for a reasonable period the funds which will come to the Foundation from this specific bequest should be used, in part at least, to continue the charitable and sectarian contributions which I have been making personally since the Foundation was established. Many of these charitable and sectarian beneficiaries have long derived their chief support from the generosity of Jewish citizens and in that connection have counted on my contributions. It would be a hardship to many of these beneficiaries if my contributions were suddenly terminated. Accordingly, I am taking the liberty of suggesting that although the Falk Foundation's fundamental policies and programs should not be changed, the specific bequest which will come to the Foundation through my *Last Will and Testament* should be drawn upon to continue for a period of five years or so the contributions which I have been making to charitable and sectarian organizations and thus give these organizations ample time in which to finance their activities without the aid of my customary contributions.

Respectfully yours,
Signed: Maurice Falk

And so, drawing upon the additional resources which came to the Foundation from Maurice Falk's *Last Will and Testament,* at his death in 1946 the Falk Foundation made grants to support the work of certain organized charities. Some of these became part of the program of terminal grants which climaxed the life of the Foundation.

       .‎   .‎   .‎   .‎   .‎

At the Board Meeting in April 1946, Executive Director Gow submitted a list of the organizations, charitable and sectarian, to which Mr. Falk had made personal donations and the amounts he annually donated. Unanimous Board action authorized continuing for five years these annual contributions which are headed in the list of Foundation grants, *Maurice Falk Sectarian and Civic.*

The organizations affected by this action were Rodef Shalom Congregation; The Union of American Hebrew Congregations, Cincinnati, Ohio; The Jewish Welfare, Hollywood, California; B'Nai B'Rith Home for Children; The Salvation Army; National Conference of Christians & Jews; Pittsburgh Symphony Society; Tuberculosis League of Pittsburgh; National Jewish Hospital at Denver; Children's Hospital of Pittsburgh; and United Jewish Fund. The total of these grants continuing for five years was $41,875.

Grants to B'Nai B'Rith Home for Children was cancelled because the Home was discontinued. Four organizations listed for five-year donations later received additional grants. Those to the Pittsburgh Symphony have been described earlier in this chapter, and those to Children's Hospital of Pittsburgh in the chapter, *Grants to Medicine.* Later grants to the Salvation Army and to the United Jewish Fund are recorded in this chapter.

       .‎   .‎   .‎   .‎   .‎

When the Board of Managers was planning its first programmed grants to economic research in 1931 the question of contributing to the Pittsburgh Welfare Fund was considered. The Board concluded that whatever the Foundation gave, and perhaps something should be given because of the grave unemployment then in Pittsburgh, it should be made clear that such a donation was outside the program of Falk Foundation grants. Mr. Frank Bell moved a gift to the Welfare Fund of $15,000 in honor of Maurice Falk, Mr. Ernest Weir seconded the motion, and all members of the Board agreed.

During the prewar and postwar periods, and beginning with 1931, $442,000 was donated by the Falk Foundation for the "social welfare work" of the United Fund of Allegheny County.

In the war years, 1941 to 1945, Falk Foundation grants to welfare causes were channeled through the United War Fund and the Red Cross Fund. These grants totaled $106,600.

In 1963, $75,000 was granted the United Fund—$50,000 of this to extend support to the United Fund for five years, through 1968. And finally, in 1964, among the Falk Foundation's terminal grants, an endowment grant was made to the United Fund of $500,000, to help them meet such capital needs as building and equipment.

᙭ ᙭ ᙭ ᙭ ᙭

In the spirit of honoring the personal gifts of Maurice Falk, The Maurice and Laura Falk Foundation granted the United Jewish Federation of Pittsburgh (prior to 1955 the United Jewish Fund of Pittsburgh) $376,500 between 1946 and 1963, $100,000 in 1963, and an endowment of $500,000 in 1964. The terminal grant was earmarked to help meet capital needs and minimize the need for smaller grants which the Foundation might have contributed in future annual subscriptions had Foundation activities continued beyond thirty-five years.

        ✄   ✄   ✄   ✄   ✄

The Salvation Army in Pittsburgh was one of the charities among the beneficiaries continued for five years after the death of Maurice Falk. In 1963, when The Salvation Army campaigned for a building fund of $2,600,000, the Falk Foundation as its share donated $25,000. The total funds were to help The Salvation Army in its plans to expand, relocate, or renovate its facilities in Allegheny County, Pennsylvania.

        ✄   ✄   ✄   ✄   ✄

In July 1961 the Falk Foundation Board was pleased to grant $25,000 to the Young Women's Christian Association of Pittsburgh toward the cost of completing the YWCA's new building on Wood Street between Third and Fourth Avenues, in response to a request from Mrs. Henrietta Campbell and her committee. The new downtown headquarters replaced an older building in the so-called Hill District, razed during the City's rehabilitation program. The new building houses administrative offices, swimming pool, space for health and physical education, meeting and club rooms, food service, and accommodations for transient guests.

        ✄   ✄   ✄   ✄   ✄

And so, the Falk Foundation out-of-program diversified grants to cultural welfare and its nonsectarian grants to organized charities, small and large, have united with grants and donations from other donors to help build in Pittsburgh for all its citizens a stronger community.

THE MAURICE
AND LAURA FALK
FOUNDATION

❧ ❧ ❧ ❧ ❧

Part Five

CONCLUSION

❧ ❧ ❧ ❧ ❧

They received, each for his own memory, praise that grows not old . . . a home in the minds of men, where their glory remains fresh to stir to speech or action as the occasion comes by . . . woven into the stuff of other men's lives. —THUCYDIDES

The Board of Managers and the Executive Director of The Maurice and Laura Falk Foundation on the terminal date of the Foundation. Standing, left to right: James A. Frank, 1956–1965; J. Steele Gow, 1929–1965; Louis Caplan, 1949–1965; Thomas E. Millsop, 1957–1965; Davitt S. Bell, 1949–1965. Seated, left to right: Arthur E. Braun, 1929–1965; Leon Falk, Jr., 1929–1965; Eugene B. Strassburger, 1929–1965.

CHAPTER SIXTEEN

The Men

Supreme examples of Maurice Falk's ability to select men of leadership and understanding, sensitive to his will and purpose, are the men he chose to manage and direct the affairs of the Foundation. Of the original Board of Managers, only three served the entire thirty-five years: Arthur Braun, Leon Falk, Jr., and Eugene B. Strassburger. On the roll of self-perpetuating membership, the four who succeeded those whose terms ended with their deaths were appointed after Maurice Falk himself died in 1946. Executive Director J. Steele Gow started with the Foundation in December 1929 and remained throughout its life. All members of the Board, including those elected after Maurice Falk's death, were men known well to him, prominent in the economic and cultural life of Western Pennsylvania—men whom he trusted because they had shared his efforts and his victories.

Each of them contributed valuable time, imagination, and energy to the affairs of the Foundation, attending regular monthly meetings and special meetings, spending many hours on Foundation concerns, supporting consistently the plans and efforts of the Director. By their own choice, they served without pay.

Short biographies of the members of the Board of Managers and a short biography of the Executive Director follow. These in no way do full justice to the important careers of each of these men, their service and accomplishments.

        ❦   ❦   ❦   ❦   ❦

213

Leon Falk, Jr. was reelected, annually, chairman of the Foundation's Board of Managers, since the election of the first officers at the first meeting of the Board, December 14, 1929. Mr. Falk is a graduate of Phillips Exeter Academy and has a Bachelor of Science degree from Yale University and a Doctor of Laws degree from the University of Pittsburgh, where he is vice chairman of the Board of Trustees and a director of the Presbyterian-University Hospital.

Mr. Falk, as his father and uncle before him did, has made important contributions to the business and cultural life of Pittsburgh and the nation. He holds and has held directorships in many businesses, in scientific, educational, and medical institutions, and he has been a consultant in government welfare, at home and abroad, in war and in peace. He is chairman of the board of the Maurice Falk Medical Fund and the creator of Chatham Center, an office, motor hotel and apartment unit in Pittsburgh's Lower Hill District, which helps beautify a decayed area in Pittsburgh and adds substantially to the rebuilding in Pittsburgh known widely as the "Pittsburgh Renaissance."

⋅⋅⋅ ⋅⋅⋅ ⋅⋅⋅ ⋅⋅⋅ ⋅⋅⋅

Arthur E. Braun was the Board's treasurer for thirty-five years. Throughout a long career in business and banking Mr. Braun has been one of Pittsburgh's most highly repected citizens. Maurice Falk was a director in the Farmers Deposit National Bank with Mr. Braun (who was also president of the Bank) and with others of highest leadership, such as the late Judge James H. Reed and Dr. George Hubbard Clapp. Mr. Braun recalls the informal gatherings of the Bank directors around a table where Maurice Falk, a great reader of newspapers, led discussion on events at home and abroad.

Maurice Falk was a good judge of human nature [Mr. Braun says], loyal to his friends, and not given to disparagement of others. He had sound judgments and his opinions were always listened to with respect. He was particularly impressed with the philosophy of Julius Rosenwald, his friend in Chicago who established a foundation with a time limit for total distribution of the principal. He was definite in opposition to discrimination for racial or religious reasons and he worked diligently to eliminate prejudice of any kind.

Arthur Braun's directorships, academic degrees, and other honors read like a litany of service to the best life in Pittsburgh. He is notably a member of the Board of Trustees of Chatham College, Carnegie Institute of Pittsburgh, University of Pittsburgh, Skin and Cancer Foundation of Pittsburgh, Western Pennsylvania Conservancy, and other important Pittsburgh institutions. It would be difficult to find anyone whose sage advice is more often sought on matters of human welfare.

       ✎   ✎   ✎   ✎   ✎

Eugene Bonn Strassburger, also a member of the original Board, was born in Pittsburgh in 1886. His father, Samuel Strassburger, and Maurice Falk's father, Charles Falk, were in business together in Old Allegheny City in the 1850's.

Mr. Strassburger has bachelor's degrees from the College and the Law School of Harvard University, and an honorary doctorate from Duquesne University of Pittsburgh, where he has lectured for many years in the Law School. He is past president of Rodef Shalom Congregation of Pittsburgh and a life trustee of the Union of American Hebrew Congregations. He has practiced law in Pittsburgh since he was admitted to the Pennsylvania Bar in 1910, and is a member of the law firm,

Strassburger and McKenna. He is a respected member of the leading legal societies and institutes of Allegheny County and Pennsylvania, council vice president of the Harvard Law Alumni, and a council member of the American Law Institute.

Mr. Strassburger's advice was of immeasurable value concerning the Foundation's grants to law research toward establishing a uniform commercial code of states' laws, and to studies of the income tax, the estate tax, and the gift tax laws. From 1956 he was secretary of the Foundation Board.

＊ ＊ ＊ ＊ ＊

Israel A. Simon was the first secretary of the Board. He had been associated with Maurice Falk in one of the earliest Falk businesses, The Duquesne Reduction Company, and was an executive secretary in Mr. Falk's central business office. He died late in 1949 and was succeeded in membership on the Board by Attorney Louis Caplan and as secretary of the Board by Attorney Eugene B. Strassburger.

＊ ＊ ＊ ＊ ＊

Louis Caplan, who succeeded Israel Simon on the Foundation's Board of Managers in 1949, was a loyal friend of Maurice Falk and was his attorney. He was sympathetic with Mr. Falk's interests in the long period of their association. He drew up Maurice Falk's *Will,* under which Mr. Falk's residuary estate was left to the Foundation. He is among Pittsburgh's leading attorneys and was for many years a partner in the firm of Sachs & Caplan. He is a member of the Federal Judicial Conference for the Third Circuit and the American Law Institute. And Attorney Caplan is a former president of the Allegheny County Bar Association.

Mr. Caplan is a past president, and now an honorary president, of the American Jewish Committee; a member of the Board of Governors of Hebrew Union College— Jewish Institute of Religion in Cincinnati; Dropsie College in Philadelphia; and a trustee of the Pittsburgh Association for the Improvement of the Poor. He was a first lieutenant in the Quartermaster Corps in World War I. The Louis Caplan Distinguished Lectures in Law have been established at his Alma Mater, the University of Pittsburgh School of Law, which has recently conferred upon him the degree Doctor of Laws.

Since his election in 1949, the Foundation has found Louis Caplan a good counselor.

❧ ❧ ❧ ❧ ❧

Ernest Tener Weir was one of the original members of the Foundation Board and a vice president until his death in 1957. To the affairs of the Board he brought the same keen judgment, faith in other men's talents, and respect for their right to opinion, even while he differed with them, that governed his thought and action in the business world. He was a pioneer in the steel business and a founder and president of Weirton Steel Company and the National Steel Corporation. He brought to the Board of the Falk Foundation a knowledgeable awareness of economic problems and a talent for organization in approach to them. He consistently directed the attention of his colleagues to projects worth sponsoring.

❧ ❧ ❧ ❧ ❧

Thomas E. Millsop, president and later chairman of the board of the National Steel Corporation and a di-

217

rector and trustee on the boards of many important businesses and financial institutions, in West Virginia, Ohio, Pennsylvania, and Canada, succeeded E. T. Weir as a member of the Foundation's Board of Managers, shortly following Mr. Weir's death.

Mr. Millsop served his country as a flyer in World War I. His progress in the business world has been notable. He began in 1919 as a riveter for Standard Tank Car Company and by 1936 was president of Weirton Steel Company. His talents and his accomplishments have been recognized academically by honorary degrees, and businesswise by directorships in important banks and corporations throughout the Tristate Area of West Virginia, Ohio, and Pennsylvania. He is a member of the board of the Maurice Falk Medical Fund.

⁂ ⁂ ⁂ ⁂ ⁂

Nathan Bernd Jacobs, a member of the original Falk Foundation Board in 1929, died in 1956. He was an engineer and the president of Morris Knowles Engineering, Inc. Both Mr. Jacobs and his wife, Marie Oberndorf Jacobs, were devoted friends of Maurice Falk, and Mrs. Jacobs was a niece of Laura Falk.

Mr. Jacobs was a man of fine sensibilities and wide information. After his death his widow established a scholarship fund for young men or young women to study in the University of Pittsburgh's School of Engineering. The fund is a memorial to Nathan B. Jacobs, first graduate from the University in sanitary engineering.

⁂ ⁂ ⁂ ⁂ ⁂

James A. Frank, a grandson of Isaac W. Frank who was a close friend of the Falks, succeeded Nathan B. Jacobs on the Falk Foundation Board in 1956. Mr.

Frank is a graduate of Shady Side Academy in Pittsburgh and of the College of Engineering, Cornell University. His business career centers around American
Air Surveys, Inc., which he serves as executive vice president and secretary. He is also a member of the boards
of the Pittsburgh Playhouse, Young Men and Women's
Hebrew Association and Irene Kaufmann Centers of
Pittsburgh, the American Jewish Committee, the United
Fund of Allegheny County, and the Urban League. He
is active in promotion of the cultural life of Pittsburgh.

꙳ ꙳ ꙳ ꙳ ꙳

Frank Breckenridge Bell, a vice president of the original Falk Foundation Board, was president of Edgewater
Steel Company. His counsel was sought in all matters
pertaining to the highest interests of the community.
He was an important elder of the Shadyside Presbyte-
rian Church. He was a good friend to Maurice Falk,
and he was always quick to recognize and support the
careful planning of Director J. Steele Gow, which recommended grants to causes, reliable and basic, and rejected
proposals merely palliative or inconsistent with Foundation policy.

꙳ ꙳ ꙳ ꙳ ꙳

When Frank Bell died, in 1949, he was succeeded on
the Board by his son, Davitt Stranahan Bell, also a
steel manufacturer—a man with the strength and vision
of his father in Foundation councils, and a leader in
community welfare. He is president of Edgewater Steel
Company and his civic responsibilities include directorships of the Tuberculosis League and the Children's
Hospital of Pittsburgh.

⚘ ⚘ ⚘ ⚘ ⚘

At Maurice Falk's request, and as he said, "in recognition of their very faithful and close friendship," two of his friends were elected honorary members of the Board, without voting power. They attended faithfully as observers, until their deaths: Louis J. Adler died in 1937 and William B. Klee in 1948.

Their friends on the Board drew up suitable memorials which with the resolutions commemorating all Board members who have died are printed in Appendix D. of this book.

⚘ ⚘ ⚘ ⚘ ⚘

The members of the Board were men busy in their own affairs but they were steadfast in service to the Foundation. And they chose a director whose background and experience fitted him to recommend and carry out a constructive program, who could work well with them and with a donor whose silent presence at Board meetings for seventeen years was encouragement and approval.

J. Steele Gow was the son of Harry Campbell Gow and Elizabeth Steele Gow. From them and their Scottish forebears he inherited a foresightedness and wisdom upon which he built his career.

The Scots of old, like the ancient Hebrews, made their covenant with God. And both included a fierce love of a free way of life, respect for independence, common sense, and a deep sense of responsibility. Maurice Falk recognized in Steele Gow the same loyalties and strengths that the University of Pittsburgh's Chancellor Bowman had recognized. The Chancellor was quoted by Mr. Falk as saying, when the Foundation asked him to recommend a director, "I am cutting off my own right arm when I tell you no one will do but J. Steele

220

Gow." And Mr. Gow likes to tell that when he reported to his father his leaving the University for the Foundation his father said "Thirty-five years! Never take a *temporary* job."

J. Steele Gow won a Bachelor of Arts *cum laude* at the University of Pittsburgh, a Master of Education at Harvard, and a Doctor of Laws at the University of Pittsburgh. He held offices successively at the University of Pittsburgh which called forth his administrative talents: head of public relations, financial secretary, assistant to the chancellor, executive secretary of the University, and dean of administration. He holds trusteeships in many community enterprises for social welfare: Children's Hospital, Allegheny Conference on Community Development, Pittsburgh Skin and Cancer Foundation, Leon Falk Family Trust. He is a member of learned societies, including Phi Beta Kappa. He is the husband of Hazel Steele Gow and the father of three successful sons. All these vital matters are good and they are his biography —but the record of The Maurice and Laura Falk Foundation is good and it is his biography, too.

CHAPTER SEVENTEEN

Final Distribution

Between December 1929 and December 1965 The Maurice and Laura Falk Foundation moved ahead to fulfill the programs approved by the Board of Managers, in steps consistent with the policies they had determined before the first grant was made in 1932. They had agreed then to concentrate on coordinated programs that within the Foundation's tenure could be built, grant by grant, to a well-rounded consummation benefiting the greatest number of people. As time passed, they had selected for concentration two of the most pressing national problems—*economics* and *politics*—making grants for economic study to reliable institutions and leaving the experts free to seek solutions and to publish their conclusions, and making grants to established institutions for educating citizens generally in colleges and communities to realize the importance of their political responsibilities in a democracy. And they had followed initial grants with succeeding grants until the programs reached a high level of performance and accomplishment, and until other donors became interested in continuing them with substantial support after the Falk Foundation was dissolved.

It has been shown in earlier chapters that a third concentrated major program, *grants to Pittsburgh,* was given greater emphasis as the Foundation continued. Grants to Pittsburgh institutions had been made as they fitted into the two selected programs of economic research and political education. After 1960, when the programs in economics and politics had developed to rounded levels, Falk Foundation support of Pittsburgh institutions increased and the objective moved forward in pace with the accomplishment, until the *Pittsburgh* program, too, reached a height of fulfillment at the termination of the Foundation.

The Falk Foundation concentration on grants to Pittsburgh shared an impulse which stirred Pittsburgh citizens interested in business, housing, labor, education, government, and philanthropy to build a fuller, richer community life. In 1943 a committee had been formed in Pittsburgh called the Allegheny Conference on Community Development, with the purpose of restoring Pittsburgh to its proud position as an industrial capital and of reawakening its citizens to a revival of the city's own inherent cultural strength, which had been born of the frontier spirit and the heritage of citizens from many lands. The story of what has become known as the "Pittsburgh Renaissance" has been told far and wide, again and again, in newspapers, magazines, and books, and it needs no elaboration here. Leon Falk, Jr., chairman of the Falk Foundation Board of Managers, united with other young and imaginative leaders in resolve to strengthen the economic welfare of Western Pennsylvania and in every way possible to make a worn urban community a better, fairer place to live; he was a sponsor of the Allegheny Conference from the beginning in 1943 and became a member of its Executive Committee in 1959. J. Steele Gow, Executive Director of the Foundation, was also one of the original incorporators of the Conference and was for many years a member of its Executive Committee. Each member of the Falk Board of Managers, representing his own special field—education, law, industry, finance, art, philanthropy—was a voice on the Falk Foundation Board in encouragement of the great community effort.

In the final reckonings of the Falk Foundation, its *Pittsburgh* program had received the largest share of cumulative grants—nearly two-thirds of the more than thirty millions granted the three major programs.

      ⚘   ⚘   ⚘   ⚘   ⚘

Behind Foundation actions throughout the years was an awareness that the terminal date written into the *Articles of Agreement* by Maurice Falk was December 1964. But as that date drew near, the Board of Managers and the Executive Director realized that additional time would be required to file complete accounting, wind up the physical complexities of Foundation matters, and complete the processing of the final grants—in fact to spend wisely the entire remaining income and principal for the fulfillment of the Foundation's programs.

As is customary in such matters, the Board of Managers of the Falk Foundation, as trustees of Foundation funds, submitted to Orphans' Court of Allegheny County, Pennsylvania, accountings of expenditures, of investments, and of unspent balances. These accountings, submitted in April 1961 covering the period December 14, 1929 to December 31, 1960, and in July 1965 covering the period January 1, 1961 to May 31, 1965, were examined and cleared by the Court, and the Foundation's "Petitions for Distribution" were registered and approved. In preparation are those accountings covering the final period, June 1 to December 31, 1965.

The officers and staff worked through the year 1965 as a "reasonable period" in which to terminate Foundation activity with December 31, 1965, the target date for dissolving The Maurice and Laura Falk Foundation.

      ⚘   ⚘   ⚘   ⚘   ⚘

Several steps, carefully planned and followed through from the time of the earliest grants, led progressively to the termination of the trust, until on September 16, 1963, Director J. Steele Gow sent to each member of the Board of Managers a memorandum entitled "Suggestions for a Program of Grants to Complete the Distribution of the Falk Foundation's Assets," and asked the Board members to forward their suggestions of any additions for discussion of terminal grants at the meeting of October 1963.

Sixteen different items were discussed at the October 1963 meeting and at subsequent meetings, and the institutions represented by these items were approved as worthy of consideration in the making of terminal grants. To start a new program with final disbursement of funds only two years away, the Board agreed, would be impractical; grants to the institutions on the list would fulfill or round out programs already receiving support.

The items listed included institutions representing the three major Foundation programs of support. They were Falk Clinic, Maurice Falk Medical Fund, Pittsburgh Foundation, American Jewish Committee, Brookings Institution, National Bureau of Economic Research, Carnegie Institute of Technology, Chatham College, Duquesne University, University of Pittsburgh, Ellis School, Shady Side Academy, Winchester-Thurston School, United Fund, United Jewish Federation, Pittsburgh Symphony, and United Negro Colleges' Capital Fund Campaign. The latter was the only new grantee considered; the others were institutions which had received earlier grants.

Chapters Thirteen, Fourteen, and Fifteen discuss the terminal grants made to most of these institutions. The majority of these terminal grants were made before the close of 1964; all of them were planned within that year; but because the prerequisite details could not be cleared within 1964, appropriations to a few of them were acted upon by the Board during 1965, the additional year planned for the termination of the Foundation.

❦ ❦ ❦ ❦ ❦

The grants acted upon in February 1965 are part of the chapters which include earlier grants related to them in common purpose. The 1965 grant of $50,000 in "further support" to the Pittsburgh Symphony Endowment is in Chapter Fifteen, where grants to Pittsburgh are grouped, and the grant of $15,000 to the American Jewish Committee "to cover publication costs of a special volume reporting in layman's language the essence of each of the Committee's Foundation-supported 'Executive Suite' studies" is in Chapter Seven, with other grants to economic research by independent agencies. An open-end endowment to be known as The J. Steele Gow Political Internship Fund of The Pittsburgh Foundation (a grant of $60,000) is in Chapter Twelve, with other grants to Pittsburgh education. And the grant of $46,000 to Bethany College for initiation of "a pilot program in practical politics for adults" is in Chapter Twelve, with other special programs in political education.

❦ ❦ ❦ ❦ ❦

It was eminently appropriate that the largest of the terminal grants was made to medicine; for a grant to originate the Falk Clinic had been made by Maurice Falk and his brother, Leon Falk, Sr., even before The Maurice and Laura Falk Foundation was formed, and Maurice Falk's greatest personal and sustained interest was in the health fields. The final grant voted by the Falk Foundation in December 1965 was to further support of the Maurice Falk Medical Fund's expanding program of grants in the health fields ($100,000).

By decree of the Court of Common Pleas of Allegheny County, the Maurice Falk Medical Fund (included in Chapter Fourteen) had been incorporated in September 1960 as a nonprofit philanthropic organization. Initial capital of $5,000,000 had been provided in December 1960 by a grant from the Falk Foundation. In June 1964, in response to an application from the Medical Fund, The Maurice and Laura Falk Foundation gave its entire capital stock of the National Steel Corporation (its total holdings of these securities bearing a current market value of $8,601,568.50) to the Maurice Falk Medical Fund "to finance the effective development in the public interest of various important programs of research and education, including services in the mental and other health fields."

※ ※ ※ ※ ※

And finally, on December 20, 1965, the last Foundation grants were approved. They were grants to programs which had been of paramount interest to Maurice Falk even before the inception of the Falk Foundation.

※ ※ ※ ※ ※

A grant was approved December 20, 1965, in response to a request from John Slawson, executive vice president of The American Jewish Committee. The grant ($150,000) was to "support certain activities to implement the findings and recommendations of the Maurice Falk Studies," which had received an initial endowment grant in 1959 ($250,000) and subsequent grants in 1963 ($40,000 and $55,000), and in February 1965 ($15,000). The three grants made earlier than 1965 are explained in Chapter Seven.

The 1965 grant is to be expended over a four-year period to provide staff salaries and means for professional diagnoses of the problems of discrimination within individual companies and for consultation with company top management and college and university placement officers with a purpose of making suggestions for specific corrective action against discrimination in employment and promotion practices at the management level.

Thus, the findings and recommendations of Maurice Falk Studies conducted under earlier Falk Foundation grants at the Harvard Graduate School of Business, at the University of Michigan Survey Research Center, at Cornell University, and at the University of California in Los Angeles can realize values beyond those of research reports—producing constructive changes in hiring and promotion practices in large companies.

With this grant, Foundation grants to the Maurice Falk Studies under the auspices of the American Jewish Committee total $510,000.

❧ ❧ ❧ ❧ ❧

The second grant approved at the final meeting of the Foundation Board was a grant of $75,000 toward a fund to develop a Radiation Center in Presbyterian-University Hospital as an integral part of the University Health Center of Pittsburgh. Increased demands and rapid advances in techniques and technology in the field of radiation were making it imperative for Presbyterian-University Hospital and the University of Pittsburgh School of Medicine to provide up-to-date facilities and equipment for patient care and appropriate research and teaching. A National Institute of Health grant to the School of Medicine and donations from The Skin and Cancer Foundation for radiotherapy services and from the School of Medicine for teaching services augment the funds needed for the threefold work of the Radiation Center: research, teaching, and care of patients.

❧   ❧   ❧   ❧   ❧

The third grant approved at the Board's final meeting was $25,000 to the Union of American Hebrew Congregations for preparation of a "Liberal Commentary on the Pentateuch." Pittsburgh's Rabbi Solomon Freehof has long been interested in such an undertaking, and he had recommended that the Union apply to the Falk Foundation for a grant to this important work. The Commentary is to involve many scholars and poets of the Reform Jewish Community for a period of three years in production of a five-volume publication, with an editor-in-chief and an advisory board following the work to its completion. Rabbi Maurice N. Eisendrath, president of the Union of American Hebrew Congregations, expressed thus the purpose of the work in a letter to J. Steele Gow:

We want to make the Bible come to life again for the modern Jew. We want to enable our congregants—especially our younger, well-educated, intelligent men and women—to turn to the Bible and to view it as a central repository of Judaism's ideas and ideals. ... The Bible's text must be explained to modern man. It must be made acceptable to him. He must be shown how its central concepts can well withstand the winds of challenge which come from swift-changing movements and ideas. ... Surely, I do not exaggerate when I say that this is the single most important publications project which the Reform Jewish community proposes to undertake in our generation.

Rabbi W. Gunther Plaut, who will work with others on the project, has explained the substance of the work as an integration of "three levels of interest": "the scientific-historical," which attempts to explain what the biblical text meant to the ancient writers; "the traditional," which "culls from thousands of years of commentary the sparkle of the original text itself" and the reverent comments of the great scholars, such as Rashi and Ibn Ezra; and the "the level of relevance," which as Rabbi Plaut says, "would ask the question, 'What does the text say to me today?'—not always giving answers."

And Rabbi Plaut summarizes thus the attitude of approach to this scholarly undertaking to provide modern man with an understanding of what the Torah has meant and can mean today:

> A liberal commentary will of needs recognize that the Torah is a human document, but that at the same time it has for 4,000 years represented our people's reach for God, that in other words the human and the divine are intermingled. We must always be aware of this, which means that while we treat the text critically we will always treat it reverently.

ఞ ఞ ఞ ఞ ఞ

And finally, as a grant to Pittsburgh culture, $15,000 was voted by the Falk Foundation in December 1965 toward the cost of constructing a swimming pool and related facilities in the Monroeville, Pennsylvania recreation park and day camp of the Pittsburgh Young Men and Women's Hebrew Association and Irene Kaufmann Centers. Other Falk resources in the amount of $85,000 gave a total to the recreation project of $100,000. The facilities made possible by the Foundation grant and the additional gift were named in honor of Maurice Falk and Leon Falk, Sr.

ఞ ఞ ఞ ఞ ఞ

As has been said before, elsewhere in this book and by those appraising Falk Foundation grants, the full impact of grants to research and education and culture is not measurable in a short span of time. Perhaps progress in economics and politics is never fully measurable. It is possible, however, to know that because of Falk grants to economic study there are publications available to businessmen and lawyers and teachers and others who need reliable information, and to know that other foundations with greater resources have followed in support of further study in the economic field. And as for politics, it is possible to know surely that because of Falk Foundation grants there is, on college and university campuses and among the public at large, an increased awareness of the need for intelligent understanding and support of a two-party system of politics in a democracy. It is possible to know, too, that there are better teaching methods and enrichment of curriculum in political science, closer ties between the college and the community in political interests, increase of other foundations' support to political understanding—in short, an enlargement of the general interest in a vital field where the Falk Foundation pioneered.

Beyond the dollar measure in grants, or the number of grants consummated, the Falk Foundation's contribution to Pittsburgh social and cultural welfare can be evaluated in some measure by listing the institutions which have by their own choosing recognized the important and lasting help of Falk Foundation grants by naming for Maurice Falk or Laura Falk, or for both of them, buildings, auditoriums, teaching chairs and professorships, a medical library, and a medical fund. (A list of those which sustain the Falk name is in Appendix D.)

These memorials commemorate the confidence and the encouragement of Maurice and Laura Falk and the

Falk Foundation for human institutions that have within their purposes and activities a power to perpetuate human values and weave them "into the stuff of other men's lives."

❧   ❧   ❧   ❧   ❧

Some statistical facts might serve as measure of accomplishment. Hundreds of grants were awarded within the three concentrated programs chosen by the Foundation Managers and the Director for support and there were some few "out-of-program grants," such as those to philanthropy Maurice Falk had supported personally during his lifetime. Thousands of requests were rejected. Rejection was not always reflection against the soundness of the request or of the program for which support was sought. Many proposals were refused because they represented causes outside the Falk Foundation's tightly-knit programs. All requests for grants were carefully weighed and action concerning them was promptly recorded in the Board *Minutes.* And many hours were given to discussion by the Board and to sessions where the Director advised those asking for grants—perhaps, how to construct a better plan, why the Foundation could not undertake a program outside its chosen programs, or even where the request might have a chance to realize fulfillment. (The Cumulative Record of Falk Grants is Appendix E of this book.)

❧   ❧   ❧   ❧   ❧

Seventeen biennial reports and a 1965 supplemental report have been published and distributed widely by Executive Director J. Steele Gow. They record the details of grants and the policies adopted by the Board of Managers and the Director for guidance in awarding

232

them. These reports and the announcements and digests of reports and grants in the public press have fulfilled the Foundation's obligation to make public accounting of the uses of the trust and they reflect the sound planning and the understanding which guided Falk Foundation giving throughout its thirty-five years.

◦ ◦ ◦ ◦ ◦

One of the last acts of the Falk Foundation was to entrust to the care of the Archives of Industrial Society of the Division of Social Sciences, University of Pittsburgh, the files, records, and correspondence—all the official papers—of The Maurice and Laura Falk Foundation. The University's assurance that these records will be of permanent concern to the University, and the details of their preservation until they can be deposited in the University's new Hillman Library, now being erected on the Pittsburgh campus, are in a letter of request which is Appendix G of this history. It is the hope of the University and of the Foundation that these records of a Pittsburgh foundation of limited tenure may be used by those who can gather from them and communicate to others something of value.

◦ ◦ ◦ ◦ ◦

And finally, at the last Board meeting, partly in the downtown Foundation offices and at the Shadyside home of A. E. Braun, with all Managers and the Executive-Director present, The Maurice and Laura Falk Foundation brought its deliberations and actions to a close.

And so the wheel set in motion December 1929 had by December 1965 gone full circle.

◦ ◦ ◦ ◦ ◦

233

On Friday, December 31, 1965, The Maurice and Laura Falk Foundation closed its doors. A quotation from J. Steele Gow's *Final Biennial Report, 1963-1964,* climax of the Foundation's accounting to the public, reflects the understanding and the spirit with which the Board of Managers and the Staff of The Maurice and Laura Falk Foundation performed the duties entrusted to them by Maurice Falk:

The final paragraph of this section of this last official report (Part I. "The Final Two Years 1963 and 1964") has the obligation and the privilege to record the Falk Foundation's indebtedness to the scores of institutions and organizations which have helped it in many ways, and to the hundreds, even thousands, of individuals who have been involved in its manifold operations. The Foundation is especially indebted to the recipients of its grants for the effective use they have made of the funds entrusted to them, and it is also indebted to those applicants who have so graciously accepted its decision when their requests were declined. Further, it is indebted to the many persons to whom it turned for advice and help in planning its grant programs and, later, in evaluating the results. Finally, it owes a great debt to the general public for good will and for the many evidences of approval of the Foundation's objectives and the methods employed to reach them.

꙳　　꙳　　꙳　　꙳　　꙳

The Maurice and Laura Falk Foundation has fulfilled the imagination, the thought, the energy, and the accomplishments of Pittsburghers. Grants to support basic research in economics and political education for teachers, their students, and the general public; to help publish the research and ideas of sound institutions and individuals and distribute these widely; to foster learning and health and enrich life in Pittsburgh, the Nation, and other lands; to encourage others to invest in these causes—all have been warp and woof of a design to expend an individual trust within thirty-five years. Surely

the meaning and force of these Pittsburgh accomplishments will go on extending and strengthening the will
of Maurice Falk to benefit the society which made possible his own good fortune and the individuals who
were very deeply his concern.

APPENDIX A

Articles of Agreement

Made and concluded this 14th day of December, A. D., 1929, by and between MAURICE FALK, of the City of Pittsburgh, County of Allegheny and State of Pennsylvania, the creator of this trust, hereinafter referred to as the creator of said trust, party of the first part; and A. E. BRAUN, LEON FALK, JR., I. A. SIMON, E. T. WEIR, NATHAN JACOBS, FRANK B. BELL, EUGENE STRASSBURGER AND FARMERS DEPOSIT TRUST COM-PANY, all of the City of Pittsburgh, County of Allegheny, and State of Pennsylvania, hereinafter referred to as the Board of Man-agers, parties of the second part, WITNESSETH AS FOLLOWS NAMELY:

WHEREAS it is the desire of the creator of the said trust to dedicate and devote the portion of his estate hereby conveyed to the said Trustees as a memorial to his deceased wife, Laura, who lived a good and useful life and to whose counsel and devotion the creator of the trust hereby founded owes much of his success, she being truly a helpmate, whose comfort and encouragement made his life happy, and her memory is accordingly lovingly en-shrined in his heart;

AND WHEREAS the creator of the trust believes that one, who by good fortune has accumulated wealth beyond his personal, economical requirements, should hold in trust that wealth to be expended for the benefit of and in helpfulness to mankind;

AND WHEREAS in consideration of the premises, it is proposed to create this trust under the name and title of THE MAURICE AND LAURA FALK FOUNDATION, to be managed, controlled and operated, and the funds expended, for the purposes and to the ends and for the accomplishments hereinafter provided.

NOW, THEREFORE, in consideration of the premises and of the mutual covenants and agreements hereinafter provided, it is stipulated and agreed by and between the creator of said trust and said Trustees, hereinafter referred to as the Board of Managers:

1st. The name of said trust shall be THE MAURICE AND LAURA FALK FOUNDATION.

2nd. The purposes and ends of said trust, and the accomplishments to be thereby obtained, are the uplifting and upbuilding of the unfortunate, the amelioration of the sufferings of the afflicted, and the encouragement, improvement and betterment of mankind, and for these purposes and aims to devote and apply the estate and the property by this instrument vested in said Board of Managers, and the income to be derived therefrom, to educational, religious, charitable, philanthropic and public uses, as determined and decided from time to time by said Board of Managers.

3rd. The property to constitute said trust and Foundation as herein provided shall consist of the property, stocks, bonds, securities and assets, set forth in the schedule hereto attached, marked Exhibit "A," and such other stocks, bonds, securities, property and assets, as the creator of said trust, or anyone else, may from time to time hereafter transfer to said Board of Managers and be accepted by them. Said stocks, bonds, and securities shall be transferred to said Board of Managers to be held by them in trust and disposed of as hereinafter provided.

4th. The creator of said trust hereby nominates and appoints and agrees that A. E. Braun, Leon Falk, Jr., I. A. Simon, E. T. Weir, Nathan Jacobs, Frank B. Bell, Eugene Strassburger and Farmers Deposit Trust Company, aforesaid, shall be the Trustees and Board of Managers of said Trust and Foundation, under and by virtue of this Agreement, said Trustees to be known as the Board of Managers of said THE MAURICE AND LAURA FALK FOUNDATION. Any vacancy occurring in said Board of Managers occasioned by death, removal, resignation, refusal or inability to serve, or otherwise, may be filled by the remaining members of the Board of Managers, or, in case of their failure to act within three (3) months after the occurrence of said vacancy, upon the application of the Board of Managers, by the Court of Common Pleas of Allegheny County, Pennsylvania, and every such new Trustee so appointed from time to time shall have, possess and exercise all the powers, authority and discretion by this instrument conferred upon the present Board of Managers, as fully and effectually as though he or it were named by this instrument as one of the original Board of Managers.

5th. Said Board of Managers, except as hereinafter limited, shall have the power and authority and are directed to distribute from time to time for educational, religious, charitable, philanthropic and/or public uses and purposes, or any or all of them, each year, such amounts of income or principal of said estate as they in their discretion may appoint, order or direct, and said Board of Man-

238

agers shall not be restricted in any manner or to any extent in their selection of the uses, objects and purposes to which the said trust fund and its income shall be applied from time to time. Said Board of Managers may use and apply the said income of said fund from time to time, or any part of the principal thereof, as in their judgment may seem wise and proper, and they may allow the income to accumulate and become part of the principal from time to time, thereby providing for the needs and demands for relief that might thereafter arise; but it is suggested by the creator of the trust, though not absolutely directed, that it is preferable as far as practicable and reasonable, that the income, at least, should be distributed each year. Said Board of Managers are authorized and empowered, within their discretion, but are not so compelled, to withhold from distribution any portion of said principal for a period of fifteen (15) years from the date of this agreement, but beginning at the end of said period of fifteen (15) years, they are directed to begin the distribution of said principal as well as the income of this Foundation, so that the same shall be fully distributed on or before thirty-five (35) years from the date of this Agreement; it being the purpose and intent of the creator of this trust that the total income and whole estate shall be distributed to such beneficiaries as the Board of Managers in their discretion shall determine, within or by the end of said period of thirty-five (35) years. The said Board of Managers may use and apply the said trust fund and the income therefrom to said uses, objects and purposes, and in such proportions respectively, as they may determine, either directly or through any municipalities, or through any religious, educational, charitable, benevolent, philanthropic or public institutions, corporations, associations, activities and agencies, or in aid of any municipalities, or in aid of such religious, educational, charitable, benevolent, philanthropic or public institutions, corporations, associations, activities or agencies, as they, the said Board of Managers, at any time and from time to time, may determine and direct. The said Board of Managers shall make a report annually of their administration of the trust, and may publish the same in the newspapers of the City of Pittsburgh, Pennsylvania, or mail copies thereof to a number of prominent men interested in religious, educational, charitable, benevolent, philanthropic and public institutions or agencies.

6th. The said Board of Managers shall have the power and authority, within their discretion and exercise of judgment, to sell and dispose of any of the property, stocks, bonds, or securities, transferred to said Foundation by this instrument, or subsequently acquired, and may invest and reinvest the income or funds thereby obtained, or the income from time to time accumulated, in any other stocks, bonds, property, or securities, which in their discretion they may determine is wise and proper. The said investments are not limited to those which are commonly known as those in which trust funds are authorized to be invested under the laws of the State of Pennsylvania. The said Board of Managers shall not be responsible for any loss arising out of said investments made by them in the exercise of their judgment and discretion. Said Board of Managers shall have power and authority to give a proxy to any one selected by said Board to vote any of the stocks and securities held in said trust at any meeting of any corporation having issued such stocks or securities.

7th. The creator of said trust agrees and directs that said Board of Managers, and its successors in the trust, shall have and exercise, subject to the limitations herein provided, all the rights and powers incident to the ownership of all the properties real and personal, held by them from time to time belonging to the trust, as fully and absolutely as though they were the owners of said properties in their own right. The said Board of Managers and its successors shall have power to deposit the moneys and securities belonging to the trust from time to time in such banks and safe deposits and trust companies as they may from time to time select.

8th. The creator of said trust hereby authorizes the Board of Managers of said Foundation from time to time to fix whatever, if any, compensation shall be paid to them or to any of them for the services they may render to the trust at such amount as said Board may from time to time determine. All of the expenses of said Board of Managers to be paid out of said trust funds. The creator of said trust hereby designates Leon Falk, Jr., as the first Chairman of said Board of Managers, to serve for one year from the creation of this trust, and as many successive years as he may be elected as Chariman by said Board of Managers. Said Board of Managers shall have power to appoint a Vice-Chairman and may from time to time appoint a Secretary and from time to time fix the duties to be performed by said Secretary. Said Board of Managers shall have power and authority to engage or employ any other person or persons they may desire to employ or engage for the performance of any services to said Foundation, including an Executive Director, and may fix the compensation of such person or persons, and shall likewise have power and authority to incur any other expense or to do any other act or acts which they may consider necessary and proper to the effective administration of said trust. The compensation of the Board of Managers, if any, the Secretary's salary, and all other compensation, and all other expenses of administration of the trust, shall first be paid each year, or provision made therefor, out of the income of said Foundation before any distribution is made therefrom for any one year.

9th. Except as herein otherwise provided, the decisions and acts of a majority of the voting members of the Board of Managers of said Foundation shall be and constitute an exercise of the trust powers and discretions conferred upon said Board of Managers, and the decisions and acts of said majority of said Board of Managers shall constitute and be taken as the decisions and acts of the entire Board.

Meetings may be held where notice has been given to all the members of the Board of Managers and three of said members attend said meeting, but to make any action taken at such meeting effective written assent to such action must be obtained from such number of members as are not in attendance, which, together with the votes of those in attendance, will show that a majority of the members of said Board assented to such action. Any member of said Board may vote at any meeting by letter as well as personally, but such letter must clearly state the action upon which the vote is cast and the vote thereon.

The trust company appointed, or that may be hereafter appointed, as a member of the Board of Managers, shall have no vote as a member of said Board, said trust company having been appointed as a member of said Board of Managers on account of the convenience in securing a depositary for, and someone to look after, the securities in said trust, and keep the books, and in obtaining financial advice on the investments, and the sole duty and obligation of said trust company shall be to keep the books of accounts of the trust and to act as depositary of its funds, certificates of stock, bonds, securities, and other properties and assets. Said trust company is authorized, empowered and directed, to act or refrain from acting, from time to time, and in all matters and respects pertaining to the trust, in conformity with the instructions of its Board of Managers, evidenced by resolution certified by the Secretary of the Board of Managers to have been adopted at a meeting of the Board regularly convened and held, or by a writing signed by a majority of the voting members of the Board of Managers, or, in the event of the organization of the corporation here-

241

inafter provided for, in conformity with the instructions of said corporation, evidenced by a resolution certified by its Secretary, under its corporate seal, to have been adopted by its Board of Directors at a meeting thereof, regularly convened and held, and said trust company shall be fully protected in so acting or refraining from acting.

10th. If any person or persons at any time is or are disposed to make gifts or bequests to the said Foundation, power and authority is hereby conferred upon the said Board of Managers to receive such gifts and bequests and to apply the principal and income therefrom to the purposes of this trust, under the powers, authorities, and discretions contained in this Agreement; provided, that said gifts or bequests are not made upon any terms or conditions that would conflict with the uses, purposes and provisions of this Agreement and the administration thereof by said Board of Managers, except that restrictions in such gifts and bequests may be agreed to by said Board of Managers and accepted subject thereto.

11th. The creator of said trust authorizes and empowers the Board of Managers of said Foundation, or a majority of them, if they desire so to do, to form and organize a corporation for the uses and purposes provided for said Foundation by this Agreement, such corporation to be organized under the laws of Pennsylvania, or any other State, or under the laws of the United States, as may be determined by said Board of Managers; said corporation when organized to have power to administer and control the affairs and property of said Foundation, and to carry out the uses, objects and purposes of said trust. Said corporation, if organized, shall be named THE MAURICE AND LAURA FALK FOUNDATION. Upon the creation and organization of such corporation, the Board of Managers of this Foundation, or a majority of them, are authorized and empowered to convey, transfer and deliver, to said corporation, all the property and assets to which said Foundation may be or become entitled. It is the purpose of this provision that the said corporation, if incorporated and organized as by this paragraph provided, shall take the place of the Board of Managers and Trustees of this Foundation as if named in the first instance. Said corporation, if formed, shall have the same powers and authority as are vested in the Board of Managers by this Agreement. The Board of Managers of said Foundation, or a majority of them, shall be the incorporators of said corporation, together with such other persons as they may choose for the purpose, and the said Managers shall constitute and act as the first Board of Trustees or Directors of said corporation, together with such other persons as the said Managers, or a majority of them, may select. The application for charter, the provisions thereof, the organization, the by-laws, rules and regulations, and other provisions for the management of the said corporation and its affairs and property, shall be such as the Board of Managers named in this Agreement, or those then acting as such, or a majority of them shall determine.

12th. Without the assent of the entire Board of Managers said Foundation shall continue for a period of at least fifteen (15) years, but thereafter, with the assent of two-thirds (⅔) of said Board of Managers, said Foundation may at any time be wound up and the assets distributed in accordance with the provisions of this Agreement; but, as above provided, said Foundation must be wound up and the assets thereof distributed at the expiration of thirty-five (35) years from the date of this Agreement.

IN WITNESS WHEREOF the parties hereto have duly executed this Agreement the day and year first above written.

Witness on all signatures:

A. Leo Weil

Alan D. Reynolds

               (signed)

Attest:

E. J. Askey

Maurice Falk   (SEAL)

A. E. Braun   (SEAL)

Leon Falk, Jr.   (SEAL)

I. A. Simon   (SEAL)

E. T. Weir   (SEAL)

Nathan B. Jacobs (SEAL)

Frank B. Bell   (SEAL)

E. B. Strassburger (SEAL)

FARMERS DEPOSIT TRUST COMPANY,

By A. E. Braun   (signed)

APPENDIX B

Extract from the Last Will and Testament of Maurice Falk

Article VI. Section 1.

I have endeavored during my lifetime to be of service to my fellow-men and I have used for their benefit a generous portion of the means which a Divine Providence has permitted me to accumulate. I have heretofore contributed large sums for specific charitable and humanitarian purposes, and I have deemed it a privilege to be able to do so. In addition, I have established, as a memorial to my late beloved wife, Laura Falk, and as an instrumentality for carrying out my plans to aid humanity, a Trust or Foundation, known as "The Maurice and Laura Falk Foundation," which was created by me by agreement in writing dated December 14th, 1929, in which Arthur E. Braun, Leon Falk, Jr., I. A. Simon, Ernest T. Weir, Nathan B. Jacobs, Frank B. Bell, Eugene B. Strassburger and Farmers Deposit Trust Company are named as Trustees. I have already conveyed to the said Foundation a considerable portion of my estate. It is now my desire that, subject to the payment of certain annuities hereinafter referred to, my entire residuary estate shall be used, through the instrumentality of The Maurice and Laura Falk Foundation, for the benefit of mankind.

APPENDIX C

Board Members and Staff of
The Maurice and Laura Falk Foundation
with
Dates of Service

Leon Falk, Jr., Chairman	December 14, 1929–December 31, 1965
A. E. Braun, Treasurer	December 14, 1929–December 31, 1965
E. B. Strassburger, Secretary	December 14, 1929–December 31, 1965
Davitt S. Bell	July 16, 1949–December 31, 1965
Louis Caplan	July 27, 1950–December 31, 1965
James A. Frank	December 6, 1956–December 31, 1965
Thomas E. Millsop, Vice Chairman	October 24, 1957–December 31, 1965

Deceased

E. T. Weir, Vice Chairman	December 14, 1929–June 26, 1957
Frank B. Bell, Vice Chairman	December 14, 1929–May 6, 1949
Israel A. Simon, Secretary	December 14, 1929–November 17, 1949
Nathan B. Jacobs, Vice Chairman	December 14, 1929–February 14, 1956

Honorary Members (also deceased)

Maurice Falk	December 14, 1929–March 18, 1946
Louis J. Adler	March 28, 1930–June 4, 1937
William B. Klee	March 28, 1930–October 27, 1948

Depositaries

Farmers Deposit Trust Company	December 14, 1929–December 18, 1939
Farmers Deposit National Bank of Pittsburgh	December 18, 1939–December 20, 1950
Mellon National Bank and Trust Company	December 20, 1950–June 21, 1960
Pittsburgh National Bank	June 21, 1960–December 31, 1965

Executive Director

J. Steele Gow	December, 1929–December 31, 1965

245

Assistants to the Director

Jane M. Wood-Smith	1938–1942
Nancy J. Richardson	1942–1944
Margaret Happel	1944–1965

APPENDIX D

Memorials

JULIUS ROSENWALD
1862–1932

WHEREAS the death of Julius Rosenwald has taken from American philanthropy a generous benefactor who used his wealth as a trust for the advancement of his fellow man, an able counselor whose guidance of the Rosenwald Fund influenced the policies of philanthropy everywhere, a wise and courageous pioneer who, because of his faith in the generosity and intelligence of each generation to care for its own needs, advocated the non-perpetual trust and thus laid down a new series of principles for keeping philanthropy sensitive to the times it serves,

BE IT RESOLVED that by this Resolution the Board of Managers of The Maurice and Laura Falk Foundation records its acknowledgment of the great debt American philanthropy owes Mr. Rosenwald, and of the grave loss it has suffered in his death,

AND BE IT FURTHER RESOLVED that this Resolution be spread on the Minutes of the Board of Managers of The Maurice and Laura Falk Foundation and a copy thereof be transmitted to the President of the Julius Rosenwald Fund and to Mrs. Rosenwald.

The above Resolution was suitably inscribed on parchment and sent to the President of the Julius Rosenwald Fund and to Mrs. Rosenwald.

FRANK BRECKENRIDGE BELL

A member of the Board of Managers of The Maurice and Laura Falk Foundation from its establishment on December 14, 1929 until his death on May 6, 1949, Frank Breckenridge Bell was peculiarly qualified for trustee-responsibility for the Foundation's affairs. He held that organized philanthropy should be purposive, and that it serves best when it is not content with small ends easily achieved but seeks the high goal and tries the hard task. In determining the purposes and policies of the Falk Foundation he gave wise and

247

far-sighted counsel. He was realist enough to recognize that achievement will not always match objective, but he gave no quarter to compromise of aim or effort in the Foundation's work.

For almost two decades the Foundation was privileged to draw rich benefits from his able and devoted attention to its interests. His passing leaves a place on its Board difficult to fill.

In grateful appreciation of the part he played in the Foundation's development we, the Board of Managers, here record our deep affection and respect for him as a colleague and as a man, and by unanimous action we vote to convey our sincere sympathy to his family in their great loss.

ISRAEL A. SIMON

Member and Secretary of the Board of Managers of The Maurice and Laura Falk Foundation from its organization on December 14, 1929 until his death on November 17, 1949, Israel A. Simon saw the Foundation as a privileged opportunity to advance the welfare of man. He therefore held its work to be of the first order of importance; whatever else was claiming his time, he promptly turned to its affairs whenever they called for his attention. For twenty years he served the Foundation faithfully and well.

Israel Simon held a place of prominence in the industrial and business life of the Pittsburgh community. The organizer of several firms, he played a creative role in the business world. To his organizing and managerial activities he brought an aggressive energy and the courage to take risks in the quest for progress. He served on the boards of many corporations, to whose councils he brought an alert and imaginative mind.

In his human relations he was a kindly and considerate man. He had great capacity for warm and enduring friendship. For those in distress he had a quick and deep sympathy and he gave generously of his time and means to help the needy. Many whom he aided never knew that he was their benefactor. He gave from a warm heart that asked no acknowledgment to the giver.

Convened in meeting on December 5, 1949, the Board of the Falk Foundation here records its affection for Israel Simon as a man and its esteem for him as a colleague, and votes to extend to his wife, Virginia Jackman Simon, and his son, Richard S. Simon, its sincere sympathy in their great loss.

248

NATHAN BERND JACOBS

Nathan Bernd Jacobs served as a member of the Board of Managers of The Maurice and Laura Falk Foundation from its organization on December 14, 1929 until his death on February 14, 1956. For more than a quarter of a century he contributed importantly to the development of the Foundation and the progress of its philanthropy.

Fully sensitive to the obligations as well as to the opportunities of private organized philanthropy in a free society, he held that it must, if it is to be constructive, attempt the important and worthy, however difficult to achieve, and avoid the unimportant and the unworthy, however easy to accomplish. He realized that results would not always match objectives, but he gave no quarter to compromise of aim or effort. As the Foundation's work grew through the years and reached into new fields of interest, he gave increasing time to the consideration of its problems. To these problems he brought a disciplined and informed mind.

His sincerity, modesty, and kindliness personally endeared him to his fellow Board members and to the Foundation's Staff. They will miss him greatly as a friend and companion as well as a colleague.

In grateful recognition of his long and devoted service to the Foundation, its Board by unanimous action enters this Memorial Minute in its records and conveys, with its deep and sincere sympathy, a copy to his family.

ERNEST TENER WEIR

Ernest Tener Weir served as a member and vice-chairman of the Board of Managers of The Maurice and Laura Falk Foundation from its organization on December 14, 1929 until his death on June 26, 1957.

Through more than a quarter of a century the Foundation's philanthropy held a place of high importance among his interests, and to its affairs he gave constant and talented attention. His able and inquiring mind probed persistently for opportunities for constructive giving. His judgment of what was worthwhile weighed heavily in the Board's choice of objectives and programs, and the work of the Foundation as it has developed through the years bears the clear imprint of his counsel, his judgment, his foresight, and his faith.

Realizing that achievement will not always match aspiration he nevertheless had full confidence that if organized philanthropy looks high, works hard, and follows sound principles in dispensing its benefits much can be accomplished to serve man and promote the general welfare.

In grateful recognition of his long and able service, the Board of the Foundation by unanimous consent enters this Memorial Minute in its records and directs that a copy be given to his family with its sincere and deep sympathy.

LOUIS J. ADLER

Elected an Honorary Member of the Board of Managers of The Maurice and Laura Falk Foundation on March 28, 1930, Louis J. Adler brought to the counsels of the Board a deep and understanding interest in constructive philanthropy. Always sensitive to the needs for individual relief through charity, he yet saw the deeper wisdom of planned and sustained search for the social causes of human distress. He had in abundance the quiet patience which keeps faith with long-term efforts to improve the lot of man. He had the courage to pioneer for new lines of progress. Soft-spoken and kindly in discussion, he was yet strong in his convictions, once he decided which way progress lay.

The death of Mr. Adler on June 4, 1937, closed a life that was fine and useful. In tribute to that life, The Maurice and Laura Falk Foundation here records in the Minutes of this official meeting of the Board of Managers on June 21, 1937, its gratitude for Mr. Adler's faithful services to the Foundation and its profound sense of loss in his passing; and directs that this Minute be conveyed to Mrs. Adler and her children as an expression of the Foundation's sincere sympathy.

WILLIAM BENJAMIN KLEE

William Benjamin Klee was elected an Honorary Member of the Board of Managers of The Maurice and Laura Falk Foundation on March 28, 1930. His death on October 27, 1948, took from the Foundation a wise and far-seeing counselor. A regular attendant at the Board's meetings, he brought to its affairs both a sound business judgment and a sensitive understanding of the human values which philanthropic funds should seek to serve.

The Board and Staff of The Maurice and Laura Falk Foundation mourn his passing and extend to his wife and family their sincere sympathy.

MEMORIALS TO
MAURICE AND LAURA FALK

Brookings Institution Maurice Falk Auditorium,
    Washington, D. C.

Maurice Falk Institute for Economic Research in Israel,
    Jerusalem

American Jewish Committee Maurice Falk Studies

Yale Maurice Falk Fellowships in Politics

Carnegie Institute of Technology Maurice Falk Professorship
of Economics and Social Studies—Pittsburgh

Carnegie Institute Maurice Falk Endowment for Research
in the Humanities—Pittsburgh

University of Pittsburgh Maurice Falk Professorship of Politics

University of Pittsburgh Maurice and Laura Falk Library for
the Health Professions

Duquesne University Moot Court honoring Maurice Falk
    Pittsburgh

Duquesne University twin lecture halls, Science Center Building,
honoring Laura Falk and Maurice Falk—Pittsburgh

Chatham College Laura Faĺk Hall of Social Studies—Pittsburgh

Chatham College Maurice Falk Endowment for the Enrichment of
Undergraduate Teaching—Pittsburgh

Shady Side Academy Maurice Falk Scholarship in the Senior School
    Pittsburgh

Ellis School Maurice Falk Chair of History—Pittsburgh

Winchester-Thurston Maurice Falk Auditorium—Pittsburgh

Montefiore Hospital rooms dedicated to the memory of Laura Falk
  Pittsburgh

Montefiore Hospital Maurice Falk Center for Research and
Postgraduate Studies in Ophthalmology—Pittsburgh

Maurice Falk Medical Fund—Pittsburgh

APPENDIX E

Cumulative Record of Grants

(Tables begin on opposite page.)

GRANTS FROM INCOME

ECONOMIC RESEARCH STUDIES AND OTHER PROJECTS IN ECONOMICS

RESEARCH STUDIES†

	Date of Grant	Amount of Grant*	Amount Paid Prior to 1963	Amount Paid in 1963 and 1964	Payable in 1965
Allegheny Conference on Community Development, Pittsburgh, Pa.					
Economic Basis for Community Development of Allegheny County District in Pennsylvania	Oct. 10, 1944	$ 2,500.00‡	$.........	$.........	$.........
American Law Institute, Philadelphia, Pa. and National Conference of Commissioners on Uniform State Laws, Chicago, Ill.					
The Preparation of a Modern Commercial Code	June 30, 1944	285,000.00	285,000.00	....	....
American Law Institute, Philadelphia, Pa.					
A Study of Federal Income, Estate and Gift Tax Laws and the Formulation of Recommendations for Improvements in the Structure of the Laws	Mar. 9, 1948 April 24, 1963	620,000.00 187,000.00	620,000.00	.... 187,000.00	....

* Where the date of a grant precedes January 1, 1963, the amount listed may be the total of a number of grants given prior to 1963.

† All titles here listed are the titles used by the applicants in their requests for grants and are not necessarily identical with the titles of the publications resulting from the research.

‡ This grant was canceled by mutual consent when the Conference reported it was unable to proceed with a satisfactory project.

253

GRANTS FROM INCOME (Continued)

ECONOMIC RESEARCH STUDIES AND OTHER PROJECTS IN ECONOMICS (Continued)

RESEARCH STUDIES (Continued)

	Date of Grant	Amount of Grant	Amount Paid Prior to 1963	Amount Paid in 1963 and 1964	Payable in 1965
American Law Institute and American Bar Association—Joint Committee on Continuing Legal Education, Philadelphia, Pa.					
To conduct a conference and prepare a report of its proceedings on the Committee's Program of Continuing Legal Education	Dec. 20, 1961	$ 37,500.00	$ 37,500.00	$	$ . . . .
Brookings Institution, Washington, D. C.					
Distribution of Wealth and Income in Relation to Economic Progress	Jan. 8, 1932	158,013.74	158,013.74	. . . .	. . . .
The Recovery Problem in the United States	June 24, 1935	70,000.00	70,000.00	. . . .	. . . .
Industrial Price Policies and Economic Progress	April 20, 1936	35,000.00	35,000.00	. . . .	. . . .
An Evolving and Flexible Program of Economic Studies	April 11, 1937	580,000.00	580,000.00	. . . .	. . . .
Productivity, Wages, and National Income	April 11, 1937	65,000.00	56,684.45*	. . . .	. . . .
Government and Economic Life	Sept. 22, 1937	100,000.00	100,000.00	. . . .	. . . .
Wartime Control of Prices	Dec. 19, 1938	13,000.00	13,000.00	. . . .	. . . .
Bases of National Prosperity	Mar. 20, 1939	25,000.00	25,000.00†	. . . .	. . . .
Pricing for Prosperity	Mar. 20, 1939	21,000.00	21,000.00	. . . .	. . . .
Relief and Social Security‡	May 13, 1940	67,800.00	67,800.00	. . . .	. . . .
Refugee Settlement in the Dominican Republic	Oct. 8, 1940	50,000.00	50,000.00#	. . . .	. . . .

---

* The cost of the project was $46,684.45. The grantee refunded $10,000.00 of the amount paid on the appropriation.
† This project was canceled by the grantee in December, 1942, and an unused balance of $14,687.76 was refunded.
‡ This project was originally entitled *Public Relief in the United States* but was expanded to include a study of social security.
# An unused balance of $613.44 was refunded by the grantee.

254

GRANTS FROM INCOME (Continued)

ECONOMIC RESEARCH STUDIES AND OTHER PROJECTS IN ECONOMICS (Continued)

RESEARCH STUDIES (Continued)

Brookings Institution (Continued)

	Date of Grant	Amount of Grant	Amount Paid Prior to 1963	Amount Paid in 1963 and 1964	Payable in 1965
Impact of the Defense Program upon the Economic Life of the Nation	May 26, 1941	$ 11,000.00	$ 11,000.00	$........	$........
Proposed Studies of the Effect of Governmental Fiscal and Other Economic Policies on the Private Enterprise System	April 25, 1942	100,000.00	100,000.00	....	....
An Economic Program for Postwar United States	April 25, 1942	100,000.00	100,000.00	....	....
Annual Wage and Employment Guarantees	Mar. 27, 1945	26,000.00	26,000.00	....	....
A Study to Determine the Need for Changes in Federal Labor Policy and to Recommend the Changes Indicated	June 26, 1946	20,000.00	20,000.00	....	....
Concentration in American Industry	June 26, 1947	91,500.00	91,500.00	....	....
Taxes and Economic Incentives	June 26, 1947	25,000.00	25,000.00	....	....
A Study of Social Security Costs and Financing Methods	Feb. 24, 1949	12,000.00	12,000.00	....	....
A Survey of Medical Service in the United States	July 15, 1949	139,000.00	139,000.00	....	....
The Dynamic Economy	Mar. 31, 1950	37,000.00	37,000.00	....	....
The Problem of Pensions	Mar. 31, 1950	64,000.00	64,000.00	....	....
A Study of Ways and Means to Reduce the Expenditures of the Federal Government	Feb. 27, 1952	120,000.00	120,000.00*	....	....
The Price-Changing Process†	Oct. 15, 1953	40,750.00	40,750.00	....	....

* This project was canceled by The Brookings Institution in March, 1954, and the total amount of the grant refunded.
† The Brookings Institution acted as fiscal agent for Dr. H. G. Moulton, the applicant for this grant.

GRANTS FROM INCOME (Continued)

ECONOMIC RESEARCH STUDIES AND OTHER PROJECTS IN ECONOMICS (Continued)

RESEARCH STUDIES (Continued)

	Date of Grant	Amount of Grant	Amount Paid Prior to 1963	Amount Paid in 1963 and 1964	Payable in 1965
Brookings Institution (Continued)					
The Impact of Union Policies upon Industrial Management	June 10, 1955	$100,000.00	$100,000.00	$........	$........
Growth Requirements in the Steel Industry	Dec. 16, 1955	80,000.00	80,000.00*	....	....
Committee on Postwar Tax Policy, New York, N. Y.#					
A Postwar Taxation Program	April 14, 1944	228,323.00	228,323.00§	....	....
Committee on Public Debt Policy, New York, N. Y.					
A Study of the Problem of the Public Debt	Feb. 7, 1946	114,677.57	114,677.57**	....	....
Falk Project for Economic Research in Israel##					
Fordham University, New York, N. Y.					
The Development and Distribution to Other Colleges of Materials Bearing on the Interdependence of American Industry	June 13, 1951	15,000.00	15,000.00	....	....
Foundation for Economic Education, Inc., Irvington-on-Hudson, N. Y.					
A Study of Industry-Wide Collective Bargaining	Oct. 8, 1947	10,500.00	10,500.00	....	....

---

* This project was canceled by The Brookings Institution in June, 1962; the total amount of the grant was refunded.

The name of the Committee was changed in 1950 to the Committee on Federal Tax Policy.

§ Unused balances of $2,553.11, $1,291.17, and $255.03 were refunded by the grantee.

** An unused balance of $2,466.72 was refunded by the grantee.

See grant to Israel Foundations Trustees, Jerusalem, Israel.

GRANTS FROM INCOME (Continued)

ECONOMIC RESEARCH STUDIES AND OTHER PROJECTS IN ECONOMICS (Continued)

RESEARCH STUDIES (Continued)

	Date of Grant	Amount of Grant	Amount Paid Prior to 1963	Amount Paid in 1963 and 1964	Payable in 1965
Israel Foundations Trustees, Jerusalem, Israel					
Investigation of the need for economic research in Israel*	Oct. 20, 1952	$ 10,000.00	$ 8,000.00**	$........	$........
Falk Project for Economic Research in Israel†	July 1, 1953	735,575.00	698,253.00	37,322.00	....
U. S. Advisory Committee for the Falk Project for Economic Research in Israel	July 1, 1953	79,000.00	56,686.60	22,313.40	....
The Johns Hopkins University (School of Advanced International Studies, Washington, D. C.)					
In support of studies of the economic status and development of foreign countries	Oct. 8, 1959	15,000.00‡	15,000.00	....	....
National Bureau of Economic Research, Inc., New York, N.Y.					
Agriculture and the Business Cycle	Sept. 18, 1933	15,000.00	15,000.00	....	....
The Volume of Production and Productivity of Labor and Enterprise in the United States, 1899-1937	Nov. 29, 1937	217,500.00	217,500.00	....	....
The Effects of Public and Private Pension Systems in the United States on Saving and Investment	Nov. 25, 1957	164,200.00	164,200.00	....	....

---

* The Brookings Institution acted as fiscal agent for Dr. A. D. H. Kaplan, who made the investigation.
† See page 130 for listing of endowment grant.
‡ A compensating contribution in the same amount was received by the Foundation from a friend.
** An unused balance of $2,000.00 was canceled.

257

GRANTS FROM INCOME (Continued)

ECONOMIC RESEARCH STUDIES AND OTHER PROJECTS IN ECONOMICS (Continued)

RESEARCH STUDIES (Continued)

	Date of Grant	Amount of Grant	Amount Paid Prior to 1963	Amount Paid in 1963 and 1964	Payable in 1965
Social Science Research Council, New York, N. Y.					
Suggestions for a program of economic research studies	Oct. 19, 1931	$ 3,000.00	$ 3,000.00	$	$ ....
University of Pittsburgh, Pittsburgh, Pa.					
Economics of the Iron and Steel Industry	Feb. 6, 1934	33,500.00	33,500.00	....	....
OTHER PROJECTS IN ECONOMICS					
American Assembly, Columbia University, New York, N. Y.					
Wages, Prices, Profits and Productivity	Oct. 15, 1958	76,500.00	76,500.00	....	....
Automation	Mar. 28, 1961	70,000.00	70,000.00	....	....
American Jewish Committee, New York, N. Y.					
To restore drafts on the Foundation's initial endowment for the Maurice Falk Studies*	Dec. 10, 1963	40,000.00	....	40,000.00	....
In support of the "Executive Suite Project" as the first undertaking of the Maurice Falk Studies	Dec. 10, 1963	55,000.00 15,000.00	....	55,000.00	....
Brookings Institution, Washington, D. C.					
Establishment of Division of Economic Education	June 13, 1951	75,000.00	75,000.00	....	....
Conferences on Economic Policy to review conditions and discuss policy with the President's Council of Economic Advisers	Oct. 15, 1953	15,000.00	15,000.00	....	....

---

* See page 130.

258

GRANTS FROM INCOME (Continued)

ECONOMIC RESEARCH STUDIES AND OTHER PROJECTS IN ECONOMICS (Continued)

OTHER PROJECTS IN ECONOMICS (Continued)

	Date of Grant	Amount of Grant	Amount Paid Prior to 1963	Amount Paid in 1963 and 1964	Payable in 1965
Carnegie Institute of Technology, Pittsburgh, Pa.					
Benjamin F. Fairless Memorial Lectures	Oct. 2, 1962	$ 5,000.00	$ 5,000.00	$.........	$.........
Alfred P. Sloan Foundation, New York, N. Y.					
The production and distribution of motion picture films for economic education	Oct. 8, 1947	230,000.00	230,000.00	....	....
University of Pittsburgh, Pittsburgh, Pa.					
Workshop in Economic Education	Jan. 22, 1953	2,000.00	2,000.00	....	....
Western Pennsylvania Council on Economic Education, Pittsburgh, Pa.					
1963 Summer Seminar-Workshop	April 5, 1963	8,500.00	....	8,500.00	....
Subtotals*—Economics		$5,501,339.31	$5,138,388.36	$350,135.40	....

---

* Unadjusted for refunded, reduced, and canceled grants. See page 135.

259

GRANTS FROM INCOME (Continued)

EDUCATION FOR POLITICS

PROGRAMS AT THE UNDERGRADUATE LEVEL

	Date of Grant	Amount of Grant	Amount Paid Prior to 1963	Amount Paid in 1963 and 1964	Payable in 1965
Allegheny College, Meadville, Pa.	June 16, 1952	$ 75,150.00	$ 75,150.00	$	$ ....
Amherst College*					
Bethany College, Bethany, W. Va.	Dec. 19, 1958	56,050.00	47,200.00	8,850.00	....
Boston University, Boston, Mass.	June 16, 1952	75,187.50	75,187.50	....	....
Chatham College, Pittsburgh, Pa.	April 30, 1952	48,450.00	48,450.00	....	....
College of Wooster, Wooster, Ohio	Jan. 22, 1953	68,875.00	68,875.00	....	....
Goucher College, Baltimore, Md.	May 17, 1954	47,500.00	47,500.00	....	....
Grinnell College, Grinnell, Iowa	April 9, 1959	67,687.00	57,000.00	10,687.00	....
Hamline University, St. Paul, Minn.	June 16, 1952	47,500.00	47,500.00	....	....
Howard University, Washington, D. C.	July 16, 1958	47,500.00	45,000.00	2,500.00	....
Knox College, Galesburg, Ill.	Mar. 5, 1958	47,500.00	45,000.00	2,500.00	....
Massachusetts Institute of Technology, Cambridge, Mass.	Mar. 25, 1957	76,000.00	76,000.00	....	....
Mount Holyoke College, South Hadley, Mass. and Amherst College, Amherst, Mass.	May 17, 1954	38,625.00	38,625.00	....	....
Ohio Wesleyan University, Delaware, Ohio	June 16, 1952	68,125.00	68,125.00	....	....
Pomona College, Claremont, Calif.	July 9, 1954	52,250.00	52,250.00	....	....
Rollins College, Winter Park, Fla.	Mar. 25, 1957	47,500.00	47,500.00	....	....

* See Mount Holyoke College.

GRANTS FROM INCOME (Continued)

EDUCATION FOR POLITICS (Continued)

PROGRAMS AT THE UNDERGRADUATE LEVEL (Continued)

	Date of Grant	Amount of Grant	Amount Paid Prior to 1963	Amount Paid in 1963 and 1964	Payable in 1965
University of Oregon, Eugene, Oregon	June 29, 1959	$ 71,250.00	$ 60,000.00	$ 11,250.00	$ ....
University of Pittsburgh, Pittsburgh, Pa.*	July 1, 1953	47,500.00	47,500.00	....	....
Wabash College, Crawfordsville, Ind.	Mar. 25, 1957	57,000.00	57,000.00	....	....
Washington Square College of Arts and Science, New York, N. Y.	Oct. 20, 1952	36,000.00	36,000.00	....	....
Wesleyan University, Middletown, Conn.	April 14, 1953	25,515.00	23,490.00	2,025.00	....

PROGRAMS AT BOTH UNDERGRADUATE AND GRADUATE LEVELS

	Date of Grant	Amount of Grant	Amount Paid Prior to 1963	Amount Paid in 1963 and 1964	Payable in 1965
University of North Carolina, Chapel Hill, N. C.	Mar. 25, 1957	139,500.00	139,500.00	....	....
Vanderbilt University, Nashville, Tenn.	Mar. 25, 1957	83,450.00	83,450.00	....	....

* See page 133 for listing of endowment grant.

GRANTS FROM INCOME (Continued)

EDUCATION FOR POLITICS (Continued)

PROGRAMS AT THE GRADUATE LEVEL

	Date of Grant	Amount of Grant	Amount Paid Prior to 1963	Amount Paid in 1963 and 1964	Payable in 1965
Michigan State University, East Lansing, Mich.	Dec. 14, 1954	$124,800.00	$124,800.00	$.........	$.........
University of California, Berkeley and Los Angeles, Calif.	June 29, 1959 Jan. 16, 1963	132,000.00 147,000.00	132,000.00	.... 147,000.00	....
University of Chicago, Chicago, Ill.	April 9, 1959 Jan. 16, 1963	56,000.00 59,000.00	56,000.00	.... 59,000.00	....
University of Washington, Seattle, Wash.	Dec. 19, 1958	59,232.00	37,682.00	21,550.00	....
Yale University, New Haven, Conn.*	Jan. 22, 1953	174,500.00	174,500.00	....	....

OTHER PROGRAMS IN EDUCATION FOR POLITICS

	Date of Grant	Amount of Grant	Amount Paid Prior to 1963	Amount Paid in 1963 and 1964	Payable in 1965
American Heritage Foundation, New York, N. Y. In support of the Register-and-Vote Campaign of the American Heritage Foundation	Dec. 16, 1955	10,000.00	10,000.00	....	....
Chatham College, Pittsburgh, Pa. To establish a Center for the Study of American Politics, sponsor a Conference on the Administration of Elections, etc.	July 14, 1961	7,238.00	7,238.00	....	....

262

* See page 133 for listing of endowment grant.

GRANTS FROM INCOME (Continued)

EDUCATION FOR POLITICS (Continued)

OTHER PROGRAMS IN EDUCATION FOR POLITICS (Continued)

	Date of Grant	Amount of Grant	Amount Paid Prior to 1963	Amount Paid in 1963 and 1964	Payable in 1965
College of Wooster, Wooster, Ohio To conduct the program "Dialogues in Politics"	July 14, 1961	$ 6,300.00	$ 6,300.00	$.........	$.........
Governmental Affairs Institute, Washington, D. C. Toward the costs of compiling and publishing voting statistics for United States elections between 1920 and 1964	Dec. 19, 1958	47,300.00	47,300.00	....	....
Grinnell College, Grinnell, Iowa To finance a program of student internships in political news gathering	Dec. 10, 1963	4,500.00	....	4,500.00	....
Metropolitan Pittsburgh Educational Television Station WQED, Pittsburgh, Pa. To finance telecasts on the role of political parties and the presidential nominating process	Oct. 14, 1954	43,050.00	43,050.00*	....	....
Professor James W. Miller, Michigan State University, East Lansing, Mich. To finance a survey and appraisal of the work in progress under Falk Foundation grants to colleges and universities for political education programs	Dec. 14, 1953	3,500.00	3,490.91**	....	....

---

* An unused balance of $1,225.65 was refunded by the grantee.
** An unused balance of $9.09 was canceled.

GRANTS FROM INCOME (Continued)

OTHER PROGRAMS IN EDUCATION FOR POLITICS (Continued)

	Date of Grant	Amount of Grant	Amount Paid Prior to 1963	Amount Paid in 1963 and 1964	Payable in 1965
Mount Holyoke College, South Hadley, Mass., and Amherst College, Amherst, Mass.					
In support of the cataloguing and storing of political records and literature at the Amherst-Mount Holyoke Political Studies Center	June 21, 1960	$ 8,550.00	$ 8,550.00	$	$ . . . .
National Center for Education in Politics (formerly Citizenship Clearing House), New York, N. Y.*					
Survey of courses in practical politics in American colleges and universities	Nov. 7, 1950	50,000.00	50,000.00	. . . .	. . . .
In support of a program of activities to encourage the education of college men and women for political participation	April 30, 1952	424,972.00	413,027.20**	. . . .	. . . .
To commission an author to state the case for citizen participation in politics	Jan. 22, 1953	15,000.00	15,000.00	. . . .	. . . .
In support of an Undergraduate Political Internship Program	April 9, 1959 April 15, 1964	139,550.00 140,000.00	139,550.00	. . . . 140,000.00	. . . .
Ohio Wesleyan University, Delaware, Ohio					
To finance the development of tests to evaluate the results achieved by the Ben A. Arneson Institute of Politics	June 16, 1952	5,000.00	5,000.00	. . . .	. . . .

---

* See page 131 for listing of canceled endowment grant.
** An unused balance of $5,000.00 was refunded by the grantee; an unpaid balance of $11,944.80 was canceled.

GRANTS FROM INCOME (Continued)

EDUCATION FOR POLITICS (Continued)

OTHER PROGRAMS IN EDUCATION FOR POLITICS (Continued)

	Date of Grant	Amount of Grant	Amount Paid Prior to 1963	Amount Paid in 1963 and 1964	Payable in 1965
Pennsylvania Association of Colleges and Universities, Harrisburg, Pa.					
To finance a Conference on Higher Education to Prepare College Students for Political Responsibilities of Citizenship	April 30, 1952	$ 3,000.00	$ 3,000.00†	$.........	....
Professor Rhoten A. Smith, University of Kansas, Lawrence, Kansas					
To finance a survey and appraisal of the work in progress under Falk Foundation grants to colleges and universities for political education programs	Mar. 5, 1958	10,000.00	9,707.53‡	....	....
University of Pittsburgh, Pittsburgh, Pa.					
In partial support of the 1957 Pittsburgh meeting of the Executive Committee of the International Political Science Association and for publication of the proceedings	Mar. 25, 1957	7,000.00	7,000.00	....	....
To establish a Center for Politics, sponsor a Conference on the Administration of Elections, etc.	July 14, 1961	6,588.00	6,588.00	....	....
For a study of the political forces at work in Latin America as they affect U. S. policy and programs	July 21, 1964	14,840.00*	....	14,840.00	....

---

* A compensating contribution in the same amount was received by the Foundation from a friend.
† An unused balance of $117.79 was refunded by the grantee.
‡ An unused balance of $292.47 was canceled.

265

GRANTS FROM INCOME (Continued)

EDUCATION FOR POLITICS (Continued)

OTHER PROGRAMS IN EDUCATION FOR POLITICS (Continued)

	Date of Grant	Amount of Grant	Amount Paid Prior to 1963	Amount Paid in 1963 and 1964	Payable in 1965
Wesleyan University, Middletown, Conn.					
In support of the preparation of a guide for surveying the politics and governmental organization of local communities	May 17, 1954	$ 4,500.00	$ 4,500.00	$..........	$..........
FALK FOUNDATION'S ACCOUNT FOR RESEARCH IN POLITICS					
For the development of teaching materials for political education programs	June 21, 1960	15,000.00	15,000.00*	....	....
Subtotals**—Education for Politics		$3,042,534.50	$2,605,586.14	$424,702.00	....

---

* Allocated to The Eagleton Institute of Politics, Rutgers University, New Brunswick, New Jersey.

**Unadjusted for refunded, reduced, and canceled grants. See page 135.

GRANTS FROM INCOME (Continued)

DISTRIBUTION OF PUBLICATIONS

	Date of Grant	Amount of Grant	Amount Paid Prior to 1963	Amount Paid in 1963 and 1964	Payable in 1965
Brookings Institution, Washington, D. C. and Falk Foundation's Distribution of Publications Account					
Distribution of various reports and summaries of studies made under Falk Foundation grants	Mar. 5, 1934	$129,524.98	$129,524.98	$........	$........
Falk Foundation's Distribution of Publications Account	April 4, 1938	373,500.00	362,573.29	10,926.71	....
	April 5, 1963	10,000.00	....	10,000.00	....
	April 15, 1964	15,000.00	....	1,473.35	13,526.65
	Nov. 24, 1964	5,000.00	....	....	5,000.00
Public Affairs Committee, Inc., New York, N. Y.					
Preparation of pamphlet-digests of economic and other social science research studies made under the grants of the Falk Foundation and other organizations	Sept. 9, 1935	65,000.00	65,000.00	....	....
Dr. Agnes L. Starrett, University of Pittsburgh, Pittsburgh, Pa.					
To commission Dr. Starrett to write and publish a history of the Falk Foundation	April 15, 1964	30,000.00	....	....	30,000.00
Subtotals*—Distribution of Publications		$628,024.98	$557,098.27	$ 22,400.06	$ 48,526.65

---

* Unadjusted for refunded, reduced, and canceled grants. See page 135.

267

GRANTS FROM INCOME (Continued)

OTHER FIELDS

	Date of Grant	Amount of Grant	Amount Paid Prior to 1963	Amount Paid in 1963 and 1964	Payable in 1965
American Assembly, Columbia University, New York, N.Y. President Eisenhower's Commission on National Goals	June 21, 1960	$ 25,000.00	$ 25,000.00	$	$ . . . .
American Red Cross, Pittsburgh, Pa. Social welfare work in Allegheny County, Pennsylvania	Feb. 7, 1946	11,000.00	11,000.00	. . . .	. . . .
Boy Scouts of America (Allegheny Council), Pittsburgh, Pa. Construction of four troop lodges in Guyasuta Reservation	June 29, 1959	30,000.00	30,000.00	. . . .	. . . .
Carnegie Institute, Pittsburgh, Pa. Rehabilitation of the building of the Carnegie Institute	Sept. 9, 1955	25,000.00	25,000.00	. . . .	. . . .
Carnegie Institute of Technology, Pittsburgh, Pa. Annual support of The Maurice Falk Professorship of Social Relations prior to payment of endowment*	Sept. 19, 1938	60,000.00	60,000.00	. . . .	. . . .
Falk Educational Development Fund for The Maurice Falk Professorship of Social Relations	July 15, 1948	105,000.00	105,000.00	. . . .	. . . .
Children's Hospital, Pittsburgh, Pa. Psychiatric training and service program	Mar. 20, 1956	120,000.00	120,000.00	. . . .	. . . .

* See page 130 for listing of endowment grant.

GRANTS FROM INCOME (Continued)

OTHER FIELDS (Continued)

	Date of Grant	Amount of Grant	Amount Paid Prior to 1963	Amount Paid in 1963 and 1964	Payable in 1965
Duquesne University, Pittsburgh, Pa. The Maurice Falk Moot Court in the Rockwell Hall of Law and Business	Dec. 14, 1954	$100,000.00	$100,000.00	$.........	$.........
Harvard University, Cambridge, Mass. Harvard Law School—Israel Cooperative Research for Israel's Legal Development	Mar. 19, 1954	10,000.00	10,000.00	....	....
Junior Achievement, Pittsburgh, Pa. Establishment of a downtown headquarters for the Pittsburgh Branch	July 27, 1950	10,000.00	10,000.00	....	....
Metropolitan Opera Association, New York, N. Y. General support of the Metropolitan Opera Association	Dec. 11, 1951	2,500.00*	2,500.00	....	....
Metropolitan Pittsburgh Educational Television Station WQED, Pittsburgh, Pa. Toward an emergency fund to meet operating requirements	Dec. 20, 1961	10,000.00	10,000.00	....	....
Montefiore Hospital, Pittsburgh, Pa. Construction, equipment, and experimental development of air-conditioned oxygen-therapy rooms	June 10, 1935	20,000.00	20,000.00	....	....
National Fund for Medical Education, New York, N. Y. Support of medical education in the United States	Oct. 15, 1953	5,000.00	5,000.00	....	....

* A compensating contribution in the same amount was received by the Foundation from a friend.

269

GRANTS FROM INCOME (Continued)

OTHER FIELDS (Continued)

	Date of Grant	Amount of Grant	Amount Paid Prior to 1963	Amount Paid in 1963 and 1964	Payable in 1965
Pennsylvania George Junior Republic, Grove City, Pa.					
Toward the cost of a dormitory-cottage	June 7, 1962	$ 15,000.00	$ 15,000.00	$	$ . . . .
Pittsburgh Bicentennial Association, Pittsburgh, Pa.					
Program in the field of education	Mar. 5, 1958	25,000.00	25,000.00	. . . .	. . . .
Pittsburgh Board of Education, Pittsburgh, Pa.					
Construction of a special building for the education of physically handicapped children	June 18, 1957	15,000.00	15,000.00	. . . .	. . . .
Pittsburgh Child Guidance Center, Pittsburgh, Pa.					
Expansion of professional staff and services	April 13, 1955	40,000.00	35,900.00	4,100.00	. . . .
Pittsburgh Council for International Visitors, Pittsburgh, Pa.					
Hospitality services to visitors from foreign countries	Dec. 21, 1960	1,500.00	1,500.00	. . . .	. . . .
Pittsburgh Foundation, Pittsburgh, Pa.					
General operating expenses	Mar. 27, 1945	7,400.00	7,400.00	. . . .	. . . .
Toward expenses as host to Sixteenth Annual National Conference of the Council on Foundations	Nov. 24, 1964	3,000.00	. . . .	3,000.00	. . . .
Pittsburgh Symphony Society, Pittsburgh, Pa.					
For emergency support of the 1950-1951 program of concerts	Dec. 20, 1950	10,000.00	10,000.00	. . . .	. . . .

GRANTS FROM INCOME (Continued)

OTHER FIELDS (Continued)

	Date of Grant	Amount of Grant	Paid Prior to 1963	Paid in 1963 and 1964	in 1965
Pressley House, Pittsburgh, Pa. Construction of a Treatment Center and re-adaption of present building for dormitory use	April 5, 1963	$ 35,000.00	$.........	$ 35,000.00	$.........
Red Cross War Fund Social welfare work with the Armed Forces	Jan. 30, 1942	19,100.00	19,100.00	....	....
Saint Anthony's School, Oakmont, Pa. Construction of three classroom-shops for education of retarded children	July 16, 1958	35,000.00	35,000.00	....	....
Salvation Army of Pittsburgh, Pittsburgh, Pa. Contribution toward $2,600,000 Building Fund Campaign in Allegheny County, Pa.	Oct. 8, 1963	25,000.00	....	25,000.00	....
United Fund of Allegheny County, Pittsburgh, Pa.* Social welfare work in Allegheny County, Pa.	Oct. 19, 1931 Oct. 8, 1963 Dec. 10, 1963	442,000.00** 25,000.00 50,000.00	417,000.00	25,000.00 25,000.00 50,000.00	....

---

* Prior to 1956, this organization was named the Community Chest of Allegheny County.

** The above figure represents the total of the grants given in the prewar and postwar periods. In the war years from 1941 to 1945, inclusive, grants in this classification were channeled through the United War Fund and the Red Cross War Fund and are recorded elsewhere in this listing.

271

GRANTS FROM INCOME (Continued)

OTHER FIELDS (Continued)

	Date of Grant	Amount of Grant	Amount Paid Prior to 1963	Amount Paid in 1963 and 1964	Payable in 1965
United Jewish Federation of Pittsburgh, Pittsburgh, Pa.*					
Social welfare work**	June 26, 1946	$376,500.00	$376,500.00	$.........	$.........
	April 5, 1963	25,000.00	....	25,000.00	....
	Oct. 8, 1963	25,000.00	....	25,000.00	....
	Dec. 10, 1963	50,000.00	....	50,000.00	....
United War Fund					
Social welfare work with the Armed Forces	Sept. 24, 1941†	76,500.00	76,500.00	....	....
University of Pittsburgh, Pittsburgh, Pa.					
Falk Medical Clinic's operations	April 15, 1946	42,500.00	42,500.00	....	....
A library to be named The Maurice and Laura Falk Library for the Health Professions	Mar. 25, 1949	25,000.00‡	25,000.00	....	....
A mental health program in the field of child psychiatry and child development	Nov. 7, 1950	250,000.00	250,000.00	....	....
Remodeling the interior of the Falk Clinic	July 9, 1954	100,000.00	100,000.00	....	....
Expansion of the Institute of Local Government	Dec. 14, 1954	75,000.00	75,000.00	....	....
Establishment of an integrated Student Counseling Center and Placement Service	Oct. 15, 1956	100,000.00	100,000.00	....	....
Seminars in the social sciences, business administration and student affairs as part of the inauguration ceremony of the twelfth chancellor of the University	Dec. 6, 1956	22,500.00	22,500.00	....	....

---

* Prior to 1955, this organization was named the United Jewish Fund, Pittsburgh, Pa.

**See page 132 for listing of endowment grant.

† See page 127.

‡ The total amount given for this purpose was $800,000.00; the balance of $775,000.00 was paid from principal. See page 133.

GRANTS FROM INCOME (Continued)

OTHER FIELDS (Continued)

University of Pittsburgh (Continued)

	Date of Grant	Amount of Grant	Amount Paid Prior to 1963	Amount Paid in 1963 and 1964	Payable in 1965
Purchase of the building of the Municipal Hospital of Pittsburgh, to be named Jonas E. Salk Hall	June 18, 1957	$150,000.00*	$150,000.00	$ · · · · · · ·	$ · · · · · · ·
Planning for the establishment of a School of Public and International Affairs and an Administrative Science Center	Oct. 24, 1957	100,000.00	100,000.00	· · · · · · · ·	· · · · · · · ·
Various institutions and organizations					
Continuation for five years of certain sectarian and civic donations which Mr. Maurice Falk was making at the time of his demise	April 15, 1946	41,875.00**	41,750.00	· · · · · · · ·	· · · · · · · ·
Western Pennsylvania Conservancy, Pittsburgh, Pa.					
To meet the costs of physical development of Raccoon Valley Wildflower Reserve and to initiate and develop an educational program in botany	Oct. 2, 1962	66,000.00	66,000.00	· · · · · · · ·	· · · · · · · ·
White House Conference on Children and Youth, Washington, D. C.					
The 1960 Conference on Children and Youth	Oct. 8, 1959	10,000.00	10,000.00	· · · · · · · ·	· · · · · · · ·
Subtotals†—Other Fields		$ 2,817,375.00	$ 2,550,150.00	$267,100.00	· · · · · · · ·
Totals†—Grants from Income		$11,989,273.79	$10,851,222.77	$1,064,337.46	$48,526.55

* The total amount given for this purpose was $300,000.00; the balance of $150,000.00 was paid from principal. See page 133.
** A contribution to the B'Nai B'Rith Home for Children was canceled by the closing of the home.
† Unadjusted for refunded, reduced, and canceled grants. See page 135.

273

GRANTS FROM PRINCIPAL

	Date of Grant	Amount of Grant	Amount Paid Prior to 1963	Amount Paid in 1963 and 1964	Payable in 1965
American Jewish Committee, New York, N. Y. Endowment for the Maurice Falk Studies	Oct. 8, 1959	$250,000.00	$250,000.00	$........	$........
American Friends of the Hebrew University, New York, N. Y. Endowment for the account of The Maurice Falk Institute for Economic Research in Israel, The Hebrew University, Jerusalem	April 5, 1963	500,000.00	....	500,000.00	....
American Law Institute, Philadelphia, Pa. Endowment to reactivate and staff the Editorial Board serving the Uniform Commercial Code project	Mar. 28, 1961	125,000.00	125,000.00	....	....
Brookings Institution, Washington, D. C. Construction of an auditorium to be named The Maurice Falk Auditorium	Oct. 8, 1959	300,000.00	300,000.00	....	....
Carnegie Institute of Technology, Pittsburgh, Pa. Endowment of The Maurice Falk Professorship of Social Relations	Nov. 29, 1937	600,000.00	600,000.00	....	....
Maurice Falk Endowment for Research in the Humanities	June 12, 1964	125,000.00	....	125,000.00	....
Chatham College, Pittsburgh, Pa. Construction of The Laura Falk Hall of Social Studies	April 30, 1952	350,000.00	350,000.00	....	....
Maurice Falk Endowment for the Enrichment of Undergraduate Teaching	Jan. 16, 1964	250,000.00	....	250,000.00	....
Community Chest of Allegheny County, Pittsburgh, Pa. Special endowment fund	July 21, 1964	500,000.00	....	500,000.00	....
Duquesne University, Pittsburgh, Pa. Construction of the Maurice Falk Lecture Hall and the Laura Falk Lecture Hall	Jan. 16, 1964	200,000.00	....	200,000.00	....

274

GRANTS FROM PRINCIPAL (Continued)

	Date of Grant	Amount of Grant	Amount Paid Prior to 1963	Amount Paid in 1963 and 1964	Payable in 1965
Ellis School, Pittsburgh, Pa. Endowment for Maurice Falk Chair of History	Mar. 29, 1960 April 15, 1964	$ 50,000.00 50,000.00	$ 50,000.00	$......... 50,000.00	$......... ....
Maurice Falk Institute for Economic Research in Israel, The Hebrew University, Jerusalem, Israel*					
Maurice Falk Medical Fund, Pittsburgh, Pa. To endow the Fund in honor of Mr. Maurice Falk	Dec. 21, 1960	5,000,000.00	5,000,000.00	....	....
To increase the original endowment fund Transfer of 220 shares of Oakland Corp. Voting Common Stock	June 12, 1964 Nov. 24, 1964	8,601,568.50 22,000.00	....	8,601,568.50	.... 22,000.00
Montefiore Hospital, Pittsburgh, Pa. The Maurice Falk Center for Research and Post-graduate Studies in Ophthalmology	Nov. 24, 1964	137,500.00	....	137,500.00	....
Mount Mercy College, Pittsburgh, Pa. Construction of proposed science building	June 12, 1964	50,000.00	....	50,000.00	....
National Bureau of Economic Research, New York, N. Y. In support of general research program	Dec. 10, 1963	100,000.00	....	100,000.00	....
National Center for Education in Politics (formerly Citizenship Clearing House), New York, N. Y. Toward the endowment of the Center's Under-graduate Political Internship Program	June 7, 1962	500,000.00**	....	....	....

* See American Friends of the Hebrew University.

**This grant was canceled when the Center reported it was unable to meet the conditions of the grant.

GRANTS FROM PRINCIPAL (Continued)

	Date of Grant	Amount of Grant	Amount Paid Prior to 1963	Amount Paid in 1963 and 1964	Payable in 1965
Pittsburgh Child Guidance Center, Pittsburgh, Pa.					
To establish a Josephine S. Falk Research Pavilion	Jan. 16, 1963	$400,000.00	$.........	$400,000.00	$.........
Pittsburgh Symphony Endowment, Pittsburgh, Pa.					
Toward the capital resources of the Endowment	June 12, 1964	100,000.00	....	100,000.00	....
Shady Side Academy, Pittsburgh, Pa.					
Endowment for The Maurice Falk Scholarship and to provide an increase in the salary of a teacher in the Senior School selected by the Academy for outstanding service to the institution	Oct. 8, 1959	90,000.00	90,000.00	....	....
Endowment to provide income to be used for increases in the salary of a member or members of the faculty in recognition of excellence in teaching in the Junior and Middle Schools	April 15, 1964	50,000.00	....	50,000.00	....
United Jewish Federation of Pittsburgh, Pittsburgh, Pa.					
Special endowment fund	July 21, 1964	500,000.00	....	500,000.00	....
United Negro Colleges Development Campaign, New York, N. Y.					
Toward the $50,000,000 development campaign for major capital, plant, and program improvements in 32 private educational institutions in the South	Jan. 16, 1964	50,000.00	....	50,000.00	....

GRANTS FROM PRINCIPAL (Continued)

	Date of Grant	Amount of Grant	Amount Paid Prior to 1963	Amount Paid in 1963 and 1964	Payable in 1965
University of Pittsburgh, Pittsburgh, Pa.					
A library to be named The Maurice and Laura Falk Library for the Health Professions	Mar. 25, 1949	$775,000.00*	$775,000.00	$.........	$.........
Purchase of the building of the Municipal Hospital of Pittsburgh, to be named Jonas E. Salk Hall	June 18, 1957	150,000.00**	150,000.00	....	....
Toward purchase of Woman's Hospital building and equipment in the Health Center	May 15, 1961	200,000.00	200,000.00	....	....
Endowment of the Maurice Falk Professorship of Politics	Jan. 16, 1964	500,000.00	....	500,000.00	....
Renovation of Falk Clinic building and construction of a covered passageway connecting Clinic with Presbyterian-University Hospital and Nurses' Residence	Nov. 24, 1964	1,000,000.00	....	....	1,000,000.00
Winchester-Thurston School, Pittsburgh, Pa.					
Construction of an auditorium to be named The Maurice Falk Auditorium	June 21, 1960 April 15, 1964	150,000.00 50,000.00	150,000.00	.... 50,000.00	....
Yale University, New Haven, Conn.					
Endowment to provide income for fellowship awards under the Falk Graduate Fellowship Program in Political Science	Mar. 28, 1962	500,000.00	500,000.00	....	....

---

* The total amount given for this purpose was $800,000.00; the balance of $25,000.00 was paid out of income funds. See page 128.
**The total amount given for this purpose was $300,000.00; the balance of $150,000.00 was paid out of income funds. See page 129.

GRANTS FROM PRINCIPAL (Continued)

	Date of Grant	Amount of Grant	Amount Paid Prior to 1963	Amount Paid in 1963 and 1964	Payable in 1965
Young Women's Christian Association of Pittsburgh, Pittsburgh, Pa.					
Toward the costs of constructing a new metropolitan headquarters	July 14, 1961	$ 25,000.00	$ 25,000.00	$.........	$.........
Totals*—Grants from Principal		$22,251,068.50	$ 8,565,000.00	$12,164,068.50	$1,022,000.00
Gross Totals**—All Grants		$34,240,342.29	$19,416,222.77	$13,228,405.96	$1,070,526.65

* In addition to these grants from principal for specific projects there were transfers accumulating to $750,000.00 from principal cash to income cash for payments on various grants listed under "Grants from Income."

**Unadjusted for refunded, reduced, and canceled grants. See page 135.

278

	Amount of Grant	Amount Paid Prior to 1963	Amount Paid in 1963 and 1964	Payable in 1965
LESS REDUCTION OF GRANTS:				
Brookings Institution	$ 8,315.55	$	$	$
Productivity, Wages, and National Income Investigation of the need for economic research in Israel	2,000.00			
Citizenship Clearing House				
Program of activities to encourage the education of college men and women for political participation	11,944.80			
Professor James W. Miller				
Survey and appraisal of the work in progress under Falk Foundation grants to colleges and universities for political education programs	9.09			
Professor Rhoten A. Smith				
Survey and appraisal of the work in progress under Falk Foundation grants to colleges and universities for political education programs	292.47			
LESS CANCELED GRANTS:				
Allegheny Conference on Community Development				
Economic Basis for Community Development of Allegheny County District in Pennsylvania	2,500.00			
B'Nai B'Rith Home for Children	125.00			
National Center for Education in Politics, New York, N.Y.				
Endowment of the Center's Undergraduate Political Internship Program	500,000.00			

279

	Amount of Grant	Amount Paid Prior to 1963	Amount Paid in 1963 and 1964	Payable in 1965
LESS RETURNS ON AMOUNTS PAID ON GRANTS:				
Brookings Institution				
Productivity, Wages, and National Income	$ 10,000.00	$	$	$
Bases of National Prosperity	14,687.76			
Refugee Settlement in the Dominican Republic	613.44			
A Study of Ways and Means to Reduce the Expenditures of the Federal Government	120,000.00			
Growth Requirements in the Steel Industry	80,000.00	30,000.00	50,000.00	
Citizenship Clearing House				
Program of activities to encourage the education of college men and women for political participation	5,000.00			
Committee on Federal Tax Policy				
A Postwar Taxation Program	2,553.11			
	1,291.17			
	255.03			
Committee on Public Debt Policy				
A Study of the Problem of the Public Debt	2,466.72			
Metropolitan Pittsburgh Educational Television Station WQED				
Telecasts on the role of political parties and the presidential nominating process	1,255.65			
Pennsylvania Association of Colleges and Universities				
Conference on Higher Education to Prepare College Students for Political Responsibilities of Citizenship	117.79			
	238,210.67	188,210.67	50,000.00	
LESS COMPENSATING CONTRIBUTIONS RECEIVED BY THE FOUNDATION FROM FRIENDS	2,500.00	2,500.00		
	15,000.00	15,000.00		
	14,840.00	....	14,840.00	....
Net Totals	$33,444,604.71	$19,210,512.10	$13,163,565.96	$1,070,526.65

APPENDIX F

Cumulative Record of Publications

For the high quality of these publications the Foundation is indebted to the institutions and organizations which planned, produced, and published the research.—J. STEELE GOW

The following books, listed alphabetically, have been published by research organizations to report the findings of studies made under grants received from the Falk Foundation:

America's Capacity to Consume
Leven, Moulton, and Warburton. Brookings Institution, 1934.
272 pp., $3.00.

America's Capacity to Produce
Nourse and Associates. Brookings Institution, 1934.
608 pp., $3.50.

American Agriculture, 1899-1939: A Study of Output, Employment, and Productivity
Harold Barger and Hans H. Lansberg. National Bureau of Economic Research, Inc., 1942.
435 pp., $3.00.

Automation and Technological Change
The American Assembly, Columbia University. Prentice-Hall, Inc., 1962.
184 pp., $1.95 paperback, $3.95 clothbound.

Banking Institutions in Israel: 1950-1961
Meir Heth. (In Hebrew.) Falk Project for Economic Research in Israel, 1963.
279 pp., IL.5.00.

Big Enterprise in a Competitive System
A. D. H. Kaplan. Brookings Institution, 1954.
269 pp., $4.00.

Can Inflation Be Controlled?
Harold G. Moulton. Anderson Kramer Associates, 1958.
302 pp., $4.95.

Consumption Patterns in Israel
Nissan Liviatan. (In Hebrew and English.) Falk Project for Economic Research in Israel, 1964.
88 pp., IL.3.00, $2.00.

Controlling Factors in Economic Development
Harold G. Moulton. Brookings Institution, 1949.
397 pp., $4.00.

The Cost and Financing of Social Security
  Lewis Meriam, Karl T. Schlotterbeck, and Mildred Maroney.
  Brookings Institution, 1950.
  193 pp., $3.00.

Direct Export Premiums in Israel: 1952-1958
  David Pines. (In Hebrew with English summary.) Falk Project for Economic Research in Israel, 1963.
  144 pp., IL.5.00.
  Research Paper 16. (English summary.) 19 pp., IL.0.75.

Discussion Draft of a Study of Definitional Problems in Capital Gains Taxation
  Stanley S. Surrey, Chief Reporter, working with the Tax Committee and the Tax Advisory Group of The American Law Institute. The American Law Institute, 1960.
  511 pp., $7.00.

The Distribution of Wealth and Income in Relation to Economic Progress
  (Textbook combination of *America's Capacity to Produce, America's Capacity to Consume, The Formation of Capital, and Income and Economic Progress.*) Brookings Institution, 1936.
  888 pp., $2.50.

Distribution's Place in the American Economy Since 1869
  Harold Barger. National Bureau of Economic Research, Inc., Princeton University Press, 1955.
  222 pp., $4.50.

The Dynamic Economy
  Harold G. Moulton. Brookings Institution, 1950.
  238 pp., $2.00.

An Economic Analysis of Established Family Farms in Israel: 1953-1958
  Yair Mundlak. (In Hebrew and English.) Falk Project for Economic Research in Israel, 1964.
  172 pp., IL.3.00.

Economics of the Iron and Steel Industry
  Daugherty, DeChazeau, and Stratton. University of Pittsburgh (McGraw-Hill Book Company), 1937.
  2 vols., 1188 pp., $6.00 per volume.

Employment in Manufacturing, 1899-1939: An Analysis of Its Relation to the Volume of Production
  Solomon Fabricant. National Bureau of Economic Research, Inc., 1942.
  360 pp., $3.00.

Estimates of Israel's International Transactions, 1952-1954
  Nadav Halevi. (In Hebrew and English.) Falk Project for Economic Research in Israel, 1956.
  139 pp., $2.00.

Falk Project for Economic Research in Israel, A Ten Year Report: 1954-1963
  Don Patinkin. Falk Project for Economic Research in Israel, 1964.
  110 pp., free.

Financial Intermediaries in Israel: 1950-1954
Rachel Floersheim. (In Hebrew with English summary.) Falk Project for
Economic Research in Israel, 1962.
161 pp., IL.2.50.

The Formation of Capital
Harold G. Moulton. Brookings Institution, 1935.
207 pp., $2.50.

Goals for Americans
President's Commission on National Goals. Prentice-Hall, Inc., 1960.
372 pp., $1.00 paperback, $3.50 clothbound.

Going Into Politics: A Guide for Citizens
Robert E. Merriam and Rachel M. Goetz. Harper & Brothers, 1957.
216 pp., $2.50.

Government and Economic Life
Lyon, Watkins, Abramson, and Associates. Brookings Institution, 1939,
1940.
2 vols., 1301 pp., Vol. I, $3.00; Vol. II, $3.50.

Governmental Costs and Tax Levels
Lewis H. Kimmel. Brookings Institution, 1948.
153 pp., $2.50.

The Guarantee of Annual Wages
A. D. H. Kaplan. Brookings Institution, 1947.
269 pp., $3.50.

Health Resources in the United States
George W. Bachman and Associates. Brookings Institution, 1952.
344 pp., $5.00.

Immigration to Israel: 1948-1953
Moshe Sicron. (In Hebrew and English.) Falk Project for Economic
Research in Israel and Central Bureau of Statistics. Special Series No.
60, 1957.
137 pp., IL.2.50, $2.00.
Statistical Supplement, IL.1.75, $1.50.

The Impact of Collective Bargaining on Management
Sumner H. Slichter, James J. Healy, and E. Robert Livernash. Brookings
Institution, 1960.
982 pp., $8.75.

Income and Economic Progress
Harold G. Moulton. Brookings Institution, 1935.
191 pp., $2.00.

The Income Structure of the United States
Maurice Leven. Brookings Institution, 1938.
177 pp., $1.50.

Industrial Pensions
Charles L. Dearing. Brookings Institution, 1954.
310 pp., $3.75.

Industrial Price Policies and Economic Progress
Edwin G. Nourse and Horace B. Drury. Brookings Institution, 1938.
314 pp., $2.50.

Industry-Wide Bargaining
Leo Wolman. The Foundation for Economic Education, 1948.
63 pp., $0.50.

Israel's National Expenditure:1950-1954
Harold Lubell and Others. Falk Project for Economic Research in Israel and Central Bureau of Statistics. Special Series No. 74, 1958.
93 pp. and Appendices, 58 pp., IL.2.00, $2.00.
Research Paper 5. (In Hebrew, Chapters 1 and 2.) 35 pp., IL.0.80.

Israel's National Income: 1950-1954
Daniel Creamer and Others. (In Hebrew and English.) Falk Project for Economic Research in Israel and Central Bureau of Statistics. Special Series No. 57, 1957.
115 pp., IL.2.00, $2.00.

Israel's Terms of Trade Under Its Clearing Agreements
Avraham Kessler. (In Hebrew.) Falk Project for Economic Research in Israel, 1964.
123 pp., IL.3.00.

The Labor Force in Israel
Avner Hovne. (In Hebrew and English.) Falk Project for Economic Research in Israel, 1961.
88 pp., IL.3.00, $2.00.

Labor Policy of the Federal Government
Harold W. Metz. Brookings Institution, 1945.
296 pp., $2.50.

Leadership in a Small Town
Aaron Wildavsky. The Bedminster Press, 1964.
388 pp., $7.50.

Local Political Surveys
E. E. Schattschneider and Victor Jones. Holt, Rinehart and Winston, Inc., 1962.
229 pp., $3.75.

Long-Term Projections of Supply and Demand for Agricultural Products in Israel
Yair Mundlak and Others. (In Hebrew and English.) Falk Project for Economic Research in Israel, 1964.
2 vols., 927 pp., IL.4.00 per volume.

The Mining Industries, 1899-1939: A Study of Output, Employment, and Productivity
Harold Barger and Sam H. Schurr. National Bureau of Economic Research, Inc., 1944.
452 pp., $3.00.

A National Labor Policy
 Harold W. Metz and Meyer Jacobstein. Brookings Institution, 1947.
 164 pp., $2.25.

The New Philosophy of Public Debt
 Harold G. Moulton. Brookings Institution, 1943.
 93 pp., $1.00.

Our National Debt: Its History and Its Meaning Today
 Committee on Public Debt Policy, 1949.
 182 pp., $2.50.

Output and Productivity in the Electric and Gas Utilities, 1899-1942
 Jacob Martin Gould. National Bureau of Economic Research, Inc., 1946.
 195 pp., $3.00.

The Output of Manufacturing Industries, 1899-1937
 Solomon Fabricant. National Bureau of Economic Research, Inc., 1940.
 685 pp., $4.50.

Postwar Fiscal Requirements (Federal, State and Local)
 Lewis H. Kimmel and Associates. Brookings Institution, 1945.
 166 pp., $2.00.

Preparing College Men and Women for Politics
 Dr. and Mrs. Thomas H. Reed. Citizenship Clearing House, New York
 University, 1952.
 180 pp., free.

Price Making in a Democracy
 Edwin G. Nourse. Brookings Institution, 1944.
 541 pp., $3.50.

Productivity, Wages, and National Income
 Spurgeon Bell. Brookings Institution, 1940.
 344 pp., $3.00.

The Public Sector Accounts of Israel: 1948/49-1954/55
 R. M. Barkay. (In English, mimeograph.) Falk Project for Economic
 Research in Israel and Central Bureau of Statistics, 1957.
 2 vols., 362 pp., IL.3.00, $3.00.

The Recovery Problem in the United States
 Moulton, Leven, Pasvolsky, Hardy, *et al.* Brookings Institution, 1937.
 710 pp., $4.00.

Refugee Settlement in the Dominican Republic
 Dana G. Munro. Brookings Institution, 1942.
 410 pp., $4.00.

The Regulation of the Security Markets
 Atkins, Edwards, Moulton. Brookings Institution, 1946.
 123 pp., $2.00.

Relief and Social Security
 Lewis Meriam. Brookings Institution, 1946.
 912 pp., $5.00.

285

The Supply of Professional Manpower from Israel's Educational System
H. V. Muhsam and Others. (In Hebrew with English summary.) Falk
Project for Economic Research in Israel, 1959.
136 pp., IL.3.50.

A Tax Program for a Solvent America
The Committee on Postwar Tax Policy. Ronald Press, 1945.
278 pp., $3.00.

A Tax Program for a Solvent America—1947
The Committee on Postwar Tax Policy. Ronald Press, 1947.
232 pp., $3.00.

Taxes and Economic Incentives
Lewis H. Kimmel. Brookings Institution, 1950.
217 pp., $2.50.

Transportation Industries, 1889-1946: A Study of Output, Employment, and Productivity
Harold Barger. National Bureau of Economic Research, Inc., 1951.
228 pp., $4.00.

The Trend of Government Activity in the United States Since 1900
Solomon Fabricant. National Bureau of Economic Research, Inc., 1952.
288 pp., $4.00.

Trends in Employment in the Service Industries
George J. Stigler. National Bureau of Economic Research, Inc., Princeton
University Press, 1956.
167 pp., $3.75.

Trends in Output and Employment
George J. Stigler. National Bureau of Economic Research, Inc., 1947.
67 pp., $1.00.

Uniform Commercial Code
The American Law Institute and National Conference of Commissioners
on Uniform State Laws. American Law Institute, 1952.
816 pp., $3.50.

Wages, Prices, Profits and Productivity
Edited by Dr. Charles A. Myers. The American Assembly, Columbia
University, 1959.
193 pp., $2.00.

Wartime Control of Prices
Charles O. Hardy. Brookings Institution, 1940.
216 pp., $1.00.

The following pamphlets have been published by organizations under grants from the Falk Foundation:

The Action Program of the Citizenship Clearing House
George H. Williams and Lawrence L. Pelletier. Citizenship Clearing
House, New York University, 1954.
23 pp., free.

Appraising the Responsiveness of Market Demand
(Chapter VII of *Price Making in a Democracy*) Edwin G. Nourse. Brookings Institution, 1942.
34 pp., $0.25.

Areas of Applicability of Low-Price Policy
(Chapter VI of *Price Making in a Democracy*) Edwin G. Nourse. Brookings Institution, 1942.
51 pp., $0.25.

Basic Criteria of Price Policy
(Chapter XI of *Price Making in a Democracy*) Edwin G. Nourse. Brookings Institution, 1943.
52 pp., $0.25.

Better Minds for Better Politics
George H. Williams and James W. Miller. Citizenship Clearing House, New York University, 1954.
15 pp., free.

Between Automatic and Authoritarian Price Making
(Chapter I of *Price Making in a Democracy*) Edwin G. Nourse. Brookings Institution, 1942.
38 pp., $0.25.

Bibliography on Political Participation, (A Selected and Annotated)
Hugh Bone. Citizenship Clearing House, New York University, 1954.
21 pp., free.

California Politics
Joseph P. Harris. Citizenship Clearing House, New York University. Stanford University Press, 1955.
66 pp., $1.00.

Collapse or Boom at the End of the War?
Harold G. Moulton and Karl T. Schlotterbeck. Brookings Institution, 1942.
40 pp., $0.25.

Competition as Method and as Goal
(Chapter III of *Price Making in a Democracy*) Edwin G. Nourse. Brookings Institution, 1942.
30 pp., $0.25.

Curtailment of Non-Defense Expenditures
Henry P. Seidemann. Brookings Institution, 1941.
54 pp., $0.25.

Democracy as a Principle of Business
(Appendix B of *Price Making in a Democracy*) Edwin G. Nourse. Brookings Institution, 1942.
24 pp., $0.25.

Depreciation Policy and Postwar Expansion
Lewis H. Kimmel. Brookings Institution, 1946.
66 pp., $0.50.

287

Discrimination Without Prejudice
  Survey Research Center, Institute for Social Research, The University of Michigan. American Jewish Committee, 1964.
  45 pp., free.

Distribution Costs—Wasting at the Bunghole
  (Chapter VIII of *Price Making in a Democracy*) Edwin G. Nourse. Brookings Institution, 1942.
  25 pp., $0.25.

Do We Want a Federal Sales Tax?
  Charles O. Hardy. Brookings Institution, 1943.
  47 pp., $0.25.

Domestic Servants in the United States, 1900-1940
  George J. Stigler. National Bureau of Economic Research, Inc., 1946.
  44 pp., $0.50.

Economic Systems: Free Enterprise, Communism, Socialism, Hybrids; Regulations Compatible with Private Enterprise
  (Chapter VI of *Controlling Factors in Economic Development*) Harold G. Moulton. Brookings Institution, 1948.
  55 pp., $0.50.

Effects of the Defense Program on Prices, Wages, and Profits
  Meyer Jacobstein and Harold G. Moulton. Brookings Institution, 1941.
  43 pp., $0.25.

Employment and Compensation in Education
  George J. Stigler. National Bureau of Economic Research, Inc., 1950.
  73 pp., $1.00.

Fifth Report—1959 and 1960
  (In Hebrew and English.) Falk Project for Economic Research in Israel, 1961.
  242 pp., free.

Financing Defense: Can Expenditures Be Reduced?
  Committee on Federal Tax Policy, 1951.
  31 pp., free.

Financing Defense: Is an Excess Profits Tax the Solution?
  Committee on Postwar Tax Policy, 1950.
  25 pp., free.

Financing Defense: The Tax Program
  Committee on Federal Tax Policy, 1951.
  34 pp., free.

First Annual Report—1954
  (In Hebrew and English.) Falk Project for Economic Research in Israel, 1955.
  92 pp., free.

Fourth Report—1957 and 1958
  (In Hebrew and English.) Falk Project for Economic Research in Israel, 1959.
  198 pp., free.

288

Free Enterprise and "Laissez Faire"
(Chapter II of *Price Making in a Democracy*) Edwin G. Nourse. Brookings Institution, 1942.
26 pp., $0.25.

Free Enterprise, Price Policy, and Democracy
(Chapter V of *Price Making in a Democracy*) Edwin G. Nourse. Brookings Institution, 1942.
34 pp., $0.25.

Fundamental Economic Issues in National Defense
Harold G. Moulton. Brookings Institution, 1941.
32 pp., $0.25.

Guide to Michigan Politics
Joseph G. LaPalombara. Citizenship Clearing House, New York University, 1955.
70 pp., $0.25.

Investments in Manufacturing Made Through the Investment Center
Zwi Citron and Avraham Kessler. Falk Project for Economic Research in Israel.
Research Paper 2. (In Hebrew with English summary), March, 1958.
32 pp., IL.0.50.
Mimeograph (in English), including an Evaluation of the Basic Data, a Summary of Comparison of Development of Approved Firms with Non-Approved Firms, and supplemental statistical tables, April, 1958.
69 pp., IL.1.00, $1.00.

Israel's Tariff Structure and Functions
Arnon Gafni, Nadav Halevi, and Giora Hanoch. Falk Project for Economic Research in Israel.
Research Paper 3. (In Hebrew with English summary), April, 1958.
35 pp., IL.0.60.

Is There Enough Manpower?
Harold W. Metz. Brookings Institution, 1942.
25 pp., $0.25.

Labor Savings in American Industry, 1899-1939
Solomon Fabricant. National Bureau of Economic Research, Inc., 1945.
38 pp., $0.50.

Massachusetts Politics
Earl Latham. Citizenship Clearing House, New York University, 1956.
74 pp., $0.75.

National Income Originating in Israel's Agriculture (1952-1954)
Michael Noam. Falk Project for Economic Research in Israel and Central Bureau of Statistics, Special Series No. 48, 1956, 106 pp.,
together with *Technical Notes,* Supplement to Special Series No. 48, 95 pp., IL.1.00.

Our National Debt After Great Wars
Committee on Public Debt Policy, 1946.
12 pp., $0.25.

Our National Debt and the Banks
Committee on Public Debt Policy, 1947.
18 pp., $0.25.

Our National Debt and the Budget
Committee on Public Debt Policy, 1947.
20 pp., $0.25.

Our National Debt and Interest Rates
Committee on Public Debt Policy, 1947.
19 pp., $0.25.

Our National Debt and Life Insurance
Committee on Public Debt Policy, 1948.
13 pp., $0.25.

Our National Debt and the National Welfare
Committee on Public Debt Policy, 1948.
25 pp., $0.25.

Our National Debt and Our Savings
Committee on Public Debt Policy, 1948.
20 pp., $0.25.

Postwar National Income: Its Probable Magnitude
Joseph Mayer. Brookings Institution, 1944.
34 pp., $0.50.

Postwar Re-Employment: The Magnitude of the Problem
Karl T. Schlotterbeck. Brookings Institution, 1943.
27 pp., $0.25.

Postwar Tax Policy and Business Expansion
Lewis H. Kimmel. Brookings Institution, 1943.
46 pp., $0.50.

*Proceedings, Work Conference on Higher Education for Preparing Students
for Political Responsibilities of Citizenship*
Sponsored by Pennsylvania Association of Colleges and Universities, June
16-18, 1952, Lancaster, Pa.
92 pp., free.

Productivity and Economic Progress
Frederick C. Mills. National Bureau of Economic Research, Inc., 1952.
36 pp., $0.75.

The Profit Motive and "Maximum" Profits
(Chapter IV of *Price Making in a Democracy*) Edwin G. Nourse. Brookings Institution, 1942.
30 pp., $0.25.

Provisional Estimates of Israel's National Expenditures, 1952 and 1953
Harold Lubell. (In Hebrew and English.) Falk Project for Economic Research in Israel and Central Bureau of Statistics, Special Series No. 44, 1956.
50 pp., IL.0.60.

Provisional Estimates of Israel's National Income, 1952 and 1953
Daniel Creamer. (In Hebrew and English.) Falk Project for Economic Research in Israel and Central Bureau of Statistics, Special Series No. 29, 1955.
22 pp., IL.0.60.

Report No. 1 of The Permanent Editorial Board for the Uniform Commercial Code
The Permanent Editorial Board for the Uniform Commercial Code. The American Law Institute and National Conference of Commissioners on Uniform State Laws, 1962.
141 pp., free.

The Rising Trend of Government Employment
Solomon Fabricant. National Bureau of Economic Research, Inc., 1949.
30 pp., $0.50.

Second Annual Report—1955
(In Hebrew and English.) Falk Project for Economic Research in Israel, 1956.
187 pp., free.

Should Price Control Be Retained?
Harold G. Moulton and Karl T. Schlotterbeck. Brookings Institution, 1945.
43 pp., $0.50.

Sixth Report—1961-1963
(In Hebrew and English.) Falk Project for Economic Research in Israel, 1964.
130 pp., free.

A Student's Guide to Practical Politics
Lee C. McDonald. Institute of Practical Politics, Pomona College, 1955.
20 pp., free.

Third Annual Report—1956
(In Hebrew and English.) Falk Project for Economic Research in Israel, 1957.
106 pp., free.

The Timing of Price Changes
(Chapter X of *Price Making in a Democracy*) Edwin G. Nourse. Brookings Institution, 1943.
35 pp., $0.25.

Wages as Cost and as Market
(Chapter IX of *Price Making in a Democracy*) Edwin G. Nourse. Brookings Institution, 1942.
43 pp., $0.25.

The following books and pamphlets have been issued by various organizations as reprints, translations, or summaries of publications reporting the findings of studies made under grants from the Falk Foundation:

Aggregation Over Time in Distributed Lag Models
  Yair Mundlak. Falk Project for Economic Research in Israel.
  Research Paper 10. (Reprinted from *International Economic Review,*
  Vol. 2, No. 2, May, 1961), October, 1961.
  10 pp., IL.0.50.

America's Factories
  Public Affairs Committee, Inc., 1941. (Pamphlet based on *The Output
  of Manufacturing Industries, 1899-1937*)
  31 pp., $0.10.

Brookings Primer of Progress
  J. Walter Thompson Company, 1936. (Illustrated summary of *Income
  and Economic Progress*)
  21 pp. Printed in limited edition for free distribution.

The Composition of Gross Farm Income Since the Civil War
  Bulletin 78, National Bureau of Economic Research, Inc., 1940. (Report
  based on an uncompleted study entitled *Agriculture and the Business
  Cycle*)
  24 pp., $0.25.

Consistent Estimation of Distributed Lags
  Nissan Liviatan. Falk Project for Economic Research in Israel.
  Research Paper 15. (Reprinted from *International Economic Review,*
  Vol. 4, No. 1, January, 1963), July, 1963.
  9 pp., IL.0.75.

The Development of Production and Prices in the Vegetable Branch
  I. Honigbaum. Falk Project for Economic Research in Israel.
  Research Paper 7. (Reprinted from *The Economic Quarterly,* in Hebrew
  with English summary, Vol. 7, No. 25-26, January, 1960), March, 1960.
  12 pp., IL.0.50.

Empirical Production Function Free of Management Bias
  Yair Mundlak. Falk Project for Economic Research in Israel.
  Research Paper 9. (Reprinted from *Journal of Farm Economics,* Vol.
  XLIII, No. 1, February, 1961), September, 1961.
  13 pp., IL.0.50.

Errors in Variables and Engel Curve Analysis
  Nissan Liviatan. Falk Project for Economic Research in Israel.
  Research Paper 11. (Reprinted from *Econometrica,* Vol. 29, No. 3, July,
  1961), December, 1961.
  27 pp., IL.0.50.

*Estimation of Production and Behavioral Functions from a Combination of
    Cross-Section and Times-Series Data*
  Yair Mundlak. Falk Project for Economic Research in Israel.
  Research Paper 13. (Reprinted from *Measurement in Economics: Studies
  in Mathematical Economics and Econometrics in Memory of Yehuda
  Grunfeld,* Stanford University Press, 1963), November, 1963.
  29 pp., IL.0.75.

292

Factory Employment and Output Since 1899
   Occasional Paper 4, National Bureau of Economic Research, Inc., 1941.
   (Report based on *Employment in Manufacturing, 1899-1939*)
   39 pp., $0.25.

Government and Economic Life
   Brookings Institution, 1940. (Interpretative summary of *Government and Economic Life*)
   66 pp., $0.25.

Government in Relation to Agriculture
   Brookings Institution, 1940. (Reprint of Chapter XXIII of *Government and Economic Life*)
   85 pp., $0.25.

Gross Farm Income and Indices of Farm Production and Prices in the United States, 1869-1937
   Technical Bulletin No. 703. United States Department of Agriculture, 1940. (Report based on an uncompleted study entitled *Agriculture and the Business Cycle*)
   154 pp., $0.20.

Hausse Des Salaires ou Baisse Des Prix?
   Payot, Paris, 1938. (French translation, by Gael Fain, of *Income and Economic Progress*)
   266 pp., 36 fr.

Income and Economic Progress
   Public Affairs Committee, Inc., 1936. (Pamphlet-digest of *Income and Economic Progress*)
   34 pp., $0.10.

*Income and Economic Progress** (pocket edition)
   National Home Library Foundation, 1936.
   165 pp., $0.25.

Industrial Price Policies
   Public Affairs Committee, Inc., 1938. (Pamphlet-digest of *Industrial Price Policies and Economic Progress*)
   32 pp., $0.10.

Israel and The General Agreement on Tariffs and Trade
   Nadav Halevi and Giora Hanoch. Falk Project for Economic Research in Israel.
   Research Paper 1. (Reprinted from *The Economic Quarterly,* in Hebrew with English summary, Vol. 5, Nos. 17-18, November, 1957, pp. 154-162), January, 1958.
   12 pp., IL.0.30.

   Mimeograph (in English), including Country Studies, a Summary of Main GATT Provisions, statistical tables, and bibliography, December, 1957.
   73 pp., IL.1.00, $1.00.

---

*This study was authored and first published by The Brookings Institution.

Manufacturing Output, 1929-1937
Occasional Paper 1, National Bureau of Economic Research, Inc., 1940.
(Report on selected sections of *The Output of Manufacturing Industries, 1899-1937*)
28 pp., $0.25.

Productivity of Labor and Machines in Israel's Cotton Spinning Mills
Ruth Klinov-Malul. Falk Project for Economic Research in Israel.

Research Paper 4. (Reprinted from *The Economic Quarterly*, in Hebrew, Vol. 5, No. 19, April, 1958, pp. 303-328), July, 1958.
30 pp., IL.0.60.
Research Paper 4. (In English), September, 1958.
48 pp., IL.0.80, $0.75.

Productivity of Labor in Peace and War
Occasional Paper 7, National Bureau of Economic Research, Inc., 1942.
(Report utilizing materials gathered in studies of production and productivity in manufacturing, extractive industries, and public utilities.)
28 pp., $0.25.

Productivity, Wages, and National Income
Brookings Institution, 1940. (Pamphlet-summary of *Productivity, Wages, and National Income*)
21 pp., $0.25.

Readjustments Required for Recovery
Public Affairs Committee, Inc., 1937. (Pamphlet-digest of *The Recovery Problem in the United States*)
32 pp., $0.10.

Steel—Problems of a Great Industry
Public Affairs Committee, Inc., 1937. (Pamphlet based on selected sections of *Economics of the Iron and Steel Industry*)
32 pp., $0.10.

Survey of Family Savings, 1957/58 (Preliminary Report) and
Survey of Family Savings, 1957/58 and 1958/59 (Preliminary Report)
Falk Project for Economic Research in Israel *Research Papers 6 and 8* respectively. Falk Project for Economic Research in Israel, Central Bureau of Statistics, Bank of Israel, The Israel Institute of Applied Social Research, and Department of Economics, Hebrew University.

Research Paper 6. (In English and in Hebrew), (Reprint from Bank of Israel Bulletin No. 10, October, 1959), December, 1959, 25 pp., free.
Research Paper 8. (In English only), (Reprint from Bank of Israel, Annual Report 1959, August, 1960), September, 1960, 11 pp., free.

A Tax Program for a Solvent America (short version)
The Committee on Postwar Tax Policy. The Committee on Postwar Tax Policy, 1945.
44 pp., free.

Technical Progress and Agricultural Depression
Bulletin 67, National Bureau of Economic Research, Inc., 1937. (Partial report of an uncompleted study entitled *Agriculture and the Business Cycle*)
32 pp., $0.50.

Tests of the Permanent-Income Hypothesis Based on a Reinterview Savings Survey
Nissan Liviatan. Falk Project for Economic Research in Israel.

Research Paper 12. (Reprinted from *Measurement in Economics: Studies in Mathematical Economics and Econometrics in Memory of Yehuda Grunfeld*, Stanford University Press, 1963), October, 1963.
37 pp., IL.0.75.

Wage Differentials and Specification Bias in Estimates of Relative Labor Prices
Uri Bahral. Falk Project for Economic Research in Israel.

Research Paper 14. (Reprinted from *The Review of Economics and Statistics,* Vol. XLIV, No. 4, November, 1962), July, 1963.
9 pp., IL.0.75.

Your Income and Mine
Public Affairs Committee, Inc., 1938. (Pamphlet-digest of *The Income Structure of the United States*)
31 pp., $0.10.

The following reprints, digests, and reports have been published by the Falk Foundation for free distribution:

The Annual Wage—Where are We?
(Reprinted from *American Economic Review,* Volume XXXVII, No. 5, December, 1947.)

Digest of "America's Capacity to Produce" and "America's Capacity to Consume." 1935.

Digest of "The Formation of Capital." 1935.

Digest of "Income and Economic Progress."
(A reprint of an article entitled *Economic Progress Without Economic Revolution* from the November, 1935, issue of *Fortune.*) 1935.

Educating the Citizen for Politics
The Maurice and Laura Falk Foundation. The Maurice and Laura Falk Foundation, 1957.
23 pp., free.

The First Two Years
(Report of the Falk Foundation's activities for 1930-1932.) 1933.

The Falk Foundation Report for 1933 and 1934. 1935.

The Falk Foundation Report for 1935 and 1936. 1937.

The Falk Foundation Report for 1937 and 1938. 1939.

The Falk Foundation Report for 1939 and 1940. 1941.

The Falk Foundation Report for 1941 and 1942. 1943.

The Falk Foundation Report for 1943 and 1944. 1945.

The Falk Foundation Report for 1945 and 1946. 1947.

The Falk Foundation Report for 1947 and 1948. 1949.

The Falk Foundation Report for 1949 and 1950. 1951.
The Falk Foundation Report for 1951 and 1952. 1953.
The Falk Foundation Report for 1953 and 1954. 1955.
The Falk Foundation Report for 1955 and 1956. 1957.
The Falk Foundation Report for 1957 and 1958. 1959.
The Falk Foundation Report for 1959 and 1960. 1961.
The Falk Foundation Report for 1961 and 1962. 1963.

The Final Two Years
(Report of the Falk Foundation's activities for 1963-1964.) 1965.

Proceedings of the Dinner Meeting of The Maurice and Laura Falk Foundation Held in Observance of its Tenth Anniversary, Hotel Schenley, Pittsburgh, September 24, 1940. 1940.

The following motion picture films for economic education have been produced under the joint financing of The Maurice and Laura Falk Foundation and the Alfred P. Sloan Foundation, Inc.:

Albert in Blunderland
(Life in a regimented economy.)

Dear Uncle
(Taxes.)

The Devil and John Q
(Inflation.)

Fresh-Laid Plans
(How one economic control leads to another.)

Going Places
(The role of the profit motive in the American economy.)

Inside Cackle Corners
(The function of the profit motive.)

It's Only the Beginning
(Industrial research.)

Make Mine Freedom
(The creative role of freedom in economic enterprise.)

Meet King Joe
(Technology as a factor in economic progress.)

Why Play Leapfrog?
(The relation of wages to prices.)

APPENDIX G

Preservation of
The Maurice and Laura Falk
Foundation Archives

UNIVERSITY OF PITTSBURGH
PITTSBURGH, PENNSYLVANIA 15213
DIVISION OF THE SOCIAL SCIENCES

Office of the Dean   June 14, 1965

Dr. J. Steele Gow
Executive Director
The Maurice and Laura Falk Foundation
Grant Building, 3315
Pittsburgh, Pennsylvania 15219

Dear Dr. Gow,

I should like to request, on behalf of the University of Pittsburgh, that the Officers and Board of Directors of The Maurice and Laura Falk Foundation consider entrusting the Foundation's records to the Archives of Industrial Society of the University.

The following terms are proposed to assure appropriate care for the Foundation's records:

1. The University of Pittsburgh recognizes a firm and lasting commitment to the Archives of Industrial Society. All manuscripts and records accepted by the Archives for permanent retention will be assured of perpetual care by the University.

2. As soon as its construction has been completed, the Hillman Library will provide space for the housing of the records of the Falk Foundation. In the meantime, it is understood that the Foundation's records will be kept in safe storage by the University until the move to adequate space in Hillman Library has been arranged.

3. Eventually, all records will be catalogued and arranged for

convenient use by scholars and others who have a legitimate reason for consulting them.

4. The entire collection of files, records, books, pamphlets, films, and other publications and materials of the Falk Foundation will be kept intact for a period of not less than five years, and any culling thereafter of duplicate or unnecessary materials from this collection will be done in consultation with a designee of the Foundation.

5. All books, pamphlets, films, and other publications reporting studies made under Falk Foundation grants, including biennial and other reports on the Foundation's works, will be kept together in the Archives as a unit.

6. The Archives of Industrial Society and the University of Pittsburgh request that the complete records of the Falk Foundation be donated to the Archives for permanent retention.

7. It is understood that the Foundation's records will not be transferred to the University until the Foundation terminates its activities and closes its office.

It would be an honor for the University to care for the records of the Falk Foundation.

My very best wishes.

Sincerely,

(Signed) Richard L. Park

Richard L. Park
Dean

RLP:sb
cc: Vice Chancellor C. H. Peake

❧ ❧ ❧ ❧ ❧

Falk Foundation Minutes (Book II, Page 856)

Mr. Gow summarized the letter to the Foundation from Dr. Richard L. Park, Dean of the Division of the Social Sciences of the University of Pittsburgh, under date of June 14, 1965, requesting that at a suitable time the Foundation's files, records, publications, documents, etc. be placed on permanent deposit in the University's Archives of Industrial Society which are to be housed in the Hillman Library on completion of its construction, presently scheduled for June 1967. On Mr. Gow's recommendation, it was moved, seconded, and unanimously voted that this request be, and it hereby is, approved on the understanding that the terms set forth in Dean Park's letter, a copy of which is attached hereto as a part of these minutes, are to govern the care and management of these records, files, etc.

INDEX

Abbott, C. C.: 84.
Adams, Sherman: 147-148.
Adler, Louis J.: 220, 247, 252.
Agricultural economics research: 74-75.
Agriculture and the Business Cycle: 74.
Albert in Blunderland: 99.
Alfred P. Sloan Foundation: 29, 98-100.
Allegheny (City): 5-6.
Allegheny College: 122-123, 126.
Allegheny Conference on Community
    Development: 223.
Altschul, Eugen: 74.
America at the Polls: 141, 143.
America Votes: 143.
American Assembly: 69-70.
American Chemical Company of Newark: 7.
American Heritage Foundation: 138.
American Heritage Register and Vote
    Campaign: 138.
American Jewish Committee: 87-90, 225-228.
American Law Institute: 34-35.
America's Capacity to Consume: 26-27.
America's Capacity to Produce: 26-27.
Amherst College: 115, 123, 147-148, 166.
Amherst-Mount Holyoke Political Studies
    Center: 147.
Ami, Joseph: 56.
Anderson, Paul: 170-171; picture: 170.
Annual Wage and Employment Guarantees: 30.
Arensberg, Charles C.: 178.
Arnon, Yaakov: 62.
Automation and Technological Change: 70.
Ayres, Leonard P.: 83-85.

Bach, George Leland: 159.
Bachi, Roberto: 62.
Badger, Sherwin: 84-85.
Bagley, Eleanor S.: 85.
Barach, Joseph: 181, 184.
Barger, Harold: 76.
Barkdull, Howard L.: 38.
Barrett, Joe C.: 38.
Becker, Aharon: 57.
Beckhart, B. H.: 84.
Belfour, Stanton C.: xiii, 150, 199.
Bell, Daniel W.: 83.
Bell, Davitt Stranahan: 185, 219, 247;
    picture: 212.
Bell, Frank Breckenridge: 7, 13, 15, 17, 33,
    185, 208, 219, 247, 249-250; picture: 2, 92.
Bell, Robert K.: 38.
Benezet, Louis T.: 126.
Benjamin F. Fairless Memorial Lectures:
    160-161.
Bergman, A. D.: 57.
Berlin, University of: 76.
Bethany College: 123, 150-153, 226; Board of
    Fellows: 151-152.
The Bethany College Institute for
    Responsible Citizenship: 150-153.

Better Minds for Better Politics: 104.
Bingham, W. V.: 18.
Blaw-Knox Company: 7.
B'Nai B'Rith Home for Children: 207.
Bogen, Jules: 84.
Boggs, J. Caleb: 152.
Bone, A. R., Jr.: 152.
Boston University: 106, 122-123.
Bovard, James M.: 201.
Bowman, John G.: 8-9, 15, 220.
Boyle, Hugh: 168.
Braun, Arthur E.: xiii, 13, 15, 171, 213-215,
    234, 247; pictures: 2, 92, 212.
Bridgeport University: 106.
Brookings Institution: 22-23, 48, 65, 79, 185,
    225; Dominican Republic study: 32-33;
    Institute for Government Research: 18;
    picture: 22, 25, 27; publications in
    economics: 26, 30-31.
Brosin, Henry: 189.
Brown, E. E.: 83.
Brown University: 76-77, 79, 83, 106, 162.
Brussels, University of: 110.
Buchanan, John Grier: 35-36.
Buhl, Henry: 18-19.
Buhl Foundation: 17-19, 65, 170-171, 205.
Bunn, Charles: 38.
Burgess, W. Randolph: 82-83, 85.
Burns, Arthur F.: 76, 161.
Burton, Courtney: 152.
Button, John: 57.
Byrne, Mrs. Herbert: 191.

California, University of: 88, 110, 119, 124,
    127-128, 130, 141-142, 166, 195, 228.
Calkins, Robert DeBlois: 29, 48.
Cambridge University: 76.
Campbell, Henrietta, (Mrs. Robert D.): 209;
    picture: 170.
Caplan, Louis: xiii, 11, 36, 43, 185, 216-217,
    247; picture: 212.
Cardoza, Benjamin M.: 35.
Carnegie Corporation: 17, 35, 71, 107, 158, 201.
Carnegie Foundation for the Advancement of
    Teaching: 17.
Carnegie Institute (Pittsburgh): 201.
Carnegie Institute of Technology: 158-162,
    202, 215, 225.
Carroll, Holbert: 165.
Carroll, Sister M. Thomas Aquinas: 172.
Cases in Practical Politics: 139.
Casner, James A.: 42.
Catholic University: 172.
Center for Politics: 146.
Chatham Center: 214.
Chatham College: 121-123, 127, 146, 169-172,
    202, 215, 225.
Chazeau, Melvin de. *See* de Chazeau, Melvin.
Chicago, University of: 28-29, 35, 37, 52, 76,
    110, 128, 189.

300

305